Kearby's Thunderbolts

I0809248

Kearby's Thunderbolts

The 348th Fighter Group in World War II

John C. Stanaway

Schiffer Military/Aviation History
Atglen, PA

Cover artwork by Steve Ferguson, Colorado Springs, CO.

THEN THERE WERE SIX— The front cover depicts a scene from the October 11, 1943, Congressional Medal of Honor mission, which is described in Chapter 6. The title of the cover alludes to the last Ki-61 Tony shot down by Kearby that day.

Book Design by Ian Robertson.

Copyright © 1997 by John C. Stanaway.
Library of Congress Catalog Number: 96-72653

All rights reserved. No part of this work may be reproduced or used in any forms or by any means – graphic, electronic or mechanical, including photocopying or information storage and retrieval systems – without written permission from the copyright holder.

Printed in China.
ISBN: 0-7643-0248-5

We are interested in hearing from authors with book ideas on related topics.

Published by Schiffer Publishing Ltd.
77 Lower Valley Road
Atglen, PA 19310
Phone: (610) 593-1777
FAX: (610) 593-2002
E-mail: Schifferbk@aol.com
Please write for a free catalog.
This book may be purchased from the publisher.
Please include $2.95 postage.
Try your bookstore first.

CONTENTS

Introduction

Since the first version of this story came out a few years ago, some new information has surfaced about the eventual fate of Colonel Neel on his last mission, flown on March 5, 1944. My good friend, Dr. Frank Olynyk, and a new friend, Bob Piper, who was the Historian for the Royal Australian Air Force, both sent me what was essentially the same piece of information on the recovery of Kearby's remains at the crash site.

One of the things that became clear was that Kearby was not flying his own P-47, "Fiery Ginger" on that mission. It had been assumed from General George Kenney's comments in his famed book, GENERAL KENNEY REPORTS, that Kearby was flying his own aircraft, but subsequent information from surviving members of the 348th Fighter Group indicated that "Fiery Ginger" had developed mechanical problems (reportedly, a balky fuel pump) and that Kearby used Jesse Ivey's 42-22668. Both Olynyk and Piper offered verbal descriptions by the original search parties that indicated the wreckage was badly decomposed by mid-1946. The Australians who discovered the wreckage apparently were initially unable to read the tail number as it could have been either 42-22662 or 42-22668. A number 72 was on the fuselage, which further identified the wreckage as Ivey's P-47 (22668) and the one that Kearby was flying.

Another interesting fact that was brought to my attention by Piper was the curious disparity of distance between the reported site of Kearby's going down at Dagua and the discovery of the wreckage near Annanberg, a distance of about 140 miles on a direct route to Allied bases at Gusap, Nadzab and Tsili. Is it possible that Kearby could have recovered from his spin to almost make it back to safety? Perhaps it is a bit too much speculation, but the idea that Kearby could have been intact enough to valiantly try to survive is a poignant thought. On the whole, the 348th story is just as rich and enigmatic as that of its famed commander, Neel Kearby. Jesse Ivey is gone, now, as are the devoted wingmen, Dunham and Blair, who searched in vain for their fallen leader on that last mission. We have only their written statements about that unfortunate event, and a dwindling number of first-hand accounts of the rest of the 348th legacy.

PART I: Kearby's Thunderbolts

Chapter 1

Wewak Relics: '29 Australian War

Graves' Unit was left with an unenviable task. The war in the Pacific had been over for more than six months in late March 1946 when the job of locating missing Allied military personnel in the New Guinea area was left mainly to Australian authorities. The Royal Australian Air Force was responsible for locating missing aircraft and personnel.

Within the Wewak area there were reports of at least six crash sites (two A-20 Havoc/Bostons, one B-25 Mitchell, one P-40, one light reconnaissance aircraft and a P-47 Thunderbolt). An RAAF search party comprising Flying Officers L.S. Cogswell, J.D. Coape-Smith and Sergeant C. Dixon set out from Madang on an overland

Wide angle view of the Wewak area. 43rd Bomb Group strike photo. (AFM)

search of the Ramu Valley area as far away as Annanberg with a patrol officer and five police boys from Madang.

Annanberg was a fair sized settlement located on a bend of the Ramu River somewhat less than a hundred miles northwest of Madang. The plan was for the search party to trek by foot and be met on the river at Annanberg on May 4th by RAAF trawler. Heavy rains and flooding of the rivers on the way delayed departure of the party until April 23. A few days into the trek brought word of aircraft wrecks in two different parts of the search track and it was decided to split the search party into two groups, one led by Cogswell and Bentinck toward Annanberg and the other with Coape-Smith and Sgt. Dixon in another direction.

On the sixteenth day after Coape-Smith's party set out they traveled by canoe twenty-eight miles down the Ramu River to Annanberg. After searching for missing aircraft in the Annanberg area, Coape-Smith received word on May 10 of a wreckage site at Pibu, a small village about five miles north of Annanberg. He set out with Sgt. Dixon and contacted some natives who knew of the plane. They took him to a village leader who gave him a skull and a few bones wrapped in bark.

The accounts from the natives were jumbled because the natives could neither read nor write and the sequence of events was badly confused in their minds. What seemed to be derived from their testimony was that approximately two years before, an aircraft fell in flames and the pilot parachuted from a low height only about 100 yards from the village. Some of the natives went to the pilot only to discover that he was already dead.

In some sort of order of events, the Japanese arrived to take whatever seemed of value from the body, the natives buried the dead pilot and the matter was informally reported to Graves Registration via some of the police boys. The RAAF search party found the wreckage and identified it as an American Republic P-47 Thunderbolt, tail number 222662 (later corrected to 222668, after careful examination of the damaged and fire scarred tail). Designation Unknown X-1598 was given to the pilot's remains which were transferred to the American Graves Registration Service Mausoleum in Manila.

It took more than two years of conscientious research to be certain that the pilot who rested in death at the Manila mausoleum and the missing airman who flew P-47D-4 number 222668 were one and the same. His family sent their concurrence with the conclusion reached by the office of the Quartermaster General and requested that the body be returned home.

The airman's body was brought to the U.S. aboard the Army transport, Private John R. Towie, and arrived home on June 16, 1949. Six Army colonels flew out to Dallas, Texas, to act as pallbearers. The airman was finally buried at Hillcrest Memorial Park in Dallas on July 23, 1949.

Curious as it may seem, practically no one outside the people attending the funeral were aware that the body of the American airman had been found. It is curious because the airman was not only the fourth-ranking fighter ace in the Southwest Pacific he was also the holder of the Congressional Medal of Honor as well as numerous other decorations. He was a full colonel and group commander as well as a high-ranking staff officer of the Fifth Fighter Command. He had pioneered the acceptance of the P-47 fighter plane in the Pacific as well as being the key instrument of its performance record and leading his 348th Fighter Group to some impressive victories at the end of 1943.

Such as the facts may be, those who knew him venerate his memory and can rest assured that his mortal remains were recovered to find a hero's grave. Finally, Colonel Neel Earnest Kearby, great leader of fighter pilots and victor of more than twenty air battles, was home again.

348th P-47 from above. July-September 1943.

Chapter 2

"Gentlemen, I give you the 348th Fighter Group"

On paper, the 348th Fighter Group began life at Mitchel Field, New York, in September 1942. It was born and transferred the same day, September 30, 1942, to Bradley Field at Windsor Locks in Connecticut. On October 29, 1942, the group moved once again, this time to Westover Field, Massachusetts, where it received the first of its P-47 Thunderbolt aircraft.

Neel Kearby as a flight cadet. (USAF)

September 1942 was cold and rainy in northeast America. The weather seemed to reflect the bleak and gray situation of the war for the allies. German domination of Europe was at its most complete point, with U-boats threatening the very coasts of the United States. Japanese forces were operating with deadly effectiveness in struggles around New Guinea and Guadalcanal. Conversely, American and British forces were hard pressed simply to maintain their positions in North Africa and the China-Burma-India theater. Into this dismal scene the 348th was preparing to enter with its new P-47s.

The P-47 was a 13,000 pound bull of a fighter that was yet unblooded at the end of 1942. It had been included in the USAAF inventory for less than ten months when it was introduced to the 348th Fighter Group. The P-39s and P-40s that formed the bulk of American resistance to axis air domination were barely able to defend themselves, much less take the offensive against the redoubtable Zero, Messerschmitt 109 and Focke Wulf 190.

By the final days of 1942 the great American hope was the P-38 twin-engine fighter with the P-47 as a promising question mark in squadrons training in the United States. American fighter designs tended to be unconventional with the exception of the Curtiss P-40 which conformed closely to current European designs. Other types of fighters proved to be faster with better rates of climb and higher altitude ceilings. The Zero was faster and more maneuverable than the P-40, and enjoyed greater range. Japanese pilots were often openly disdainful of the American fighter.

However, like most other American designs, the P-40 was a remarkably rugged airplane with a flashing diving speed. Later models carried six super-heavy and fast-firing .50 caliber guns that could shred a target with a well-aimed burst. The P-47 increased the margin of these advantages with a much better performance at high altitude, faster level speeds and the potential for longer range which was pioneered by the 348th Fighter Group.

Neel Kearby with his wife Virginia, for whom "Fiery Ginger" was named, and Bill Leverette and his wife on the right. The Leverettes and Kearbys were good friends. Coincidentally, Leverette shot down seven Germans on the Mediterranean front in a single combat, just two days before Kearby did virtually the same thing in the Pacific. (Leverette)

The 342nd Fighter Squadron was the first to be assigned to the group. It was organized at Bradley Field on October 4, 1942, with its cadre drawn from the 56th and 80th Fighter Groups which were stationed nearby. Original pilots included names that would later be prominent in the history of the group: George Burgess, George Dougherty, David Eastham and Randall Hilbig would become air leaders while Bob Gibb, Marvin Grant, Bob Knapp, Larry O'Neill and Ed Popek would also become aces.

Enlisted men on the original cadre roster of October 4, 1942, included David Crockett as First Sergeant, Master Sergeants Dave Smith and Joe Baxter as Engineering Chiefs and Technical Sergeant Marion Iddings, one of the line chiefs. Iddings was a rugged and good-natured rock of a veteran from western Indiana who got into the heart of the 342nd Squadron from the beginning and made his mark on the group as a whole.

One of the officers who quickly became aware of the value of personnel like Iddings was Captain William M. Banks who was made squadron commander on November 2, 1942. He and Iddings began a mutually satisfying professional and personal relationship that lasted until Banks' death more than forty years later. Banks was squadron commander for only about three weeks when he was outranked and uprooted by Captain Raymond K. Gallagher who took the squadron helm through the first days of combat.

Around the middle of November the 342nd began receiving its first aircraft in the form of twenty-five P-47Bs and P-47Cs. Other personnel came into the squadron at the same time, including Second Lieutenant Altamont J. Cornwell who was responsible as Engineering Officer for a remarkable standard of ingenuity in keeping the 342nd's aircraft in the ring with the Japanese.

On October 28, 1942, the 342nd moved to Westover Field near Chicopee Falls, Massachusetts. More names that would be linked with the combat record of the 348th began to appear on the roster of the 342nd Squadron. In December, First Lieutenant Walter Benz of Miami, Florida, came into the squadron as a flight leader. He had been with the 326th Fighter Group at the same station and simply moved across the field to stow his gear in quarters with the 348th. As it happened, he stayed on to command the group just after the war ended.

Captain Edward Roddy was the Operations Officer for the 342nd by November and would become another of the group's aces. His assistant was First Lieutenant William D. "Dinghy" Dunham who had been recently a test pilot for the First Fighter Command in New York. He had also been a flying comrade of the new 348th commander, Major Neel E. Kearby, with the 53rd Fighter Group in Panama. Dunham and Kearby had become close friends and Dunham impressed Kearby with his easy facility as a fighter pilot, so he was persuaded to join the new fighter unit with the untried P-47.

There is no doubt that at the end of 1942 the P-47 was still an open issue. Whatever it could do against an enemy was left for eager young pilots to discover. The Thunderbolt was promised to the European theater as a high-altitude escort and was scheduled to be combat ready by May 1942. The airplane was nearly a year late in being deployed and the 348th was to be one of the units taking the P-47 to England.

Major Kearby became the first commander of the 348th Fighter Group in October, but he was less than encouraged when he found the group headquarters and little else attached to the unit. He would

Kearby boarding his stateside 348th P-47. (Captain Thorne Spaulding via Krane collection)

Captain Bill Banks, B Flight leader.

have been even less heartened if he had arrived a few weeks before when the quarters and buildings at Bradley Field were dubbed "Skunk Hollow" for good reason. However, in the two weeks before Kearby arrived, the group was moved to a newly built area just outside the base and at least now there was indoor plumbing, central heating and formal mess facilities.

The day after Kearby arrived the first group aircraft showed up in the form of one P-47B, one P-47C and a Piper Cub. If he couldn't have a snappy looking formation from the start at least he could begin training his pilots on the Thunderbolt and begin to overcome the difficulties of flying the new powerhouse.

By November the group acquired an executive officer, Captain William Hovis, an adjutant Second Lieutenant William parent and Second Lieutenant Bernard Roth as Intelligence Officer. Other officers were assigned to group posts who were necessary to administer the incipient stages of training an active fighter group.

During the same time the other two squadrons were organized and began training. The 340th Squadron was commanded in turn by Lieutenant LeRoy V. Sutter and Lieutenant Stevens before Captain Frank Oksala took over on November 6, 1942. Captain Meade Brown, another original group pilot who later became an ace, was the Operations Officer.

Captain Bill Dunham, C Flight leader.

Captain Ed Roddy, also C Flight leader.

Oksala moved up to 348th Headquarters and Captain Charles H. MacDonald took command of the 340th Squadron on November 17. MacDonald was an officer of unusual ability as a fighter unit leader and took the squadron into its first days of combat. He was a popular commander who left the 348th a year later to become even more famous as the guiding hand of the legendary 475th Fighter Group; the "Satan's Angels" which would carry on a tacit but friendly rivalry with the 348th.

The 341st also worked up to training status with Captain David Campbell taking command on November 15. Captains Sam Blair and John T. Moore would become aces of the squadron as well as commanders. Other notable pilots of the original 341st cadre were Lieutenants Arthur Weeks, Clarence Blend, Charles Cronk, Glenn Perryman and William Foulis who would also become an ace.

November also saw the mass movement of the group to Westover Field where training had its own special difficulties. Air traffic was as congested over the base as any other busy east coast station, adding to the confusion of young pilots simply trying to manipulate their P-47s. There also seemed to be a perpetual haze that made navigation and observation hazardous endeavors for neophyte pilots learning to fly high performance aircraft.

The first casualty of the difficult training conditions occurred in the 340th Squadron on December 1, 1942. Lieutenant Charles G. Hay was in the circuit over Westover when something went wrong in the murky weather and he crashed to his death.

Another luckier accident happened in the 342nd Squadron on December 19. Lieutenant Russell D. Lynn was on a cross country flight in a P-47B when his engine quit somewhere over Massachusetts. It was not well known at the time how dangerous a bailout from a P-47 could be, but Lynn was in no mood to consider alternatives while riding the leaden weight of a Thunderbolt without power. He released the canopy and popped out into the New England sky to land safely and be inducted into the caterpillar club, an association of successful parachutists.

Formation flying was the first order of training. First in two's and three's, then in the standard four-plane flight the pilots learned the basic grouping in which they would meet the enemy. Then there was practice in navigation and instrument flying before the pilots took up high-altitude flying which was to be the P-47's main regime since it developed maximum efficiency at 20,000 to 40,000 feet. After they had attained an acceptable degree of proficiency the pilots began gunnery training and finally the aerobatics and mock combat that young fighter pilots love so much.

There were some dangers in acquiring all the skills necessary to successfully pilot the Thunderbolt. Lieutenant Larry O'Neill discovered some of those dangers to his own peril during a high altitude aerobatics mission over Cape Ann on March 19, 1943. He took off at about 10:15 in the morning and started a lengthy climb along the Atlantic coast.

He made one serious error, however, that would dictate future practice in the 348th Fighter Group. While he set the oil cooler flaps at neutral, shut the intercoolers, put the supercharger at 10,000 rpm's with the engine on full power, he also turned the oxygen on to emergency. That last item wasted the precious oxygen at a terrific rate before O'Neill ever became aware of it.

The last thing that he remembered was the altimeter passing 20,000 feet when he drifted into unconsciousness like a porous cup losing all its liquid. He woke up minutes later and all the instruments on the panel before his eyes were unwinding with crazy speed. Out the divided windscreen was not the blue of the open sky but undulating gray and blue-green of the sea waves.

His mind was still unable to register the data that his eyes were receiving, except for the fear that was already pumping adrenaline into his nerves. Somehow, his training took hold and he revived enough to roll in a little trim and pull back hard enough on the control column to raise the nose enough to pull up into a zoom climb.

The screaming P-47 began to shudder at the top of the zoom with the first indication of a high-speed stall before O'Neill kicked the plane over on the left wing and managed with the help of a bit of aileron trim to level off at 3,000 feet. He looked around and saw only water, but oriented himself with the gyro compass and headed in the direction of land. The oxygen meter read below 100, but at the lower altitude even that minimal amount flowed easily into the mask. The shaken pilot landed safely at the Bedford Airdrome.

Major Kearby was obliged to learn about the P-47 with the rest of his pilots since his recent flying experience had been in a low altitude P-39 while he commanded the 14th Pursuit Squadron in Panama. He quickly learned to appreciate the advantage of the P-47. Although it was certainly clumsy at lower altitudes with a rate of climb almost legendary in its modesty, the big fighter changed nature at higher levels. Kearby was one of the first to realize that the P-47 could not only dive like a rocket, but that it would zoom with authority, aided by the power of its dive inertia.

The P-47 had also been designed to absorb a six-ton impact and therefore had some claim to impunity when attacking well-defended targets. One story suggests that a P-47 flew through a brick factory, shedding its wings along the way, and landed on the other side of the building with an uninjured pilot in the cockpit.

Also endearing to Kearby was the armament, which was comprised of eight .50 caliber machine guns in the wings. Most P-47 pilots shared this affection for the fighter which Kearby learned to fly and trust in anticipation of joining the European war.

Westover improved by the end of 1942 in terms of facilities for enlisted personnel. The 348th was on garrison rations and the enlisted ranks lived in two-story wooden barracks, for the most part. A newspaper, THE WESTOVER FLYER, was published for the benefit of base personnel, and the basic amenities of civilian life were roughly duplicated.

One of the things that kept the 348th thoroughly military was early morning reveille. Postwar variation in individual schedules made the barbaric practice impractical for anything but basic training, but the bleating notes were widespread during World War II.

A 340th Squadron NCO, Sergeant Panconi, had a habit of sleeping through the call and was challenged by the Charge of Quarters one morning early in 1943. He simply replied to the effect that he was going to be a flop as a soldier because he didn't know one tune from another.

Private Ed Launer wrote a column for the newspaper and picked up the story for a 340th Squadron contribution. Launer had been fortunate simply to be in the Army (if fortunate is the word) because of disqualifying physical conditions, especially his eyes. He did not elect the Army Air forces or the 348th Fighter Group, but took to the experience with some enthusiasm on the feeling that the group was destined to be a great one.

During the 348th Fighter Group's term at Bedford Airdrome from January 13 to April 28, 1943, the training schedule was intensified to the point that all air and ground personnel would be prepared for combat. It was still assumed that Germany would be the enemy the 348th would face and everyone braced for the contest with Messerschmitt and Focke Wulf.

Officers not only attained proficiency with their P-47s in aerial combat but also learned to handle the .45 caliber pistol, assimilated the basics of first aid and got in plenty of the physical training that developed the body while dulling the mind with its unremittingly dead repetition. There was also lots of aircraft recognition drill, gas mask instruction and the famous sex hygiene films for enlisted and commissioned alike.

In spite of the drudgery of ground training there was always the dangers associated with flying training. One 342nd pilot was

Lt. Bob Gibb, an ace of the 342nd, was later killed in action over Korea.

Lt. Larry O'Neill

lost in a crash on March 1, 1943, and the 341st had a double tragedy on April 12 when two P-47s collided during a training maneuver and the pilots were lost in the subsequent crashes.

But the training process did go on and the 348th was becoming honed to a combat edge. It was clear that Kearby was getting the results he wanted with the advanced proficiency shown by the 348th formations at the beginning of March 1943.

A new commander of the New York Air Defense Wing was appointed late in January 1943 in the person of Brigadier General Earl E. Partridge. At the time there were between six to ten fighter groups in the wing, including the 348th. Most of the groups were equipped with P-47s and were destined for Europe. At least two of the units—the 56th and 352nd Fighter Groups—became famous while fighting with the Eighth Air Force out of England.

There was a reception supper for General Partridge at the stately Hotel New Yorker on the evening of March 4, 1943. It was the usual military affair with each unit being represented in block sections at the tables with junior officers waiting dutifully behind their respective chairs until senior officers were seated.

The customary black cigar was smoked by every man after the dinner and the rounds of speeches and toasts began. Sometime during the late hours of the affair someone stood up, raised his glass and offered, "Gentlemen, I give you the 348th Fighter Group." Partridge nodded and took a sip of his wine with a polite smile.

He may have had a moment of wanting to retract his endorsement of that toast when he paid the 348th an unannounced visit a month later at Bedford. General officers should know better than to make surprise appearances and Partridge paid for it with a bit of inconvenience and embarrassment.

For one thing, Kearby had left for six days leave on April 3, just two days before Partridge arrived. Everything went wrong from the beginning and the 348th staff was caught flatfooted in a bout of handwringing, bowing and scraping. Group records state that a fatal accident occurred two days into the general's visit which hardly served to lighten the mood of the occasion. There were other decidedly more minor mishaps that Partridge tried to laugh off in the spirit of salvaging morale.

The final piece of missed timing came when Partridge was preparing to leave and was left standing waiting for his assigned transportation which, as it happened, failed to arrive. If the group officers in charge were concerned about their careers before they probably hoped for something as lenient as a Fort Leavenworth rock pile when the taxi that was hastily called was turned away at the gate. Nobody had thought to contact the guards at the gate to authorize the taxi on the base.

Partridge finally called up his own staff car from New York City and left Bedford in the dust without much more comment. When Kearby returned on April 9 he may have noticed some anxiety on the faces of his officers, but apparently never discovered the reason.

In any event, the 348th was about to receive orders for overseas shipment. In February, Major Bob Rowland, another luminary who would become an ace and eventually command the 348th, replaced Bill Hovis as executive officer when he moved up to Headquarters, New York Air Defense Wing.

During the same time events on world battlefronts were having their effect on the 348th. General George Kenney's Fifth Air Force was desperately shorthanded at the time that he was trying to defend Port Moresby as well as prevent the Japanese from reinforcing their northern New Guinea garrisons.

General Kenney was attempting to do everything with an air force that was outnumbered about two to one, and with worn out fighters of limited range. What he really wanted was at least three groups of P-38 fighters with the speed, range and altitude to help do the job. In addition, the P-38 had already proved itself to have an impressive rate of climb, having the ability to reach Japanese bomber formations with about a half-hour's warning.

In spite of all the P-47's lamented short range and slow climb, Kenney preferred it to the P-40. He thought the P-47 was probably a perfectly good fighter, "...in spite of some of the adverse comments from England." He protested when he was promised another P-40N group in July. His anguished cries were answered when he was promised, instead, a P-38 group in place of the P-40s — and a P-47 unit originally scheduled for England.

By the end of March it was decided by the Operations Division, War Department Staff that the 348th would be diverted to the Fifth Air Force. The Group's P-47s were unlikely to be ready for shipment since they were plagued by difficulties. Certain engine adjustments had to be made to prevent piston and ignition failure. There were also troublesome radio noises and, worst of all, fire hazards appeared and had to be eliminated.

Flight and ground personnel were scheduled to depart early in May and the aircraft would be ready by June 12. TSgt Iddings had been to the Republic school to learn how to repair the P-47 and was back in the 342nd Squadron in time for the scramble to prepare for movement to a combat area. The 342nd and Headquarters moved

Major Gallagher, 342nd FS Commander.

Lt. Walter Benz D Flight Leader.

back to Westover from Bedford while the 340th and 341st returned from Green Field, Rhode Island, where the two squadrons had conducted their winter training, on April 26.

Two pilots who joined the 340th during its training were captains Hervey Carpenter and Max Wiecks. Both men had already been to the operational theater to which the 348th was assigned and had been seasoned in combat with the P-39 Airacobra. Carpenter would take command of the squadron after MacDonald left and Wiecks would have the honor of claiming the 348th's first confirmed air victory.

Even with the hectic preparation for overseas movement the 348th continued to train and sharpen its skills in becoming a deadly combat unit. By the end of March the pilots had averaged about 185 hours in P-47s and were expert enough to have almost as much confidence in the type as Kearby, who, incidentally, was promoted to Lieutenant Colonel in November 1942.

On May 9, 1943, the group moved to Camp Shanks, New York, in the final stage of preparation for overseas shipment. One 340th member who would not be going was Pvt. Ed Launer. The squadron journalist who had fought just to stay in the Army in spite of disqualifying physical defects was mustered out while his unit was racing around like squirrels in a cage, preparing to go to war.

Even though he was in the 348th only a few months, Launer was right about its eventual greatness and maintained his association with his old comrades through the years.

If there had been any lingering doubts about which war the 348th would be entering, those doubts disappeared during the first days of the voyage. The 348th had boarded the Army transport HENRY GIBBONS on May 14 and sailed the next day. The ship headed south into the Atlantic and on the twenty-first of May passed through the Panama Canal enroute to the Pacific.

There was no doubt about the matter now. The final stop would be somewhere in range of the Japanese. More than one pilot tried to hunt up recognition books to brush up on identification of Japanese aircraft types. Nearly everybody was eager to find available performance specifications on the Mitsubishi A6m Zero

Chapter 3

The 348th Comes to the SWPA

By June of 1943 the V Fighter Command had fewer than 450 fighters of all types including fifty-nine P-47s. Whatever the judgment may have been in the SWPA (Southwest Pacific Area) regarding the P-47 there were a number of brand-new fighters being assembled on the docks and they were certainly more promising than the worn-out P-39s and P-40s which sometimes could not even reach the combat area due to malfunctions.

There were shortages of everything on the New Guinea front and maintenance took an appallingly long time in the service life of fighter aircraft. The Service Command was doing remarkable things in modifying aircraft for the conditions of the theater. Command technicians were converting P-40s and P-39s to late model standards, modifying landing gear and fuel systems and adapting gunnery systems to the needs of the local battle conditions.

Perhaps the most ambitious and useful activity of the Service Command was the attempt to extend the range of fighter aircraft. By the middle of August 1943 a project was underway to install a "Fifth Air Force leak-proof tank" with fifteen to twenty gallons more integral fuel capacity. Less than a month later General Kenney had started a production line in Sydney to rework all spare wings and eventually replace those on aircraft in the squadrons.

A concurrent and even more urgent project was the development of a belly tank for the P-47. One of the things that Kenney did not like about the P-47 was its range which he insisted was even more restricted than that of the P-40. He bemoaned the fact that engineers back home were more concerned with the European theater than with the problems he faced in the wide Pacific. The necessary decision to beat Germany first had made the SWPA a poor relative.

"(They are developing planes with no) more range than is needed to defend London or to make a fighter sweep across a ditch no bigger than Chesapeake Bay," was the way he is quoted as having voiced the complaint.

The answer for the P-47 came in the form of external belly tanks developed in the SWPA. No tanks had been sent with the 348th aircraft and it was discovered that a Materiel Command's 200 gallon tank was unusable because of the tail buffeting it caused. At the beginning of July the 27th Depot Repair Squadron at Port Moresby was ordered to design as quickly as possible a suitable tank. At first, the 110-gallon tank used on P-39s and P-40s was modified to accommodate the P-47. Kenney asked Patterson Field to supply enough kits to make the modification and received the reply that requirements of other theaters would restrict delivery to a point that would delay entry of the P-47 into combat for another two months.

Colonel Neel Kearby: A tall, drawling Texan who was considered the master fighter pilot. (C.R. Cronk)

ABOVE & FOLLOWING: Kearby leads an eight plane formation early in the 348th's operational career. Identifiable numbers: 73, 56, 54, 70, 51, 61 and 59.

Finally, an effective 200-gallon tank was developed at Brisbane by the beginning of August. The tank was, in fact, superior to the tanks being developed in the United States and became standard in the Southwest Pacific. The 27th Repair Squadron installed the new tank and found it could be adapted to the P-47 with few modifications of existing booster pumps and motors.

During this time the 348th was making its way toward its first operational base in New Guinea. On June 4 the men on the HENRY GIBBONS heard the anchor drop and splash into the water off Bora in the Society Islands. Sergeant Joe Moor was part of the 342nd medical detachment and had seen enough of the pervasive seasickness during the voyage. The Free French island was the most beautiful he had ever seen and was a pleasant change from the constant lines of sick men at the head.

Local natives came out to the ship in their dugouts to sell fresh fruit. Moor was impressed by the classic blue-green of the water and the colorful fruit loaded in the boats. Payment was made by tossing coins in the water for the natives to dive for and retrieve in the best tradition of Hollywood films.

The rest of the trip was entirely uneventful and the destination was effectively tipped when booklets on customs of Australia were passed out. Brisbane was reached on June 14 and the nurses and air

ABOVE & BOTTOM: Early squadron commanders (340th) Charles MacDonald and (341st) David Campbell.

personnel were disembarked. The ground echelon stayed on the boat until it reached Townsville on the northern Australia coast at dusk on June 23.

Those men of the air echelon who trudged off the boat—about sixty-five pilots and mechanics in all—were assigned quarters at Eagle Farms; the major aircraft testing and assembly facility. While they waited for the promised one-hundred P-47s of the 348th allotment there was the social scene to be explored. There was, of course, the local pub scene as well as the unique sights of north Australia and even the horse track at Albion Park.

By the time most of the 348th personnel had acquired a taste for the indigenous liquor and learned to scout out whatever female population remained in the vicinity, the P-47s began to arrive. It took minimum time to assemble the fighters, fly them to Archer Field for ten hours of checkflight and boresighting and get them accepted for squadron service. On the flip of a coin the 342nd Squadron got the first P-47s, then the 341st and finally the 340th.

During this time Joe Moor had been making his way to Port Moresby with the rest of the 342nd. They were taken off the transport to a lighter which ferried them to a pier where they were picked up by black soldiers and driven by truck to the foothills northwest of Port Moresby. Moor was reminded of this night after the war when he learned of the famous "Red Ball Express," a detachment of trucks driven by determined black soldiers to keep the American Army supplied during critical periods in the European fighting.

The driver of Moor's truck was right next to him and began to smile a little conspiratorial smile. Between jostles on the rudimentary road Moor wondered what the man was up to. He showed Moor a moment later when he pushed up the sleeve of his jacket and there glittering in the moonlight were at least six watches. Nobody in the 348th had much money so there was no sale.

It was the evening of June 23, 1943, on the island of New Guinea, heading north to meet the Japanese. Moor thought to himself that it was a fine entry into Doug MacArthur's war.

Moor and the rest of the 342nd Squadron arrived at Ward's Drome, five miles northwest of Port Moresby. It was terribly hot and dusty and Moor reflected that he and his squadronmates did not get a change of gear before the switch of assignments from a colder European climate. With some sense of humor they unpacked wool olive drab issue, heavy overcoats and long-john underwear. There was little for them to wear in the tropics.

The first of the eighty-five erected P-47s arrived soon afterward and Moor was on ambulance duty to meet them at the revetment. There was some pronounced excitement amongst the RAAF groundcrewmen at the mammoth size of the seven-ton P-47. "Where is the rest of the crew?" Moor heard one of the astonished Australians exclaim. The P-40 fighters that they usually serviced were about half the size of the massive Thunderbolt.

Major David Campbell took the 341st Squadron into the area of his old 35th Squadron. The 35th would take the 341st under its wing and teach it the ways of New Guinea combat and camp life and then turn over its lovely new mess hall and well-ordered camp to find other less agreeable living quarters. The 35th people were glad to see Campbell again, but chafed at the prospect of being evicted from their relatively comfortable quarters. It was the old army maxim that soldiers should never get too accustomed to any one place, since they are almost certain to be relocated eventually.

At the end of July there were twenty-five P-47D-2's erected in the 341st Squadron revetment and orientation flights were made up and down the Port Moresby coast. When the 35th Squadron grumbled its way out of the area to new camps, the 341st took over

Lt. Desilets was lost in this P-47D-2 (42-8059) - photographed 7/11/43.

Lt. Jim Nixon of the 341st and his pups.

the pyramid tents that were lined up on streets named Malaria Lane, Latrine Walk, Atabrine Row and Mosquito Drive. The squadron settled in and waited for action.

If some of the problems were being worked out and the 348th squadrons were spoiling for action there was still less than an enthusiastic response to the P-47 in the theater. General Wurtsmith headed V Fighter Command and saw the P-47 only in terms of missed opportunities to meet the Japanese in decisive aerial engagements. Other Fifth Air Force leaders saw the P-47 as the only fighter in their inventory with an aircooled engine, that it was less maneuverable than other fighter types at low altitude where Japanese aircraft mostly operated and that its range was a question mark for the present.

But Neel Kearby arrived in Australia with no thought of becoming discouraged. He reacted vigorously to the negative attitude that was almost universally directed toward the P-47. He defended the fighter so enthusiastically that some long lived feuds developed between advocates of the P-38 and the P-47. Most Fifth Air Force people pointed out that the P-38 not only had crucial performance advantages over the Zero, but that the Lockheed had remarkable range and a twin-engine configuration which gave its pilots a decided boost in morale on long, overwater flights.

Kearby responded that the P-47 was capable of extended cruise flights at high altitude and that it could convert altitude into flashing speed at lower heights, neutralizing any maneuverability advantage enjoyed by the Japanese. He closed his argument by suggesting that mass production of the P-47 would make it more plentiful than the P-38—and certainly more available.

General Kenney was not much more convinced about the value of the P-47, but remained positive about its deployment. "No matter what objections there are to the P-47," he concluded, "it has eight guns and is faster than the Zero at any altitude, so I will use it and gladly take all I can get."

By the time Kearby arrived at Port Moresby he had lost none of his aggressive attitude. General Kenney remembered that the first thing Kearby wanted to know when they met was who had the top score in aerial kills and how soon could he get into action. Kenney and the rest of the leadership of the Fifth Air Force were known to be what was termed "operators" by the crews who were doing the fighting. They were people who went into action without delay and Kearby fit right into the scheme of things. Kenney is quoted as saying that Kearby looked like money in the bank to him.

Kearby's fervor in evangelizing for the P-47 produced some predictable reactions in New Guinea. There is one apocryphal incident claiming that Kearby flew his P-47 in mock combat against Dick Bong in a P 38. There are some witnesses who vaguely recall the contest, but can add no details other than the contest seemed to end more or less in a draw. It seems incredible that such an epic demonstration should not have drawn more attention, but perhaps no particular significance was assigned to the event. Bong was already a high-scoring ace with about sixteen kills at the time while Kearby had yet to establish his record.

One thing that is certain is the fact that the contest took place around August 1, 1943. One veteran who does remember some details of the mock combat is Wallace Jordan, one of the commanders and at the time a P-38 pilot of Bong's own 9th Fighter Squadron. Jordan recalls that the two pilots squared off at an altitude and position in view of Port Moresby. He may have been less than objec-

P-47s of the 342nd Squadron in the latter part of 1943.

Ward's Drome 14 September 1943. Note Grant's P-47 on left, special tanks on right. (USAF)

tive, but Jordan gives the edge to Bong after an impressive show put up by both of the superb fighter pilots.

Jordan, by the way, served in the 9th during its tenure with both the P-38 and P-47. Using his most objective manner he gives high marks to the P-47 in terms of firepower, diving speed and roll. It would appear that the P-47 did make converts, even in that P-38 sanctum sanctorum of the 49th Fighter Group's 9th Squadron.

Whatever public relations activities Kearby used to sell the P-47 he still worked the 348th hard to prepare it for combat. He was still convinced that high-speed runs from altitude would turn the P-47 into a devastating weapon for the impending offensive against the Japanese. He was keen to give the Thunderbolt pilots another edge by training them to find the Japanese first and to strike before the enemy could react.

A training tactic implemented sometime after the 348th entered combat could be used to illustrate the sort of teamwork Kearby instilled into the group to make it an exceptionally alert battle unit. A squadron of sixteen P-47s would fly at altitude with the four flights staggered about two-thousand feet from top to bottom. The lead flight would scan ahead and below for possible targets while the second flight would fly at the tip of the formation, about five-hundred feet above the others, to concentrate behind and above. The other two flights would range to the side and rear in sight of the second flight and as protection for the lead flight. This particular formation depended on each pilot to exercise a vital observer's mission. Whether or not the formation was instrumental in the 348th's subsequent successes there was a certain deadliness in the group's ability to sight the enemy first and attack from advantage.

Despite all the problems and negative reception of the P-47 the 348th became ready by the end of July 1943. Because of the slow climb rate demonstrated by the P-47 the group was confined to the Port Moresby area where at least an hour's warning could be expected before an air attack. The first missions were the usual ones, local patrol or escort of C-47 transports. Aside from the orientation flights the 348th began operational sorties inauspiciously around the end of July or the beginning of August.

Kila Drome (3 Mile) 20 May 1943. (USAF)

Joe Moor and his twin brother Bill started their duties in the medical and dental departments of the 342nd Squadron. They were so identical that they could be told apart only by rank. At the time that they were both Staff Sergeants it must have been hellish trying to give them specific assignments or discipline. *The two brothers thought is was a splendid joke on the Army Air Forces. Joe was not so terribly amused by the state of supply during those days of New Guinea circa the latter part of 1943.** Even though General MacArthur's decisions regarding little things like furloughs or rotation back home did not make him popular with his troops, he did manage to exert enough influence on the Navy to at least keep the bare essentials coming in. If the Navy had its way the Central Pacific would be the only active theater and the Fifth Air Force would be a backwater unit.

Be that as it may, MacArthur and Kenney managed not only to hold the line in New Guinea, but arranged some impressive operations like the Bismarck Sea battle in March 1943 to affect the entire Pacific war. The Japanese considered the New Guinea front important enough to send in major land and air reinforcements throughout the end of 1942 and first months of 1943.

If the first few missions of the 348th were uneventful then the actions of the next few weeks in August and September made up for it with a vengeance. Like a tightly wound spring that is released the 348th met some of those air reinforcements over Wewak and exploded into a sensational bout of scoring that would secure its reputation in the Pacific and immortalize its commander in the history of fighter aviation.

* One of the Moors would sass a superior non-commissioned officer who would be frustrated in determining the guilty one for retribution.

** shortages in anesthetics and antiseptics, for example, kept things grim.

Chapter 4

Into Combat

TO: INTELLIGENCE OFFICER, THREE FORTY EIGHTH FIGHTER GROUP
FROM 340FS
A. Field Order No. 38 - August 16, 1943 - 340th Fighter Squadron -
16 P-47s.
B. Close escort for Transports to Marilinan and return.

C. Takeoff 1320/K, arriving at target at 1424/K. Patrolled at 13,000 feet for 35 minutes. Engaged enemy aircraft at 1500/K. Departed from target at 1555/K, landing at base 1625/K.

D. Enemy losses: 2 Oscars. Our losses: Nil.

E. through J. Nil.

K. WEATHER:

Over target: Scattered cumulus at 8,000 to 9,000 feet. C. A. V. U.
Route back: Broken clouds up to 10,000 feet.

L. GENERAL:

While patrolling target at Marilinan, with escorted Transports landed, Shadow warned of approaching enemy aircraft. In about five minutes 11 or 12 Oscars were observed at about 15,000 feet.

Our aircraft were circling Marilinan at from 10,000 to 13,000 feet. P-38s were top cover at from 18,000 to 20,000 feet. The Oscars dived on our airplanes and individual combat ensued. One Oscar dove on a P-47 and was observed by its pilot, Lt. T.J. Barber, at about 1,000 feet above him. This Oscar passed in front of the P-47 at 500 yards, at an angle of 45 degrees. The P-47 gave chase and fired two bursts at a range of about 200 yards and at an altitude of 6,000 feet. Tracer bullets made circles around the Zero. The enemy aircraft fell after two short bursts. Lt. John A. Matson, a pilot in this squadron, confirms destruction of this Zero, stating that he saw puffs made by penetrating bullets, and subsequently saw the Zero go into an unnatural diving position. The Oscar had brown wings, with red roundels on each wing.

Another Oscar was escaping a dive made by a P-38 which had overpassed. This Oscar climbed from under a P-47 piloted by Captain (Max) R. Wiecks and passed in front of his P-47 at a distance of about 500 yards, making an Immelman turn. When the turn was complete, with both planes approaching each other, the P-47 opened fire head on and continued until the planes had passed each other at a distance of not more than five yards. This pilot states that the left wing of the enemy plane was badly dipping as he passed. Lt. Charles M. Allen and Lt. Myron Hnatio, pilots in this squadron, saw the enemy airplane fall in flames and confirm its destruction.

Before completing escort mission, one P-47 developed an oil leak and returned to base with an escort, landing at 1416. These two planes did not engage the enemy.

340th FS Insignia

342nd FS Insignia

By July 1, 1943, the 340th Fighter Squadron was installed in what was to become known as "Thunderbolt Valley," a camp area near Jackson Drome, seven miles from Port Moresby. The first 340th P-47s came up to Thunderbolt Valley visual range on July 24, flown in by some of the squadron pilots. Details of 340th enlisted men had moved up by truck from Kila Drome and built up the camp from scratch. Two latrines, a mess hall, an orderly room and a shower bath were constructed as basic necessities. The characteristic pyramid tents and open-air maintenance stands of the Fifth Air Force would appear soon as would a day room and the vital officer's club.

The 340th had shared quarters with the famed "Headhunters" of the 80th Fighter Squadron at Kila from the end of June. On July 11, all personnel moved up to the new base at Jackson's Drome and were quickly settled in and itching for action. By the time the first P-47s arrived there was an exuberance among the crews to get at the enemy as soon as possible. Capt. Max Wiecks was not exempt from the enthusiasm, but knew from experience that every bit of training was needed before facing the Japanese.

Fortunately, for the first few missions, the 340th joined the other 348th squadrons in area patrols over Port Moresby and sup-

340th FS at Port Moresby. Front row: unknown, unknown, unknown, Lynn Parsons, Harry Setzer, Jim Pressly, Richard Lake. Middle row: Mike Dikovitsky, Mahoney, Ambrocenia, Maj. Charles MacDonald (CO) Carpenter, Zaage, Harry Quandt. Back row: "Doc" Bassamania, Bill Chase, unknown, Floyd Meyer, Max Wiecks and Frank Oksala.

340th FS White Flight Port Moresby. 1st row: G. Woodruff, R. Frost, Max Wiecks, Lt. Monroe, Thomas Barker Back Row: Stanley Souders, Lt. Riley, Lyle Dowsett, Richard Lake, Frank Schmidt.

plying air cover for transports going to Wau, Tsili and other forward bases. It wasn't until August 16 that the 340th got close enough to engage the Japanese and then it did well for itself and as well as the entire group.

Marilinan was a small forward base about fifty miles inland from the Huon Gulf, midway between the coastal towns of Lae and Salamaua. The 340th put up sixteen P-47s on the afternoon of the sixteenth to patrol the area as close cover for transports. All three squadrons of the 348th were patrolling somewhere in the Huon Valley when Japanese Ki-43 "Oscar" formations were sighted.

Wiecks had taken his P-47 formation to an altitude of about 11,000 feet over the Maralinan area when the controller called out an enemy formation closing in. He looked through the top of his P-47 and saw two Oscars flying off to the left, coming around to attack the P-47 flight behind. Ahead was another Oscar about 600 yards away, zooming up in an Immelman turn to face the P-47s.

OPPOSITE: 340th FS Red Flight Port Moresby, mid to late 1943. Standing: Harry Setzer, Jerome Fischer, Hervey Carpenter, (Flt. CO) Bill Bennett, Marion Burt, Sitting: Floyd Meyer, Harry Quandt, Bernard Mahoney, Guy Johnston, Norman Tufford Guy "Johnny" Johnston scored one of the first group victories on October 16, 1943. Two days later at LAE another P-47 ran up the tail of Johnston's P-47 and ruined the rudder. Fortunately, another wrecked P-47 with a usable rudder was nearby and repairs were made, enabling Johnston to return to Jackson's Drome.

"After completion of the Immelman," Wiecks later reported, "he made a turn to the left at my level. While in this turn I fired two short bursts, but the range was too far. I continued to close on him and he completed his turn and came head on at me. While in this turn I fired a steady burst approximately 700 rounds and noticed just before our planes passed the he started to fall off on his left wing."

Lieutenant Charles Allen was behind Wiecks in the flight that was jumped by the Oscars. One of the Japanese fighters latched onto Allen's tail and he was obliged to dive away. Looking back, Allen was relieved to see the Oscar break away with a P-38 making a pass from the rear.

Captain Warren Lewis of the 431st Fighter Squadron happened to be in the area when the thirteen P-38s of his squadron were attacked by the same Oscars. He noticed Allen's P-47 being chased by one enemy fighter after he had cleared his own tail and dove to make a sixty-degree deflection shot from two to three hundred yards away. His fire missed, but the Oscar zoomed right into the sights of Max Wiecks.

Lieutenant Allen watched the Oscar fall off to the left when Wiecks opened fire. After it fell about one hundred yards the glistening jungle-brown and silver Oscar burst into bright flames against the dark landscape beneath. Lieutenant Mike Hnatio was following closely behind Allen also saw Wiecks hit the Oscar, sending it spinning on fire into the jungle.

The 341st Squadron also was reported to have engaged the enemy and claimed an Oscar destroyed. The pilot who was credited with the claim, Lieutenant Leonard Leighton, was hit himself and was seen to have parachuted into the wild New Guinea country below. Some months later his body was discovered by an Allied patrol and he was confirmed as the first combat casualty of the 348th.

Major David Campbell.

Two days later the 342nd Squadron suffered its own first casualty on another transport escort to Wau in the central highlands, inland from the Huon Gulf. Major Gallagher led the sixteen P-47s of the formation through some uncertain weather between 6,000 and 12,000 feet.

Sixteen fighters went into the overcast, but two were missing when the formation emerged on the other side. Some of the pilots were decidedly inexperienced and losses were not out of the question in such a situation. As it happened, Flight Officer Wilfrid Desilets went into the overcast and was simply never seen again.

The other loss was not quite so unfortunate. Lieutenant Cyril Andrews was flying the leader's wing when they plunged into the clouds at 6,000 feet. In the dark interior of the murky haze Andrews became disoriented, his P-47 went out of control and he bailed out around 1,000 feet above the treetops.

His parachute opened, but became entangled in those hostile treetops, leaving him dangling 100 feet above the ground. Not wanting to remain hanging there as an obvious target for Japanese pa-

340th FS Yellow Flight Port Moresby. Standing: James Pressly, Lloyd Zaage, William Chase, Lynn Parsons, Guy Roberts, Sitting: Vernon Turner, Mike Dikovitsky, Joel Pitchford, Robert McNulty, Alexander Ritsch.

Campbell and Blair.

trols he cut himself free and dropped through the branches of the tree to the ground.

He immediately regretted his haste when the excruciating pain between his right hip and knee told him that his leg was fractured. He could only lie where he fell and curse his condition when any attempt to move some distance produced stark agony. Fortunately, he was near enough to a stream to reach water with his left hand and his rubber raft was beneath him to offer some protection from the ground. He was able to use some of the parachute cloth to cover himself for additional relief from the elements. the only food he had was the "D" ration bar in his jungle kit.

All through the next day Andrews drifted in and out of sleep to conserve his strength. At one point he heard the unmistakable sound of a P-47 engine and spotted what must have been Captain Ed Roddy searching the area for him and Desilets. If he had a mirror or flare gun Andrews was sure he could have signaled the plane overhead. He had heard his own plane crash nearby, but it probably couldn't be spotted any easier than he could.

It wasn't until he had spent three days and two nights of arduous crawling along the ground that some friendly natives found him and put a splint on his leg before they carried him to their village. They cared for him until local troops came along and took him to Garaina strip where he was flown out to Port Moresby. Later, Andrews found the exact spot where he went down, about twenty miles southwest of Garaina on the side of Mt. Batchelor.

In the first few days of operations the 348th had lost three P-47s and two pilots for one definite Oscar claimed destroyed and perhaps three others listed as probably destroyed or damaged. During the same time the 475th Fighter Group had claimed more than twenty-five Japanese shot down for the loss of two P-38s and one pilot. The 475th was made up of some the best pilots collected from combat-hardened squadrons. This instant crack unit completely dominated the sky in its first big shows and understandably outshone the 348th which was not supposed to be in the same league with a P-38 unit.

Thus, the opinion was reinforced that the P-47 could not really compete with the P-38 in combat against the Japanese. Kearby was out in the field selling the P-47 and was pleased that the 348th had been blooded during August. He still yearned for an all out crack at the Japanese which would prove his point that large formations of P-47s piloted by properly trained and motivated fighting men would sweep the skies wherever they appeared.

Whatever his hopes, Kearby's men still worked at the mundane tasks of settling in to New Guinea camp life. Sgt. Charles Fox

David Campbell by "Miss Jaqueline" (Letters are yellow).

of the 342nd Squadron was amazed at the temperature transformation within four months' time from the 27° below Fahrenheit of Bedford to the blast furnace temperatures of inland New Guinea.

His first meal in the mess hall at Ward's Drome gave Fox some inkling of what life for a crew chief in the Fifth Air Force would be like. He noticed a fly in his coffee and naturally dumped it and got another cup. SSgt Roscoe "Ace" Slider was sitting across the table and laughingly took Fox and the other new hands into his confidence.

"Look, here's the way it is," Slider told them, "the first couple of months you dump the coffee out when you see a fly in it. After a couple of months, you just blow the fly to the other end of the cup. At six months, when you see a fly in your coffee, you get out your knife and fork because it will be the first fresh meat you will have."

Fox just blinked at Slider's remarks, but came to realize that it wasn't all a joke. Some of the things he thought of as inedible then were delicacies later—but never the universal Australian bully beef.

Slider was an old AAF mechanic who was picked to head up the crew on Kearby's P-47 when it was maintained in the 342nd Squadron. Apparently, Slider and Kearby did not get along and the colonel knew better than to butt heads with his crew chief. He moved his P-47 named "Fiery Ginger" to the 341st Squadron by the end of the year where Ssgt Pankyo tended to the airplane until Kearby was lost.

At first, Charles Fox was an assistant crew chief on Larry O'Neill's P-47, working for Sgt. Stanley Cierakowski. Later, he headed his own crew for Lt. DeWitt Searles. Searles would eventu-

Charles Cronk by "Nip Nipper."

Cronk after 9/22/43 battle.

ally move over to the 460th Fighter Squadron when it was formed as the fourth squadron of the group, and would claim three air victories. Meanwhile, Tsgt Iddings was also becoming accustomed to the 342nd's new home in the bush and was adjusting his schedule to bring up the maintenance efficiency of the flight line. He also managed to get a few anthropology lessons from the curious natives who visited the squadron in their decidedly brief jungle attire.

One of the things that Iddings learned was that the natives weren't entirely stupid. A 342nd sergeant found it screamingly funny that the private parts of the unobtrusive indigenous male population seemed somewhat underdeveloped. Iddings, along with several others, joined this sergeant on a trip to 17-Mile strip to go swimming when a group of native men came walking along the river. The sergeant began pointing at them and making fun when the natives stopped in surprise at his laughing outburst. With a glance at the naked American standing there in the water, the native leader pointed back and led his group in a howl at the sergeant's endowment. A thoroughly embarrassed Yank went into the river for cover and swam to the other side.

Another time, Iddings was visiting some 35th Fighter Group pilots in their tent. These pilots had a houseboy who stopped in and asked his employers how they had done on the day's mission. In the most prosaic terms they announced that a large number of enemy planes had been shot down and so many Japanese troops had been killed in the strafing. It was both an impressive and incredible number.

This houseboy had been educated in a missionary school, so he was a bit more sophisticated than he would have been without exposure to western culture. He turned to the 342nd visitor, smiled and said, "They snow me."

Up to the beginning of September V Fighter Command was restricted to local defense or closely escorting bombers to Japanese bases from which the enemy could intercept at his own discretion. Freedom of action was what Kearby craved and he, among other fighter leaders, argued for the free sweeps that would allow the fighters to aggressively seek out and attack the Japanese wherever they could be found. Oddly enough, Kearby saw his first real action and made his first victory claims during one of the interceptions which he had hoped to replace with the free fighter sweeps.

Pressure on Japanese bases around the Huon peninsula had reached a climax at the beginning of September when an Allied invasion fleet set out to land at Lae on the 5th. Japanese response was immediate and desperate with a large attack on the convoy during September 4. Twelve G4m "Betty" bombers with eight divebombers covered by more than sixty fighters assaulted the Allied ships.

When the first order came early in the afternoon of September 4 it specified an interception of bogeys in the Morobe, Salamaua and Finschhafen vicinities. There was an expected Japanese response to the upcoming invasion, but it was probably not anticipated so soon. The American interception was, at first, casual and seemingly routine.

The 342nd Fighter Squadron's Yellow Flight was the first off to scramble against the bogeys around Morobe at about two o'clock in the afternoon. Seven more P-47s of Blue and Green Flights were off a few minutes later. Kearby sensed a battle in the making and led the last flight of the twenty 348th Group fighters to take off from Dobodura.

At about 2:30 around fourteen miles south of Hopoi Beach, east of Lae, at 25,000 feet Kearby's flight saw what seemed to be a flying boat with a fighter off each wing just off the water. Kearby hated to lose precious altitude, but there were signs of fighting with bombing evident in the Morobe area to the south and several fires in the water near Cape Ward Hunt even farther to the south.

Kearby decided to let down and identify the three aircraft below. When he got down to about two-thousand feet he could see the gray mottle camouflage on what could now be identified as a Betty bomber with a Zero or Oscar off either wing. The three Japanese planes were flying to the northeast and Kearby turned his flight to attack them from behind.

Kearby came in at an indicated airspeed of 400 miles per hour until he could plainly see the red insignia on the bomber and its escorts. He closed to about three-hundred yards, slightly above and to the left of the Japanese. Nervously, he checked the gunsight again and again with an impatience borne of his first real air combat.

This time even the master dogfighter got a little greedy and set his sights on both the bomber and one of the fighters with a one-half radii lead, hoping to get both of them. The first tracers arced out and seemed to circle the Oscar before Kearby settled down and concentrated on the Betty.

Tracers converged on the obviously surprised target and pieces of metal flew off in every direction before the bomber burst into flames. The P-47 roared over the small Japanese formation before any of the enemy crews could react and Kearby looked back long enough to see the Betty wrapped in flames as it settled into the froth it had churned up only a moment before when it splashed into the sea.

There was no sign of the escort when Kearby twisted around in his cockpit to look high and low, making sure that somebody didn't do to him what he had just done to the Betty. He then sighted one of the Oscars climbing away and concluded that there was no

Lt. Hodge of the 341st Squadron. (C.J. Blend)

danger being attacked from that quarter since the speed of his P-47 was sufficient to quickly take it out of range.

With a little luck there was an opportunity to get this fighter, too. Kearby turned back to attack, but the Japanese fighter executed a neat climbing turn before he could get in range. Fifth Air Force veterans sometimes compare the performance of the Oscar to that of a butterfly and this Japanese pilot could maneuver his agile little fighter well enough to make Kearby break off and then get on the tail of the number three P47 in the flight.

Kearby dived once again to the attack, but when he raised his sights he could see only the P-47 ahead of him in the clear. Apparently, the Oscar had thought better of attacking a superior number of American fighters and used the amazing maneuverability of his Oscar once again to escape. George Orr was Kearby's wingman and reported later that the first Oscar had dived into the water when Kearby fired on it.

The four P-47s continued to patrol until about fifteen minutes after three when the fuel of the second element forced numbers three and four P-47s in the flight to retire. Kearby and Orr continued to orbit the area for about another hour until their own fuel shortage caused them to return to base.

Although many of the twenty P-47s participated in the action and some probables were claimed, only Kearby claimed confirmed kills in his P-47D-2. Again, P-38s had the lion's share of kills with eighteen confirmations.

The Japanese Navy reported to the Emperor the loss of three Bettys and four Zeros on this mission. In addition, another Betty and two divebombers apparently made crash landings back at their bases. It is possible that Kearby engaged a Japanese Army formation since his description of mottled gray camouflage is more likely to have adorned a Ki-21 "Sally" bomber rather than the olive green of the Imperial Navy. Also, it is unlikely that Oscars would be escorting Navy bombers since cooperation between the Japanese services was not up to that standard.

There is no available record of Japanese Army Air Force operations in the area on that date, so it could be assumed that Kearby engaged Imperial Navy aircraft. In that case, he definitely accounted for one of the three missing Bettys.

Kearby was understandably jubilant when he got back to Ward's Drome. George Orr's account gave him credit for the fighter as well as the bomber which was observed by the entire flight to be burning on the water. There were mistakes, to be sure. Kearby knew that his own eagerness had jeopardized a nearly perfect bounce that should have netted both fighters as well as the bomber. If the Japanese had been as alert as they should have been, they perhaps could have escaped or even turned the tables on the Americans.

However, Kearby had proved his point that altitude and speed made the P-47 a formidable weapon against the Japanese. If and when he would be able to range freely with his 348th Fighter Group he could take a terrible toll of the enemy. The opportunity was not long in coming even though the wait must have been frustrating to the energetic Kearby.

In the meantime, the routine missions honed the fighting skills of the young 348th pilots. On a cover mission for transports to Tsili flown September 13, 1943, eight P-47D-2s of the 342nd Fighter Squadron again ran into a force of Oscars, Tonys and Sallys. In a running fight that lasted fifteen minutes the P-47s dived and zoomed, attacking the enemy at every opportunity with overwhelming speed and pure audacity. Kearby's training was beginning to pay off in the first small dividends when Major Bill Banks and Lieutenant Larry O'Neill scored their first victories. Another Tony was claimed as probably destroyed and all P-47s returned to base.

Kearby added to the total on the next day when he led eight other P-47s of the 341st Squadron on a similar mission. He was at the head of White Flight when it reached the Nadzab area at about 9:45 in the morning. They flew around the target for about forty-five minutes when a plot was called in to 8th Fighter Squadron P-40s in the area. Kearby decided to investigate when he realized that his P-47s were higher than the P-40s and probably closer to the bogey.

The P-47s were at twenty thousand feet, but when the bogey was sighted it was even higher and off to the right of the 348th formation. He immediately revealed himself as Japanese when he turned and raced for the clouds.

Lt. Lawrence O'Neill of the 342nd Squadron, September 1943.

Kearby reminded himself that he had a shortage of P-47 belly tanks and ordered his flights over the radio not to drop theirs while he disposed of his. When he looked around he saw that six of his fighters had dropped their tanks anyway and shrugged it off with a mixed feeling of disgust at the breech of discipline and approval of the evident fighting spirit. He learned later that the seventh P-47 pilot would have dropped his also if the thing hadn't jammed.

As it was, Kearby climbed until he identified the red discs on the enemy's wings; it was one of the fast, twin-engine Dinah reconnaissance bombers. He then closed on the Japanese from behind and slightly to the left. When the P-47 was three hundred yards away the eight heavy machine guns opened up for a single three-second burst and the Dinah fell away in flames. Kearby flew over the falling plane and looked back to see bright flames licking over the gray fuselage and orange insignia while the Japanese went down in a gentle dive.

September proved to be the blooding month for the 348th. Two pilots had been lost while claims for more than a dozen air victories had been filed, even though some had to be downgraded to probable status. Kearby was making a dent in the resistance to the P-47 among commanders and pilots who were beginning to believe something could be done with the airplane.

One of the next big tests of the 348th was another interception over the Lae convoys off Finschhafen on September 22. Eight Bettys covered by a host of Zeros again tried to get at the Allied ships, this time with a low-level torpedo attack. The P-38s once again took top honors with claims of twenty-nine confirmed when 35th Fighter Squadron P-40s got seven and the 348th downed four more.

The action began by ten o'clock in the morning when sixteen P-47s of the 341st and eleven from the 342nd headed for their station just south of Finschhafen. The twenty-seven fighters droned over the New Guinea base at altitudes around 20,000 feet for about two hours when about fifty fighters and bombers were sighted below heading for the friendly shipping that was approaching the invasion beach. In fact, the 341st Squadron was just about to leave the area when the Fighter Sector Controller reported the enemy about sixty miles away.

Captain John Moore of the 341st changed course with the rest of his squadron and followed the instructions of the controller's reports until his P-47 was over the water and in sight of the ships.

Lt. Marvin Grant and Jim Stanton by "Sylvia", "Racine Belle."

Captain Moore's subsequent report read: "...I arrived over the ships at 20,000 feet at 1245. The controller aboard ship reported they were being attacked. I looked down and saw bombs dropping in the water. (Perhaps torpedo splashes-author) Then I saw the bombers making a sharp turn to the left after dropping their bombs. We dropped our belly tanks and dove down."

"After my getting down almost in a position to make a pass at the bombers, a ZEKE got on my tail. Lt. Nixon, my wingman, made a pass at the Zeke. By that time I had overshot the bombers due to my speed, so turned to get in position again when I saw another Zeke on my tail. I dived from 5,000 to 1,000 feet and the Zeke did not follow as I was pulling away from him. By this time I realized I did not have a wingman so I started climbing back up. I saw a single P-38 dive on a Zeke to my right and below me. The Zeke dived into a cloud and the P-38 pulled back up to the right. I saw the Zeke through the opening in the cloud so dove from 4,000 to 1,000 feet before I got in range. As soon as I started firing he started a gentle turn and climb to the left, gradually increasing the turn and steepening the climb. I gave him a long continuous at about 30 degrees deflection. I was overleading him at first till he tightened his turn almost at the top of his climb and flew through my fire. I started to break away to the right when I saw him stall and go down at about a 75 degree angle into the water. I thought I saw a hole in his left wing just above the elevator when back was against the sky almost at the top of his climb.

By this time the fight had broken up as the only other planes I saw were P-38s, and I was getting short on gas, so I returned to Dobodura and landed."

Lieutenant Charles A. Cronk, Jr., was the only other 341st pilot to score when he downed two bombers. He had dropped his tank and went down at the same time that Moore had dived into the fray. When Japanese fighters appeared from all directions Cronk was able to concentrate long enough to set fire to two Sally bombers which were observed to crash into the water. Lt. Nixon probably destroyed the Oscar that he managed to drive off Moore's tail.

The 342nd Squadron was also patrolling uneventfully for about two hours with the pilots listening in frustration to the battle sounds

Captain Arthur L. Weeks, 341st Squadron, in his P-47D-3-RA, serial #42-22641 at Finschhafen. He claimed 2 zeros near Arawe on Dec. 27, 1943. Crew chief was Sgt. A. Dorko. Credit: C.J. Blend

coming over their radios. The P-47s were patrolling at about 25,000 feet; early returns had reduced their number to just eleven P-47D-2s.

Captain Walter Benz was leading one flight of four P-47s and must have wished for the opportunity to fly toward the sound of the fighting for only fifteen minutes—ten might even do it.

Suddenly, his wish came flying to meet him when he saw a single twin-engine aircraft flying toward the south about a thousand feet above him.

Benz climbed toward the bogey while it flew away toward the southeast. Just like Kearby a few days before he cautiously approached the aircraft form behind and to the left. This aircraft, too, was gray and had the broad, dirty-orange hinomaru markings on the wings. Benz closed to about fifty yards and fired a single burst into the apparently unaware Dinah. The Japanese reconnaissance plane instantly burst into flame and fell away into the water. Benz had scored the first of his eight confirmed kills.

When the battle died and their fuel was depleted the pilots of the 348th returned to Dobodura. By one o'clock in the afternoon all P-47s had landed and the 348th had its first real victory with four confirmed kills in one combat. Kearby's training and personal example was taking effect. His most flashing moment of combat was about to come.

Chapter 5

Medal of Honor

TSgt Iddings was on the 342nd flightline one day when Colonel Kearby landed FIERY GINGER and got out of the cockpit once the propeller stopped ticking over. He came up to Iddings and announced that he wanted the P-47 checked out and ready to fly again within a short time.

Iddings was swamped with work at the time and had little sympathy with high-ranking officers who wanted to add to his burden. However, with as much respect for rank as he could muster, he sang out, "We'll do the best we can, sir."

Kearby had already turned to walk away, but looked back to utter an ominous threat, "You'll do it or I'll have you busted."

It was a serious warning for a group commander to throw at an obviously overtaxed line chief, but it was also indicative of the urgency that was beginning to descend on Kearby when he began to strain for every opportunity to beat the Rickenbacker WWI record of twenty-six aerial victories.

In any event, Major Banks heard about the incident and told Iddings not to worry since if anybody busted him it would be Banks himself and no one else. Ironically enough, it was Banks who demoted Iddings for some minor infraction just eleven days before he was to make Master Sergeant. Iddings got back his full rating within a short time and laughed about the story for years afterward with his dear friend, Bill Banks.

Colonel Kearby was known to the members of the 348th Fighter Group as "The Boss." There was no doubt that he was in charge and commanded respect from every man in the outfit. Some of the people who knew him claim that he covered a keen sense of humor in a mantle of stern authority to maintain the 348th's efficiency. Others who did not know him quite as well thought of him in deific terms as the master fighter pilot and disciplinarian who could do no wrong.

His reputation as the great aerial combat expert spread even before the war began. When the United States became involved in

Neel Kearby about the time he flew the Medal of Honor mission.

Kearby being awarded some decoration by General Kenney (occasion uncertain). (Adrian Gehl via Norb Krane)

Awards ceremony, probably Nadzab, Kearby and MacDonald are standing at ease just behind table and General Freddie Smith is saluting. (Lenard)

Lt Col Tamiya Teranishi, believed shot down by Kearby on 10/11/43. (Yoji Watanabe via Henry Sakaida)

the conflict Kearby was in demand to pass on some of his technique to younger pilots. It was a priceless experience just to fly in mock combat with the great fighter mentor.

More than one notable P-47 pilot owed at least some of his success to Kearby's attention. One pilot swears that he learned to appreciate air-to-air combat ability when he faced Kearby in mock combat with P-35 fighters. While the fledgling was straining every muscle and using every bit of skill to throw his friendly adversary off his tail he was shocked to look back and see Kearby calmly lighting a cigarette.

From the beginning it was natural to assume that Kearby would excel in combat. He was not only a superb fighter pilot, but also technically polished enough to pass on his ability to others under his influence. His ultimate moment in air-to-air combat was to come during the second week of October in 1943.

The Japanese were ever more on the defensive during the latter part of 1943 on the New Guinea front. By late September the 18th Fighter sub-sector was established along the line from Lae through Nadzab to Wau, roughly covering the entire Huon Gulf coastline south of Finschhafen. Japanese efforts over the area had virtually ceased and only a few night raids with less than effective results were attempted during October.

While the bomber line was being advanced, the five fighter groups of V Fighter Command found that they were capable of a wider range of combat missions now that more Japanese targets were available to tactical strikes. More fighter sweeps were scheduled and the pilots of the 348th were able to use the P-47 on strafing and ground attack missions, the sort of combat that would bring the Thunderbolt its greatest fame late in the war.

When the 23rd Fighter Sector was established over Finschhafen targets were available not only in the northern New Guinea area but also the New Britain bases of Cape Gloucester and, exclusively for the P-38, the installations at Rabaul. There were, in virtual fact,

ABOVE & BOTTOM: *An obviously pleased Col. Kearby back from a mission late in October 1943.*

only three substantial bases remaining from which the Japanese could threaten Allied strength in northern New Guinea. These bases included Rabaul, Wewak and Hollandia.

Thus, the pilots of V Fighter Command were capable by the beginning of October to range belligerently against the enemy. One 348th mission on October 10, 1943, had four P-47s of the 341st and 342nd Fighter Squadrons on a sweep over Cape Gloucester's Borgen Bay. The pilots found twelve Japanese barges and strafed the lot of them, claimed three destroyed and several others damaged.

The next day, October 11, 1943, started off routinely enough. For example, the 341st Squadron flew several transport cover missions to Nadzab beginning at about eight o'clock in the morning. The only thing out of the ordinary mentioned in squadron records was one P-47 that landed at Tsili with engine trouble, but was off again and landed back at base by a few minutes to four in the afternoon.

Perhaps it was the ordinary nature of the day that inspired Neel Kearby to be a little more daring. He must have looked out into the sky toward the north and thought it was a perfect day for a flight to Wewak. The first attempt at a sweep over Wewak was tried the day before by 348th fighters, but an overcast up to 23,000 feet over the target had frustrated the mission.

Captain John Moore was the operations officer of the 341st Squadron and not required on any of the missions being flown that day, so he was happy to go along as Kearby's wingman. Major Raymond Gallagher, commander of the 342nd, was leader of the second element and Captain Bill Dunham agreed to go along as Gallagher's wingman.

Captain John Moore.

With all the group ranking officers in the flight there was no problem in taking off by seven-thirty in the morning. They flew from Ward's Drome to land at Tsili for refueling. The flight spent just an hour at the forward base before taking off at 9:30 to head northwest along the coast for the last two hundred and some odd miles to Wewak.

The four olive and gray P-47D-2's strained for altitude through marvelously clear blue skies. There were only a few scattered puffs of clouds between 2,000 and 8,000 feet on the approach to the target area. The Thunderbolts climbed to 28,000 feet and looked down with frightening authority at the enemy landscape below.

For the first time Kearby would be able to put his tactics into practice. He would lead his men down in a fast strike on any Japanese aircraft below, leaving the enemy falling in flames or running in terror from the spectral American attack.

When the four P-47s were just about fifty miles from the approach to their station over Wewak the Japanese radar picked them up. Lt. Colonel Tamiya Teranishi was the commander of the Japanese Army Air Forces 14th Fighter/Bomber Group and happened to be at the Wewak alert area at the time. It is not known whether the Japanese were aware that only four enemy aircraft were intruding into their skies, but Teranishi must have thought it a great opportunity to personally lead his fighters in an ambush of the impudent American force.

He ordered Ki-43 Hayabusa (Oscar) and Ki-61 Hien (Tony) fighters to intercept. The Oscars could have been from a number of units in the area and the Tonys were probably from the 68th Sentai, which with the 78th Sentai, were the only Ki-61 units in New Guinea. Teranishi selected one of the nimble little Oscars as his own mount to lead the attack.

Later, it was estimated by the Americans that about forty Japanese fighters rose to meet the four-plane flight of Thunderbolts. Considering that many of the 68th Sentai's Tonys were usually down with engine trouble and that Oscar units had suffered heavy losses at Wewak in recent months, the estimate was perhaps a bit high. It seems more likely that Teranishi led a total of about twenty to twenty-five fighters.

Meanwhile, Kearby was orbiting over the area at extreme height with the other three P-47s in tow. Between ten thirty-five and eleven o'clock that morning he watched far below and in every direction to clearly see what was going on. Over at Boram strip on the southeast corner of Wewak there were aircraft visible; one was taxiing on the runway. Two large ships were just off the coast and there were about a dozen barges chugging placidly in Hansa Bay. Four

Sergeants Patzli and Koontz standing by Gallagher's P-47.

others were moving along the Sepik River and a larger ship was several miles upstream. The view from 28,000 feet was panoramic.

At about 11:05 Kearby realized that the fuel in the formation's belly tanks was exhausted and ordered them dropped to increase speed and to conserve internal fuel. The four Thunderbolts dropped their tanks in unison and the silvery oval tubes tumbled into the blue sunlight toward the sea below. Now the P-47s were committed to action or retreat within the next few minutes after they reached the critical point in their fuel supply.

The Americans had no way of knowing, but any anxiety they may have had about engaging the enemy would be dispelled within the next few minutes. Kearby was the first to sight the enemy when he saw an Oscar below and to his left at about 20,000 feet. It was 11:15 on Kearby's clock.

The Japanese fighter, which must have been reflecting the bright sun off the outline of its green and natural metal camouflage was misidentified as a Mitsubishi Zero. Kearby didn't waste any more time than he had to before he rolled over in a screaming dive, so the identification was limited to general type and the energizing dark red meatball hinomaru markings on the wings.

Tony fighters in the gunsights of unidentified V Fighter Command pilot.

It was the kind of situation that Kearby had anticipated and trained his pilots to meet. With a tremendous shedding of inertia his P-47 built up speed and rushed with terrific velocity toward the left rear of the Japanese fighter. When the range closed to about three-hundred yards Kearby opened fire and immediately saw hits on the target. The Oscar pilot must have had no idea that he was being attacked because he took no evasive action before Kearby's .50 caliber bullets ripped into his fighter, which caught fire, rolled over and dived into the sea.

Gallagher, Dunham and Moore all witnessed the crash of the Oscar. Major Gallagher had his lather up when he saw another Japanese fighter farther out to sea. He gave chase and was just getting into range when the target fighter evaded by slipping into a large cloud. The frustrated American pulled up above the white mass and realized that he had pursued the Japanese longer than he had intended.

There was no sign of any other aircraft, so Gallagher headed in the direction of land. He missed the rest of the fight and the only thing the dejected 342nd commander managed to do was witness the crash of another Japanese fighter into the sea at the end of the engagement.

Kearby rallied the other two P-47s and began climbing back to 26,000 feet. It had already been a good mission for the 348th commander and he noticed there was just enough time to possibly repeat the success one more time.

Bill Dunham sighted an enemy fighter below at 18,000 feet. This may have been the same one that Gallagher had chased into the cloud now returning to Wewak. Dunham was getting ready to attack when a large formation of Tonys was called out.

John Moore also saw the formation and identified many "Tonys with a few Oscars and Zekes" at about 15,000 feet. There were also about twelve bombers at 5,000 feet, the whole force coming in from the sea about four miles from the coast approximately twelve miles from Borum.

The fighters must have been Teranishi's interceptors coming up to meet the 348th formation. It may have been hapless chance that the bombers were coming into the Wewak area just as an air battle was brewing, since no bomber leader in his right mind would navigate between two opposing fighter forces.

From Moore's vantage at the rear of the Thunderbolt trio things were moving quickly. He followed the other two Americans around to the rear of the Japanese formation and above it about eight thousand feet. When they rolled over to attack the Japanese fighters the P-47s picked up airspeed to an indicated 425 mph.

Kearby was almost certainly forced to restrain himself from getting too greedy about this opportunity. Even the bravest fighter pilots would have had second thoughts about taking on odds of more than four-to-one, but he probably kept telling himself not to scare the rest of the formation away. Once again there was no evasive action when he opened fire from a range of three-hundred yards behind the lead Oscar (Kearby again misidentified it as a Zero). Once again the Japanese fighter burst into flames and spun into the sea below.

Skidding slightly to the right and opening fire at another Oscar which also burst into flames, Kearby downed his third victory. This

Doing KP on 10/15/43 while others got the glory in the air. Note camp theater in the background. (T. Drozd)

one he identified as a Hamp—the clipped wing version of the Zero. The battle was going by in a flash and Kearby was not going to take the time for complete confirmation of the fighter types now that he obviously had achieved complete surprise.

From his number three man position Moore had a good view of the first moments of the main battle. Kearby's Oscar was going down toward the sea when a Tony rushed in from the rear to stop the rampage. Moore witnessed Dunham angle his fighter in to protect his leader's tail and the Tony went down in flames.

Safe from tail attacks because the redoutable Dunham and Moore were there to protect him Kearby looked up and saw another Oscar turning slightly to the left. The P-47 closed to about 500 yards behind the Japanese and Kearby opened fire, getting strikes and watching flames erupt from the doomed airplane before it turned out of his sight line.

At the same time, after he had fired two bursts which struck the Tony in the cockpit area and left wing, Dunham watched Kearby destroy the last two Oscars which fell into the sea with his own victim. Dunham was able to circle the area for the next five minutes and counted no fewer than seven circles of flames on the water which attested to the destruction of a large number of enemy planes.

Another column of dark orange flame and black smoke boiled up from the jungle to mark the death of yet another Japanese fighter. Later, it was determined that this smoke marker confirmed Moore's victory, another Tony.

After crossing fire with several other Japanese aircraft Moore noticed that his fuel was getting down to the critical point. He had witnessed three of the splashes marking the end of some Japanese fighters, but could not find the other P-47s when he searched for them.

He was alone now, and gradually climbed to 16,000 feet on a heading of 140° that took him straight along the coast toward the Allied airfields in the southeast. He had heard both Gallagher and Dunham report over the radio that they were low on fuel and headed for home.

After flying for about twenty miles on this course he saw a single P-47 and what appeared to be six Tonys about 4,000 feet below. He knew that it must be Kearby in a dangerous situation with an angry enemy all around, so he decided to come down and join the colonel. While he was diving to get on the tail of a Tony Moore noticed Kearby's fire hit one of the fighters and send it down trailing heavy smoke. It was Kearby's fifth victory.

Moore selected a flight of three Tonys and concentrated on the last plane. His guns were loaded with armor-piercing and incendiary bullets and he got in a thirty-five degree deflection shot that started the Tony smoking. Another burst caused the Tony to blossom into flame and fall off to the left into an uncontrolled spin.

There was still the problem of the first two Tonys that had pulled up sharply to the right while Moore was disposing of their comrade. They were certainly unhappy about the audacious attack by a single American and racked their fighters around with dismaying speed to get behind the Thunderbolt.

Moore did the only thing he could to avoid joining his victim now spinning into the jungle below; he grit his teeth and put the P-47 into a dive on full power. When he looked around he could see that he was just out of range. The sleek, silver and jungle-green

Lt. Wynans Frankfort (342nd FS) was shot down on October 22, 1943, and walked back to base through the jungle while others got the glory in the air.

Sam Blair late in 1943.

thing big had happened from the Ops radio that was tuned into the battle frequency. Even with this achievement already in his pocket, Kearby led Moore in a final circle of the area because of all the Tonys still visible in the sky.

Kearby made one more pass at a Tony from the 10 o'clock position, but the deflection was wrong and the enemy escaped. Another Tony was closing on his tail, so Kearby headed for a nearby cloud at an altitude of 7,000 feet. When he finally came out of the overcast there was no sign of the Japanese and Kearby was able to climb to 15,000 feet and call the rest of the flight to check in.

One of the things that came to light after the war had to do with historical research from Japanese as well as American sources. Japanese researchers who investigated the Wewak action of October 11, 1943, came to the conclusion that one of Kearby's victories was Colonel Teranishi. The time of the relevant part of the action, about 11:25, was the same time that other Japanese pilots who survived the day reported losing contact with Teranishi. It was a heavy blow to the Japanese who must have regarded Teranishi with the same respect that the Americans granted Kearby.

Japanese records for New Guinea are understandably incomplete. Much of what they couldn't carry out during the Allied advance was destroyed or simply discarded, including casualty records. What we do have was either captured by advancing Allied forces or transmitted to Japan before the retreating troops walked out of bases like Lae or Hollandia. The most direct evidence of Kearby's victory was his own gun-camera film or the testimony of the few surviving Japanese from that era.

Nevertheless, the pride of the 348th Fighter Group was high and morale burst all bounds. The unit had set a record for the most aerial kills by one pilot on a single mission in the Pacific for the entire USAAF up to that time and had the first Medal of Honor awarded to an Army fighter pilot.

Perhaps the language of the final mission report reflects the growing sense of justification in the group. It must be remembered that the report was written in the midst of the war with all the wartime prejudice and error in perception included.

One other fact unavailable to the American intelligence people during the war was the identity of one of the Tony pilots killed in the action. Captain Koyama was the leader of the 1st Chutai of the 68th Sentai when he took off on the interception with Colonel Teranishi. One of the three American victors shot the Chutai leader down.

fuselages of the Tonys with their pointed dark-brown bullet noses weren't much bigger than mosquitoes from his point of view.

A glance ahead to check his dive and Moore turned back to notice that the Tonys were still hell-bent on his tail. He must have been unnerved to realize that a P-47 in a full-power shallow dive could be successfully followed, but in this case the Tony pilots seemed up to the job.

After he finished his own Tony victim, Kearby noticed Moore's plight and went back to help him. The rear fighter was about one-thousand yards behind the first Tony and Kearby went after it in another 400 mph dive until he came within seven hundred yards and opened fire. Tracers went into the fuselage of the Japanese fighter and pieces of the Tony flew off into the space between itself and Kearby's Thunderbolt.

Kearby overflew this victim also and didn't have time to watch him crash. A greatly relieved Captain Moore, however, saw the Tony burst into flame and fall into the sea. Kearby and Moore disagree slightly in their respective combat reports about Kearby's last two victories. Moore reported that one of the Tonys shot down by Kearby occurred before he entered the area. Kearby reported that both Tonys he shot down were on Moore's tail. The difference is insignificant except that the Tony closest to Moore either broke off the engagement when his wingman was shot down or he was shot down himself.

Whatever the case may be, Kearby had flown his greatest mission and would land his P-47 to the wild cheers of 348th groundcrewmen who were already getting the first hints that some-

342nd FIGHTER SQUADRON
OFFICE OF THE INTELLIGENCE OFFICER
A.P.O. 929

12 October 1943

SUBJECT: NARRATIVE OF AIR COMBAT

TO : COMMANDING GENERAL, FIFTH AIR FORCE, ATTENTION: A.C.OF S

1.THE FOLLOWING NARRATIVE COMBAT REPORT IS SUBMITTED IN ACCORDANCE WITH AR 345-195

2.THE COMBAT DESCRIBED HEREINAFTER REPRESENTS MISSION NO.1 OF THE 342ND FIGHTER SQUADRON, 348TH FIGHTER GROUP OPERATIONS ORDER NO. 88, 11 OCTOBER 1943. ACTION INVOLVED A FOUR SHIP FLIGHT OF P47D2'S, COMPOSED OF THREE FROM THE 342ND FIGHTER SQUADRON AND ONE FROM THE 341ST FIGHTER SQUADRON.

3. ...AS THE GAS SUPPLY WAS RUNNING LOW (1145L), COL. KEARBY CALLED THE FLIGHT TO GO HOME. CAPT. DUNHAM GLANCED BACKWARD AS THEY LEFT THE AREA AND NOTED AT LEAST SEVEN SEPARATE FIRES IN THE WATER. THE FLIGHT LANDED AT LAE AT 1245L, WITH AN AVERAGE OF 50 TO 75 GALLONS OF GAS RESERVE. THEY THEN RETURNED TO PORT MORESBY LANDING AT 1515L. THE HISTORY-MAKING ASPECT OF THIS FLIGHT IS UNQUESTIONABLE. THE RESULTS OBTAINED - COL. KEARBY'S SIX VICTORIES (2 ZEKES, 2 HAPS, 2 TONYS), CAPT. MOORE'S 2 TONYS, CAPT. DUNHAM'S 1 TONY - A TOTAL OF 9 FIGHTERS DESTROYED WITHOUT A SCRATCH ON A SINGLE THUNDERBOLT DEMONSTRATES THAT THIS TYPE OF PLANE HAS COME INTO ITS OWN IN THIS THEATER, AND THAT ITS TERRIFIC SPEED BOTH IN THE DIVE AND STRAIGHTAWAY, ITS FLASHING AILERON ROLL, AND MURDEROUS FIREPOWER WILL HENCEFORTH STRIKE TERROR INTO THE HEARTS OF THE LITTLE YELLOW AIRMEN.

IN CONCLUSION, IT SHOULD BE NOTED THAT THIS PLANE FLEW WELL OVER 300 MILES, FOUGHT FOR ONE HOUR, AND RETURNED, THE WHOLE MISSION CONSUMING ABOUT THREE HOURS AND ONE HALF. ABOUT 3500 RDS. OF AMMUNITION WERE EXPENDED AND OVER 100 FEET OF FILM TAKEN.
BERNHARD A. ROTH
1ST LIEUT., AIR CORPS
INTELLIGENCE OFFICER

Walter Benz scored his first victory on Sep. 22, 1943, when he got a Dinah south of Finschhafen. Exactly one month later he got a Tony near Wewak. Credit: Krene files

Chapter 6

More October Missions

Joe Moor was getting to like life a little more in the 342nd Squadron Medical detachment. Even though the detachment was small in October 1943 with one flight surgeon, Captain Richard Weddle, and eight enlisted men, there were some compensations at Ward's Drome.

Medical emergency duty was simplified with the acquisition of two sturdy Dodge ambulances and the Flight Surgeon's jeep. The dispensary was always the best structure on whatever base the detachment found itself with screened, wooden-floored enclosures and raised litters for examining tables. There was even a server propane-fired refrigerator.

The dispensary was a popular place even for those not going at the sick call hours of eight in the morning and six in the evening. One of the most popular items was the great cache of medicinal 180 proof alcohol and 86 proof whiskey. There was always a requisition for new supplies of the alcohol while other stores were left behind in the move from one base to another.

Pilots were allowed two ounces of combat whiskey at the end of each mission, at first issued directly at the flightline. Soon afterward the practice was amended and records were kept of each pilot's due portion. When the total credit was sufficient, the pilot would claim an entire bottle of whiskey.

Moor and his medical comrades would combine medicinal alcohol, water, burnt sugar, iodine and small amounts of whiskey to distill their own brand of Guckenheimer Blend. This brew became the primary means of barter to insure necessary construction materials—not to mention ice cream, fresh fruit, candy and smoking tobacco—were always on hand.

But the life of an enlisted man at Ward's Drome was not always so amenable. Line Chief Joe Baxter told Sgt. Handy on one of the first days at the Port Moresby base to take a detail of ten or twelve mechanics on detached service to Charters Towers, Australia. The tail wheels of all P-47s based there for depot storage had to be removed because about half of the fighters going to the hot New Guinea bases were blowing out the tires on the sizzling runways. The groundcrews had to make do on the broiling ground with G.I. footwear!

Sergeant Slider told Charlie Fox, one of the crew chiefs, not to be concerned with the 'gator that walks through the tent at night because it would eat the mosquitoes. Sure enough, that first night in his tent Fox saw either a baby alligator or full-grown lizard come through and snap at the insects with its tongue. Fox didn't bother to get out of his bunk to be certain which creature it was.

Sergeants Slider and Fox were also out on the flightline the day that Kearby had his record six-in-a-day victory mission. Slider was overjoyed when Kearby did multiple rolls. When the victorious Colonel taxied past Fox's parking area at the southwest end of the strip Slider waved at him and got a return signal of five fingers held up.

Left to right: Bob Anderson, James Nixon, Charles Blend of the 341st late in 1943. (Cronk)

Probably Finschhafen, early 1944. (Note Natural metal P-47 in background)

"That's pretty good—five down for a flight of four P-47s." Slider commented just as he headed for Kearby's settling fighter.

A few minutes later Fox saw Slider jumping up and down on the wing. He was whooping and shouting about some news that made him especially animated; Kearby had told him that his P-47 got five victories in one flight. After Kearby was officially credited with six aerial victories he explained that he mentioned only five at first to avoid ridicule for such an incredible claim!

General Kenney reported that he thought Kearby would have been granted credit for a seventh victory if the gun camera had not run out of film at the critical moment. He called up the officer in charge and complained so vigorously that a second camera was installed on FIERY GINGER.

October was a good month in general for the 348th Fighter Group. By the end of the month the group had scored no fewer than fifty confirmed air kills and suffered only about six aircraft combat losses and even lighter pilot casualties. Neel Kearby was the group's only ace so far, but he had made an impressive combat debut with twelve victories scored in less than three months. With a kill ratio of ten-to-one the 348th had quickly taken its place as one of the top fighter outfits in the Southwest Pacific.

The 348th also maintained pressure on ground targets around northern New Guinea and the west coast of New Britain. At the end of October the 341st Squadron had some additional success in strafing. On October 29, 1943, the squadron strafed villages and huts at Cape Bushing and destroyed three barges off the Talasea peninsula of New Britain the next day. During the same period—between October 12 and November 11—the P-38s of V Fighter Command fought some bitter and destructive air battles over Rabaul out of effective range of the P-47s.

But the 348th sought out its own targets. On the first day of the P-38 escorted raids over Rabaul and the day after Kearby's Medal of Honor mission Lt. Colonel Bob Rowland scored his first victory on a sweep over the Wewak area. He was leading another flight of four P-47D-2s over Nubia-Wewak at 30,000 feet about thirty minutes past noon when he began a patrol along the coastline.

The four Thunderbolts had taken a roundabout route to avoid aircraft spotters at Bogadjim and Madang. Rowland hoped to duplicate the element of surprise which had evidently served Kearby so well the day before.

Within a few minutes he sighted a grayish blue twin-engine Ki-46 Dinah reconnaissance aircraft flying at 5,000 feet above the water just two-hundred yards off the coast opposite Wewak strip. Rowland automatically called out the enemy to the rest of the flight and looked up, to the right and left, and especially behind to be sure the sitting duck was not a decoy. Kearby's success from the previous day had also made the Americans suspicious that the Japanese would set a trap for any repeat performance.

Evidently the Dinah was alone and unaware of the presence of the P-47s, so Rowland maneuvered and angled for the best possible attack attitude. He then noticed that the Dinah was losing height rapidly as if it were preparing to land. It was necessary to bounce immediately if the enemy should be destroyed and Rowland rolled the P-47 smoothly over on its back into a vertical dive to lose height and gain speed. The Dinah was already calmly turning for its final approach while the P-47 screamed downward like a crazed hawk in ever increasing speed to strike its prey before it reached the relative safety of the ground.

"As I leveled out behind him I noticed that I was indicating 500 miles per hour," read the subsequent combat report filed by Rowland. "At an altitude of 3,000 feet, I closed in on him from dead astern and opened fire at approximately 250 yards. I observed hits by my incendiary bullets flashing in both his right and left wing roots. Just as I was about to pull up to avoid colliding with him he exploded in both wing roots and did a sudden push-over toward the ocean."

Rowland climbed for altitude and looked back to see the Dinah burning on the water. He reformed with the other three P47s at 24,000 feet and headed back toward Port Moresby. After refueling

341st Squadron sign (Port Moresby?). (via Bill Hess)

341st Squadron sign at Finschhafen. (via Cronk)

at Tsili the Thunderbolt formation finally landed at their home base by sundown.

The biggest mission during the period in terms of enemy aircraft claimed for the 348th was flown on October 16. Two flights of B-25s were escorted by P-47s of the 340th and 342nd Fighter Squadrons to Alexishafen. The P-47s took off a few minutes before nine in the morning and rendezvoused with the bombers in time to join them over the general target area at about eleven o'clock.

At just a few minutes after eleven, about fifteen to twenty Japanese fighters were sighted bouncing the American formations at 9,000 feet. The enemy was about 1,000 feet above when the 348th's P-47s reacted quickly by turning into the teeth of the Japanese attack.

The 340th was the first to meet the Japanese. Nine P-47s were flying at 9,000 feet over Alexishafen when about twenty Oscars and Tonys dropped down from a thousand feet above. The 340th released their belly tanks and turned to meet the enemy head on.

Max Wiecks crossed through the Japanese formation and was initially forced to dive away, but climbed back and found his way to his former altitude and position. Below him he could see the battle going on. He selected three Japanese fighters, diving and firing at one of them until the other two forced him away.

"I dived and again turned right and ran into another fighter," he wrote in his subsequent combat report. "I shot at about a 45 degree deflection and noticed tracers around him and saw one burst hit directly in the cockpit. After passing over him I looked back and saw him burst into flames. After this attack I pulled up and then

"My Ba-a-aby", 341st P-47 late 1944. (C.J. Blend)

ABOVE (Rollins via Crow) & BOTTOM (Hess): Repair on 348th P-47s at Finschhafen.

The following photos show score flags of successful squadron pilot. ABOVE: Guy Roberts after 12/21/43.

heard Lieutenant Lytle yell that Zeros were on his tail. Looking down I saw three Hamps chasing Lt. Lytle, so I dived and shot the first of the three closest to him. Lieutenant Lytle had flown through the Japanese formation and turned to find a Tony below him at 5,000 feet. He dived on the Japanese fighter before the pilot could be alerted, but he was a fraction of a second too late. A deflection shot went a bit off target when the enemy turned to avoid his fire."

Lieutenant Tom Barber was flying Lytle's wing and watched the whole thing while the Tony writhed and twisted to get clear of the P-47's line of fire. At last the deadly flashes began to appear on the silver and green fuselage of the Kawasaki fighter and it began to emit smoke a moment before it burst into flames. Barber saw it crash into the ground below.

During the time that Barber watched the Tony go down, he and Lytle became separated long enough for three Oscars to come along, latch onto Lytle's tail and for Wiecks to come to the rescue. It was something of a slight panic for Barber since he was in the midst of attacking enemy fighters without a leader and he could very well get a tonguelashing from Lytle if he came back without him. It would even be worse than that if Lytle, who was supposed to covered by Barber, did not return at all.

Andy Lytle did join up with Jesse Ivey and the two of them were on the way home when two more Japanese fighters were sighted. The two Thunderbolts immediately rolled over and attacked one from the rear. Lytle ran right up the tail of his victim and fired from close range until the left wing of the Japanese fighter crumpled and sheared off. Ivey watched the Japanese plane come apart and flutter straight down.

In spite of any anxiety he may have felt at losing Lytle, Barber used the time to fight the Japanese. He dived quickly and came up behind another Japanese fighter. With a single point blank burst from his P-47's eight guns he obliterated one Oscar which fell the short remaining distance to earth. Guy Johnson flamed a Tony for the other 340th Squadron victory.

About half an hour before this 340th Squadron formation took off, Neel Kearby assembled another special four-plane flight to sweep ahead of the second mission. The flight consisted of Frank

Perhaps this is Bob DuCharme around the time he scored on 12/17/43. #37 likely belongs to Sam Blair who got his fifth on the same day.

Sam Galik of the 341st who scored on 10/23/43. (C.J. Blend)

Oksala as Kearby's wingman and second element led by 340th commander Hervey Carpenter with wingman Captain Meade Brown.

They took off at 7:50 in the morning and landed to refuel at Lae. Forty minutes later the four P-47s were off again to sweep the Wewak area. It was a good day for a hunt with only a few scattered clouds between 2,000 and 8,000 feet.

Perhaps Kearby's flight could hear the radio chatter when the 340th Squadron engaged the Japanese at about 11 o'clock. He did see one Japanese aircraft scooting along the deck at just about that time, but decided not to come down from his altitude of 23,000 feet. The Boss would not give up his advantage so easily.

Kearby's flight cruised the area around Borum for about twenty-five minutes when a more tempting target appeared. Kearby looked off to his right at about the two-o'clock position and there was a gleaming silver and jungle-brown Oscar at 18,000 feet. This time there was no delay and Kearby led his flight down in a fast dive that gave the enemy little chance to react, much less escape.

P-47 of William Foulis in December 1943. The pilot is tentatively identified as Carroll "Red" Osborn. (C.J. Blend)

Arthur Weeks after he scored his two 341st Squadron victories on 12/17/43. (C.J. Blend)

The Oscar did try a climbing turn to the right, but Kearby was within his own killing range of 500 yards and opened fire. Hits were scored and waves of yellow-orange flames were emitting from the Oscar's engine cowling. A lucky Japanese Army pilot managed to get out of the cockpit and float down in his parachute while his plane fell into the sea. Meade Brown was close enough to witness the whole brief combat.

As a result of this day's action for the 348th, thirteen Japanese fighters were confirmed destroyed and five others were probably shot down. No Thunderbolts were lost and no B-25s were claimed by Japanese interceptors. It was a thoroughly respectable performance for an aircraft type that was deemed "practically useless" for the needs of the theater only a few months before.

Record numbers of Japanese aircraft were being claimed during this period (the 432nd Squadron of the 475th Fighter Group established a temporary record over Finschhafen on September 22, 1943, when its pilots claimed eighteen Japanese aircraft in a single engagement) and every unit of V Fighter Command managed to

Dunham's P-47 around October 19, 1943.

ABOVE & BOTTOM: Ed Popek's P-47 around January 1944 at Finschhafen.

rack up kills—when they could close with the Japanese. The P38 remained preeminent because of its range and altitude advantages. The only other competition came from Kearby's P-47s which capitalized on the type's advantages.

The Narrative Combat Report of the 342nd Squadron for its part of the October 16 mission relates the growing success of the Thunderbolt in the experiences of Captain Dunham and the rest of his flight; Lts. Upton, Pratt and Cooley:

"...Suddenly, Lt. Cooley saw behind him to the N.E. four unidentified aircraft in a long stringing dive toward some invisible target low on the water. Below him, he spotted a single silver hap flashing southward at tree-top level. Almost simultaneously, all other members of the flight saw approaching NW toward Madang at 3000 feet, five more haps of a muddy silver color, four with prominent red roundels and one with no markings, in no apparent formation.

The lower element, Lts. Pratt and Cooley swung down to make an attack from six o'clock above, closing to 300 yards, indicating well over 400 miles an hour. Lt. Pratt started firing as the hap turned steeply to the left. The Thunderbolt could not turn tightly enough to get sufficient lead and a 3 second burst achieved no results. Lt. Cooley, on Lt. Pratt's wing, had closed to almost point blank range on the tail of another hap, and had the satisfaction of seeing him explode in mid-air. Lt. Pratt meanwhile had engaged a hap and at 300 yards on a 45 degree deflection shot, observed strikes near the canopy. Flight leader Capt. Dunham and his wing man Lt. Upton, who were watching from above to rescue the other two from any difficulty, saw this latter hap emit some flame which went out as it dived toward the sea. Almost at water level, it zoomed abruptly and returned to the flight.

Lt. Pratt was making another pass, head on, at a hap, when Capt. Dunham observed an enemy aircraft maneuvering for a shot at Lt. Pratt's tail. Before he could get in position, Capt. Dunham had dived from dead astern, fried a one-second burst from 200 yards and saw the hap plunge into the sea with his engine flaming. Meanwhile Lt. Pratts head on pass had proved effective, as the hap caught on fire and passed under him straight on into the water, leaving a Lt. Cooley had returned swiftly to altitude in a steep climbing turn to the left and at 10,000 ft. observed one hap at 9 o'clock below which he dived on from 7 o'clock seeing his bullets strike the middle of his left wing, with flame following. Meanwhile, Lt. Pratt got passing shots at several haps passing by and on an 80 degree deflection shot, while steeply banking to the left, he saw strikes at the wing roots of the enemy craft followed by flame and when the craft passed from view, it was going straight down at an excessive rate of speed, smoking and flaming. As he pulled up, he saw Lt. Cooley about 1000 ft. almost directly above him pulling away from a hap that was flaming from a point midway on his left wing. As he passed the enemy plane, the flames were spreading quickly as it streaked down towards the water. Moments later, Lt. Cooley saw two aircraft hit the water simultaneously and coming from opposite directions.

Now, one hap was visible at 1000 feet streaking towards Madang. Two hundred yards offshore, he was overtaken and shot down by Captain Dunham, the pilot bailing out at 900 feet and landing 100 yards off shore..." Bill Cooley later had a laconic report of his part in the mission which characterizes the general mood of the 348th in combat: "I followed me element leader in the attack and caught a straggler and blew him up with a good burst. I pulled up and made another pass at a Hamp dead astern. After pulling up I saw him going down trailing smoke. Just then a Tony latched onto my tail as I was going for another Hamp so I dove out skidding and went into a cloud bank. His fire caught me in the tail, but I got away OK."

Mitsubishi FIM "Pete", the same type as engaged by the 348th on October 19,1943.

Chapter 7

Kearby Scores Again

Master Sergeant Charles P. Schubert had two heroes in the Southwest Pacific, and the 348th was a continuing source of pride. Two men greatly admired were General George Churchill Kenney and Colonel Neel Ernest Kearby. He was not alone in his estimation of General Kenney as a capable organizer of men and resources and a leader who knew how to get top performance from his people as well as his machines.

Colonel Kearby was a bit larger than life for Schubert. Like Kenney, Kearby was able to employ his machines to the best advantage and to encourage the most positive attitude from his pilots and ground crews. As a result, the esprit de corps of the 348th Fighter Group was as if it became etched in steel. There was an enthusiasm and pride that transcended the war and exists among 348th veterans to this day.

Schubert eventually was selected to be Technical Inspector for the group after the fourth squadron—the 460th—was added in July 1944. On his way to his auspicious post he worked hard under the influence of Colonel Kearby and got to know him perhaps a shade better than many of the 348th veterans.

Once, Schubert was happily surprised to see a B-26, a type that he had worked with previously, taxi up to the revetment where he was on duty. He was even more surprised to see the smiling faces of Colonel Kearby and another P-47 pilot in the control cabin.

"These bomber pilots are awful sissies," Kearby called down from the cockpit window, laughingly referring to the redundancy of the second pilot as well as navigator station behind the pilot seats. Kearby had been to Fifth Air Force Headquarters and, as usual, picked up whatever transportation was available.

Captain Arthur Weeks in his cockpit around the beginning of 1944. Note 342nd Squadron P-47D-2 in the background. (C.J. Blend)

Bill Dunham's P-47 between the beginning of 1944 and March 5, 1944.

Schubert later wiped his brow in amazement when he discovered that Kearby had taken the bomber off with a load of supplies and had forgotten to adjust the elevator trim. He knew very well how critical the trim on the B-26 had to be for a safe takeoff. It took the combined strength of pilot, co-pilot and a passenger reaching over the shoulder of one of the pilots to hold the control yoke and avert disaster on Kearby's flight.

Like all good commanders Kearby realized that creature comforts were important to the morale of his men. He made the effort to acquire and distribute minor luxuries that normally would not be available in the New Guinea forest. One time he sent Schubert down to Melbourne with a wad of cash from the officers of the group to buy kerosene refrigerators that would function without electricity.

Another time, around the first of October 1943, Kearby sent him down to Australia for a load of beer and whiskey to augment the medicinal hootch, and for tools, chairs and tumblers. Schubert traveled on one of the "fat cat" bomber transports that shuttled between New Guinea and Australia. One other thing that he picked up on this trip was a set of little silver eagles for newly promoted full colonel Neel Kearby.

Once, Schubert had the opportunity to travel with Kearby and asked him about his combat exploits. At least one little-known fact was revealed by Kearby during some expansive moments on the long flight. Odd as it may seem, Kearby was so eager to get into a fighter scrap that he arranged to make a P-38 sweep over the Admiralty Islands during the long-range Rabaul strikes of October and November 1943.

Schubert was surprised to learn that Kearby had agreed to go along in a flight with a high-ranking P-38 pilot to see what action they could stir up. "I really got cooled off fast over Rabaul when an engine quit on me," Kearby declared about the operation.

Some indefinite sources claim that Kearby may even have downed Japanese aircraft while flying P-38s. Since every official victory that he claimed is documented in P-47 aircraft, it is vaguely possible that Kearby actually accounted for more than the twenty-two confirmed kills with which he is credited. It must be remembered that the possibility is very remote, but the legend of Neel Kearby is broad enough to include the contingency.

As it was, Kearby scored his tenth confirmed aerial victory over Wewak on the October sixteenth mission. He was still the only ace of the 348th although John Moore of the 341st Squadron and Bill Dunham of the 342nd each had three victories. By the middle of October Dick Bong was already the leading ace of the theater with seventeen victories, followed closely by Tom Lynch and George Welch with sixteen each and Tom McGuire with thirteen. Kearby intended to close the gap.

Sometime later in 1944. The natural metal P-47 in the background would have been in the 342nd no sooner than the end of January 1944 when the first unpainted warplanes were delivered to V Fighter Command.

Since Lynch and Welch were back home on rotation, the only men to beat were Bong and McGuire. Kearby was not long in pressing the issue when he ordered another fighter sweep over Wewak on October 19, 1943. Yet one more time Kearby led three other P-47s on a high-altitude patrol over the beleaguered Japanese base.

The Thunderbolts took off from Port Moresby at eight o'clock in the morning and landed at Lae by 8:45. After they had refueled they were off again by fifteen minutes past nine and arrived over the Wewak area by eleven o'clock at 28,000 feet. Fifteen minutes later Kearby was galvanized with excitement when he saw four single-engine fighters on the deck and twelve others at about 20,000 feet over Wewak.

Three other aircraft were flying along like shimmering specks of pepper about forty miles south of Wewak and Kearby decided to attack these closer and more isolated targets first. He led the P-47s down in a head on pass, but pulled up in disgust when the three airplanes were recognized as P-38s. A quick, indignant note was scribbled on Kearby's pad that he was forced to waste gas chasing after unreported friendlies.

The P-47s turned back to search for one of the other formations of legitimate Japanese fighters, but the vagaries of aerial combat hid the enemy that was in plain sight just a short time ago. But this time the fortunes of war were with the Americans when they sighted a number of Mitsubishi Flm "Pete" floatplanes taking off from Kaeriu Island.

There were six of the little green and blue biplanes just committed to taking off when the Americans arrived over them. It was most advantageous for the attackers who were at 8,000 feet when the Petes cleared the water, leaving silvery trails of water behind them in their wake. There was little else for the hapless Japanese to do but weave to avoid the deadly fire of the charging Thunderbolts when they discovered to their horror that they were being attacked.

Lieutenant Ted Wood was on Colonel Kearby's wing when the dive started and later reported the brief fight: "We dove in and I picked my Pete and opened fire at 350 yards closing to 100 feet. I pulled up and saw him burning on the water."

Lieutenant Frank Love went into the dive following Bill Dunham and witnessed a spectacular moment: "...One flew head on to me. I fired a long burst and he went down in flames. A second started to turn into me and I fired at 90 degrees. I blew half his pontoon off and he flew into the hills and blew up."

Dunham had followed Kearby and Wood down and watched the Petes that they had fired on crash into white foam on the water. The scene below was already becoming macabre with oily black

Col. Kearby probably in a staff officer's club around Port Moresby. Note captured Japanese Arisaka rifle overhead.

Marvin Grant's P-47D-4 serial 42-22694, Sq# 64, before remarking early in 1944. (via Norb Krane files)

smoke trails pointing to flames and churning froth on the water and surviving Japanese reconnaissance biplanes twisting low over the sea in obvious near-panic.

He then saw one of the Petes off to the left make a violent turn to close the distance with his own P-47, probably to throw off his aim. "I opened fire at 400 yards," Dunham later reported, "and closed to 200 yards at which time it crashed into the sea while I was still firing."

Kearby had made short work of his first victim when he shot down a Pete on the initial pass. While he was climbing away he noticed the other three Japanese aircraft claimed by the P-47s burning on the water or the shore. He circled just long enough to find another target.

He selected one of the Petes that was trying to scurry away and dived to the attack. The Thunderbolt easily slipped into position for a ninety degree deflection shot and Kearby opened fire with the eight .50s. Strikes were immediately evident on the Japanese which began trailing smoke. Kearby overflew the Pete and was turning for another attack when he saw his target burst into flame and crash into the sea.

Kearby could find no other enemy aircraft flying in the area since his flight had certainly either shot them all down or caused them to crashland, so he called the rest of the flight together to a predetermined rendezvous point. The four P-47s joined up, but

1Lt. Robert C. Sutcliffe of the 342nd Squadron at Finschhafen in January 1944. His crew chief was "Pappy" Powers. (Marshall Vickers)

Kearby was not yet out of fighting spirit in spite of his flight's dwindling fuel supply.

He did decide to vacate the area when he looked up and saw twelve Japanese aircraft at 20,000 feet. His most rigid rule in combat was to have height and speed advantage on the enemy and, even though he would like to have tangled with the bunch above, he led his flight under the clouds at 2,000 feet.

About five miles south of Wewak Kearby and Ted Wood spent the rest of their ammunition strafing a village that showed evidence of Japanese presence. The flight proceeded to Lae and landed at half-past noon for fuel. Once again the hot runways took their toll when one of the Thunderbolts was delayed for an hour with a tire change while Kearby took off at four in the afternoon and landed at Port Moresby an hour later.

Kearby was certainly becoming one of the leading aces of the theater with an even dozen victories while "Dinghy" Dunham was about to become the second ace of the 342nd Fighter Squadron. More was to come for the 348th in the next few days of October in New Guinea.

More sweeps and patrols were the rule for the next few days until the 341st and 342nd Squadrons flew a B-25 cover mission to Wewak on October 22. Eight P-47s of the 342nd took off at eight in the morning from Tsili, followed a half-hour later by nine more from the 341st.

The 342nd was the first to meet Japanese interceptors when seven Tonys jumped the Americans at 2,000 feet about five miles off Dagua. As it was with other American fighter types, the P-47 Thunderbolt experienced some difficulty with the Kawasaki fighter. Somehow, the speed and ruggedness of the Tony made it more successful than other Japanese Army types—when its temperamental engine allowed it to operate in combat.

This time the Tonys were all too operational when they quickly attacked the rear of the P-47 formation. Captain Walter Benz looked back to see the enemy coming down on the second flight while his own flight wheeled around to take the steam out of the enemy attack. Benz went after one Tony that was twisting in a macabre combat snakedance with one of the P-47s. He dived and fired at the Tony, but could find neither plane after he pulled up.

Lt. Jerome J. Fischer by his 340th P-47 #15, "Deborah Boys Club" late 1943. Fischer scored his victory over Cape Gloucester on December 27, 1943. (Guy R. Roberts)

He was alarmed, however, when he saw one of the Tonys below near the B-25s at 2,000 feet. If the P-47 could do anything it could close distance rapidly in a dive. Before the Tony could do any damage Benz came in from behind and watched the angry flashes of his bullets striking the Tony. The Japanese simply caught fire, rolled over and went down into the water.

At the same time, Lieutenant Ed Popek followed Lieutenant Bob Martin into a pass at another Tony. Popek didn't see what happened to this Japanese fighter, but he did see two other Tonys come down fast, one on his flight and the other on the flight behind. One P-47 immediately got on the tail of the rear Tony and the other turned to help its comrade.

That was all the break that Popek needed to get on the tail of the Tony that was now at the rear of the pack. With about forty-five degrees deflection Popek fired two bursts and saw hits in the cockpit. There were three flashes under the clear canopy and the Tony went into a spin while Popek dived away. The badly smoking Tony pulled out of the spin only to dive straight into the water off Wewak.

While this fight was going on, the 341st approached the area at 5,000 feet from the direction of the sea and was jumped by five Tonys that bounced the rear flight from the cover of a rain cloud. At such a low altitude the frustrated P-47 pilots were at a disadvantage and used the superior speed of their fighters to draw away from the Japanese and climb for altitude. There wasn't much the Americans could do about it and claimed only a single probable for the loss of Lt. Harold Jacoby who was missing after the fight ended.

The 342nd also paid heavily for the combat. Lieutenant Wynans Frankfort had devoted all his attention to shooting down an Oscar in the battle area when he was hit and had to parachute into the New Guinea forest from which he was obliged to walk home. Not so lucky was Lieutenant Ernest Ness. His element leader, Lieutenant Charles Whistler, last saw him with a Tony on his tail and before Whistler could do anything he simply disappeared from sight forever.

While the exchange of three Japanese fighters for three P47s was not especially encouraging, the 348th was fighting on a par with the best V Fighter Command units. The next day fourteen P-47s of the 341st Fighter Squadron proved the group's fighting ability.

During a patrol of the Finschhafen area on October 23, the 341st was flying along at 20,000 feet about twenty miles north of the Japanese base when two formations of Oscars and Tonys, totaling sixteen fighters, came down from the direction of Saidor. The enemy was about a thousand feet higher than the P-47s and seemed unaware of their presence even though the sky was perfectly clear.

Captain Sam Blair was leading the 341st and practically jumped in his seat with excitement, even while he led his Thunderbolts to a climb above and behind the Japanese. At first he thought the fighters he saw were A6m-3 Zeros, known to the allied airmen as Hamps. Since they were painted a brown color with green dapple, it is likely that he encountered Oscars.

The first Japanese fighter that Blair set his sights on made a sudden, sharp turn to the left. Without much hesitation Blair aimed

FIERY GINGER between the end of 1943 and mid-January 1944. (Sprangers and Alder, via Krane files)

for the next Oscar in line and opened fire a bit too soon. The enemy fighter steepened its dive and began a left turn.

Another burst from Blair's guns came from closer range and a much tighter lead. Some of the .50 caliber bullets started striking the target ahead and tracers converged on its fuselage. The P-47 pilot must have been a bit overzealous and held his trigger too long because his guns jammed, but not before smoke and flame began boiling out of the Japanese fighter's engine cowl. The doomed plane rolled over and plunged straight for the water.

Lts. Ray Hayes and Glenn Perryman were right behind Blair and watched the entire combat. Blair was disgusted when he was forced out of the fight, but pleased that his first victory was confirmed by eyewitnesses.

Four other Japanese were claimed by 341st pilots before the rest of their fighters took off in no real order. The claim of five aircraft shot down for no losses was a worthy performance for any fighter unit. That same day the P-38s had a big fight over the hotbed of Rabaul and claimed about a dozen Japanese. The 431st Fighter Squadron of the 475th Fighter Group put in the best performance with four Japanese claimed for one loss.

Throughout the first few months of its combat history the 348th had benefited from the leadership of Colonel Kearby. He had organized the unit, trained it, developed tactics that would permit it to succeed against the enemy and led it with personal example to an impressive record. There was still some question as to how effective the group would be without the personal leadership of Kearby.

That question would be answered on November 12, 1943, when Kearby was transferred to Headquarters and Headquarters Squadron, V Fighter Command. His old 348th would carry on without him at the helm, but Kearby was not to be denied and found the time to attach himself to one of the squadrons while he went on to score his mounting victories.

Sergeant Schubert remembers Kearby making the offhand comment on one of his visits to the 348th that it was the worst decision he ever made to advance up to Headquarters level. Apparently, the pressure of all the administrative problems plus the difficulty of getting any combat time wore heavily on him. Kearby perhaps didn't realize how free he was as the 348th commander to pursue his combat goals with little interference from superiors.

General Kenney was ever eager to preserve leadership talent and often forced his most effective fighter people to take jobs in training or planning areas. Kenney was known and respected by his pilots as someone who could get the most aggressive pilots to the front and supply them with whatever they required to get at the enemy.

Consequently, pilots were being removed from combat before they were burnt out only to be lost when they would try "just one more mission." The end of 1943 and first months of 1944 would witness losses which affected Kenney deeply. But at the time that Kearby was moved to V Fighter Command, Kenney was merely cautious and generally ordered him to restrict combat flying.

Kearby now had time for press conferences and appreciated the uses of publicity as much as General Kenney did. One correspondent asked Kearby about his allotment of combat flying and he answered that he was rationed to two flights a week or less. He added that, "The general put a lot of emphasis on that 'or less'."

There was some element of sour grapes when Kearby talked about other matters related to his combat restriction. He insisted that he was not out to break any record, for example. "I just like to hunt," he shrugged. "It isn't that I like to kill anybody, but I do like to hunt. Since we are hunting in good, profitable ground, it makes each flight really a stimulant."

While he devoted a bit less time to combat flying than he may have wanted, Kearby was busy with other schemes. One of the plans

Port Moresby. C-108 (converted B-17) transport sometime in early 1944. 341st P-47s in background. (Cronk)

he supposedly devised was the notion of a P-47 supergroup, manned by the top aces of the theater. One of his predictions came true when P-38s became scarce after the Rabaul operations. There were plenty of Thunderbolts coming into the theater, but Kearby ran into vigorous opposition from pilots in the Southwest Pacific who were still completely sold on the P-38.

However, Kearby still found time to increase his score and must have realized some consolation for his failure to sell the P-47 during another four-plane sweep over the base at Wewak on December 3, 1943. Kearby arrived at Nadzab early on the morning of December 3 and pulled Colonel Bob Rowland and Captain Frank Oksala from the headquarters building. He also commandeered Captain Meade Brown to be his wingman and the four planes were off by 9:30.

They arrived over Wewak at 28,000 feet around 10:50 and circled their P-47s like buzzards over a prospective carcass. Rowland developed engine trouble and called out to Kearby that he was heading back. Oksala followed him back, but, before they could get out of sight, Kearby called out a formation of twenty to twenty-five Tonys and Oscars just below, flying southeast along the coast. Somehow, Rowland looked around and could not find Oksala so he headed in disgust toward home alone while the others would obviously have all the fun.

Kearby opened the scoring for the Thunderbolts when he maneuvered into the sun and began a high-speed dive. He noticed the brilliant light flashing off the fuselages of the enemy fighters, and the bright red discs of the insignia on the wings. It seemed that the Oscars were all sorts of colors—green and rust and silver—when the Thunderbolt slipped into the 7 o'clock position and opened fire from 300 yards. The closing speed was about 350 mph when the Japanese fighter began to break up and trail fire from the left wing and fuselage. Kearby just had time to see it roll over and head down before he skidded onto the tail of another Oscar.

But the Japanese were responding quickly and two more Oscars were turning sharply to Kearby's left. He turned the nose of the P-47 even more sharply and met the enemy head on. He opened fire at about the same time as his opponent from the 2 o'clock position and saw heavy strikes in the heart of the Japanese fuselage and cockpit. Quickly moving his fire to the wingman, Kearby again saw good strikes and passed over the two doomed Oscars, almost colliding with one of two other Japanese fighters coming up behind the first two.

When he looked around again Kearby saw one of the Oscars falling in flames and the other burning on the water below. He also saw Brown turning his fighter joyously about 1,000 yards inland over the smoke plume of a Tony that he had shot down. Kearby shouted the order to retreat when the superior numbers of Japanese fighters were obviously organizing to destroy the insolent American fighters. While Kearby and Brown made their speedy retreat they were joined by Oksala. Another Tony was spinning slowly toward the earth with flames trailing behind and one glance at the beaming Oksala told Kearby that he had claimed this fifth victory for the sweep.

The three Thunderbolts landed at Nadzab and refueled for the flight to Port Moresby. Things had been quiet during the day at Port Moresby and crews on the ground had sweat while they did necessary but dull work on the P-47s. They had only looked up with mild interest while an odd plane or two droned to a takeoff or landing. Then at about five minutes past five o'clock in the afternoon three olive and gray P-47s roared over the strip as if they intended to attack the place. Most people on the ground were startled since the fighters had apparently zoomed in at high speed from nowhere. Again there was surprise when what would normally have been the airplane of an upstart shavetail displayed the familiar blue and white tail and distinctive white letters on the nose, "Fiery Ginger".

Kearby pulled up into an impudent victory roll and then another and finally came around into the landing pattern after completing his third roll. Those who were keeping count realized that it represented victories number thirteen, fourteen and fifteen.

Four days later the same four pilots were back over Wewak at about the same time and altitude. This time Kearby observed three Tonys in the landing pattern far below. He immediately ordered the other P-47s down in an attack, but did not realize that they were engaged by Japanese fighters from behind and could not follow him down.

Unaware, he headed down toward the Wewak strip and was attacking all alone when he approached from behind just as the first two Tonys landed. Determination was never a stranger to Kearby and he noticed that his P-47 was indicating 500 mph when he came up behind the third Tony slightly to the right and opened fire. The Tony took hits on the canopy and rolled over at about 200 feet. However, Kearby swore audibly when his canopy hazed over due to rapid change in pressure during the Thunderbolt's fast descent.

Kearby opened the side window (referred to in his action report as an escape window, perhaps a field modification exclusive to selected P-47s) and frantically looked for his latest victim. He searched around and was dismayed to see neither his intended kill nor his wingmen. Only the unfriendly flashes of what must have been Wewak antiaircraft fire took notice of his presence. He opened the throttle in frustration and climbed back to 26,000 feet after the mist had cleared from his canopy. Since nobody who could verify his claim had seen it, what could have been victory number sixteen went into the record as a probable.

As it was, his sixteenth confirmed victory came on December 22, 1943, during yet another four-ship sweep to Wewak. This time it was with the 341st Fighter Squadron that Kearby flew and he took Lt. Blend as wingman, while Capt. Sam Blair led the second element with Lt. Charles Cronk as wingman.

Two more Oscars were sighted at 8,000 feet while the P-47s patrolled at 16,000 feet. Kearby ordered tanks dropped and fell on the enemy with Blair close behind. The two Oscars were widely separated in a loose line astern formation when Kearby came in from the usual 7 o'clock position and opened fire on the rear fighter from 300 yards with a single three-second burst. The Oscar caught fire and the pilot bailed out.

Blair came up quickly behind the lead plane and flew under the parachute of Kearby's victim in the process. The Oscar became aware and turned so tightly that Blair could only see his tracers enter the rear fuselage and smoke emitting from his target before he was forced to break lest his Thunderbolt snap into a spin. He and Blend later claimed two other Oscars when another large Japanese formation entered the fray.

Kearby encountered the same bunch of angry Japanese fighters, but his firepower was reduced when seven of his eight .50s wouldn't fire. He maneuvered around in frustration and managed to get hits on one of about seven enemy fighters before he was forced to leave the area. He had to settle for victory number sixteen.

The next day Kearby led another flight from the 341st to Wewak. Four Thunderbolts took off from Gusap at 9:40 in the morning and arrived over the target at 10:40 at an altitude of 27,000 feet.

They patrolled for no more than five minutes when two Tonys were observed below at 10,000 feet. Kearby immediately signaled for the attack and the rest is recorded in his combat report:

"...We dropped belly tanks and dived to the attack. Due to broken clouds I lost sight of the two enemy planes but sighted a bomber approaching Dagua for a landing. At this time a Tony appeared at 8,000 feet, so attacked him from 7 o'clock getting a 4 second burst from 1500 to 500 feet closing rapidly at 350 mph. I saw strikes at the wing roots and fuselage. As I pulled up I lost him but saw another Tony at 200 feet heading for Dagua. I attacked him from dead astern at 250 mph, opening fire at 1500 feet for a 10 second burst. He lazily banked to the left and crashed burning in the trees at the end of Dagua strip. No evasive action was taken by either Tony. Our flight was still together and we were on the deck with some 10 to 20 enemy planes immediately visible. Their own ack-ack at Dagua fired on them as they were down to attack us which I believe broke up their attack. We headed for home just underneath the broken clouds at 1000 feet. One Tony followed us but was unable to close as we outran him easily. We left the area at 1100/L and landed at Finschhafen at 1200/L."

Kearby had scored another victory and a probable to bring his total to seventeen confirmed air kills. At this point of the war in New Guinea only Dick Bong, who left for a furlough in the United States in November, was ahead of Kearby with twenty-one victories. Tom Lynch was also in the States with sixteen confirmed victories and Tom McGuire had just returned to operations after being wounded on his last mission. He had a total of thirteen kills which he quickly advanced to sixteen when he claimed three more Japanese on December 26, 1943.

Thus, Neel Kearby had accomplished the remarkable feat of claiming seventeen confirmed victories within four months to bid for the top-scoring honors in the theater. There was no way of telling how many victories he would score in the future despite General Kenney's restrictions. Kearby had the personal ambition of fifty confirmed kills before he allowed himself to be taken out of combat permanently. Only fate would intervene to keep him from reaching that score.

Larry O'Neill and crewchief Stanley Cierkowski by "KATHY" VENI, VIDI, VICI early in 1944. (Vickers)

PART II:
The 348th Fighter Group After Kearby

Chapter 8

Last Missions of 1943

By the middle of December 1943 the 341st Fighter Squadron had been stationed at Durand Drome—better known as 17-Mile Strip—for more than four months. The squadron joked that the weather was evenly divided between rain, mud and heat, and that the Port Moresby mosquitoes were also divided, but into dive bomber and fighter squadrons.

When the 348th was alerted for movement there was really little regret in the 341st about leaving its little home. On December 17, the squadron personnel loaded aboard transport aircraft for the flight to Finschhafen while heavy equipment and support personnel were moved by LST.

Preceding the move to Finschhafen, a change of command took place in the 341st. Major David Campbell had taken the squadron from training in the U.S. through its first months of combat and now was scheduled to become the executive officer of the famed 49th Fighter Group. He handed over control of the squadron to John Moore on November 15 and the personnel of the 341st threw him a farewell party on the twentieth.

There was a spate of action for the 348th during the final weeks at Port Moresby beginning with a spectacular victory won by the 341st over Wewak on November 5. Colonel Rowland was continuing the practice begun by Kearby when he took a flight of four P-

Col. Robert R. Rowland being congratulated by General Kenney while the 348th looks on. (Adrian Gehl via Krane files)

P-47 of the 348th probably being transferred to the 58th FG. A-20 is from the 387th Bomb Squadron, 312th Bomb Group February-March 1944.

47s on a sweep during the morning. Frank Oksala, Ed Roddy and Sam Blair were in the Thunderbolts.

Weather along the route was overcast at 25,000 feet with more broken clouds on the way and over Wewak itself. The Thunderbolts arrived at their patrol area at precisely eleven o'clock and five minutes later located three Japanese formations totaling about thirty-five aircraft at various altitudes.

Captain Oksala was flying on Rowland's wing when the signal to attack was given. He followed his leader around to maneuver from out of the sun directly behind the twelve Tonys at 16,000 feet. From an altitude of 27,000 feet to a point just about two-hundred yards behind the Tonys, Rowland and Oksala were indicating about 400 miles an hour when they opened fire on the shimmering targets ahead.

Rowland's Tony blossomed into a fireball and spun off into the sea below. Oksala had just enough time to see this aircraft, the last Tony in the lead flight of four, fall away in flames before he did the same thing to the number three Tony in the flight. He watched Rowland fly right over the two remaining Japanese in the lead while he followed his own victim in the dive to 8,000 feet.

While Oksala plummeted toward earth and almost engaged the eight Oscars below single-handedly, Rowland had pulled up and circled to the left for another pass at the first element of Tonys. He could see Roddy and Blair attacking the third flight of Tonys and continued to press his own assault.

The wingman of the lead element of Tonys came into Rowland's sights and he let go a burst from about 150 yards, closing to 50 yards and firing all the time. This Tony pilot was apparently still confused by the attack and offered little in the way of evasive maneuvers before flames erupted and trailed behind the shiny silver and green fuselage all the way down to the water.

Rowland climbed out of the combat area and looked to see if anyone else in the flight was in trouble. Blair had difficulty releasing his external tank and let Roddy go in ahead. By the time he got rid of the encumbrance, Roddy had flamed one Tony and dived on the Oscar formation to explode one of them at point blank range.

Blair made up for lost time by attacking the element leader of Roddy's Tony victim. Again, the P-47 closed to point blank range and turned the Japanese fighter into a spinning ball of flame, heading for the sea below.

All three pilots in his flight were still eager for a fight and Rowland could see them climbing for altitude advantage. He was thinking like a commander, however, and knew that the element of surprise was largely spent, and that the four audacious could get only marginal success if they lingered. He called the others together and flew to Nadzab for refueling before returning to Port Moresby.

The same crew was up on another Wewak sweep two days later and almost repeated their success. This time they were flying as a 342nd Squadron flight in the general area of Wau when Crossroads—the fighter controller—interrupted their progress toward Wewak with an enemy plot near Nadzab.

Ed Roddy was the first to see the formation of five Oscars and, by prior agreement between the four flight members, led the attack. He dived on what seemed to be a Tony in the lead a few hundred yards ahead of the Oscars. Just in time he realized that he was about to help the Japanese shoot down a P-39.

There was only time enough in his dive for Roddy to take a quick shot at the lead Oscar and then plunge into the depths. Frank Oksala was on Roddy's wing and slowed enough to shoot down an Oscar that was following Roddy down. Rowland managed to get two Oscars, one at the top of a loop, and Blair shot down another from such close range that its prop wash flipped the P-47 on its back.

The 342nd got into a sizable scrap on November 15 during a failed B-25 escort to Wewak. Fifteen P-47s were scheduled to rendezvous with the bombers, but took off late from Nadzab and could find neither the B-25s nor the B-24s that were supposed to follow them up. There was nothing to do but orbit Wewak and protect the bombers if they appeared in the area.

What the P-47s did find was a group of fifteen to twenty Oscars and Tonys taking off from Wewak and Boram strips. Like olive drab birds of prey the Americans circled at 20,000 feet and allowed the enemy to reach 8,000 feet before they attacked.

Bill Banks ordered belly tanks dropped and led the Thunderbolts down in a bounce. He exploded one Oscar himself and the Japanese pilot bailed out. Another Japanese fighter took so many hits from Banks's guns that it literally flew to pieces and crashed below.

Walter Benz led the second flight down and fired at one fighter that went down in a steep dive. Lieutenant Bob Martin fired at this same Japanese and thought that the pilot had bailed out. Benz claimed a definite Oscar that crashed about two miles southeast of Boram strip. Lieutenant Bob Sutcliffe was on Benz's wing and set fire to the wing of one Oscar which disappeared from view. He then slipped in behind another Oscar and fired a short burst which set fire to the fighter and persuaded the startled pilot to bail out.

After Bob Martin had fired at the first Oscar another came along below at 6,000 feet. The American immediately attacked and later made an exuberant report: "I dove in behind him at about 4 o'clock and hit him good in the wings and fuselage and pieces began to fly off him. He started down smoking and (Lt. William) Upton saw him bail out."

Five confirmed and three probable victories were credited to the 342nd on the mission. The P-47s broke off in pairs and returned to Gusap or Nadzab without the slightest enemy damage to their number. Other American squadrons accounted for eighteen more confirmed air victories.

The following photos show successful 348th pilots from the end of 1943 to the middle of March 1944. ABOVE: "A" (Yellow Flight) 340th FS. (Parsons)

Lyle Dowsett by his P-47 "PIZONYA" (340th). (via Hess)

Just before the 342nd moved to Finschhafen, Lt. Larry O'Neill's crewchief suffered a serious accident. Ssgt Stan Cierakowski was changing one of the frequent blown tires on the superhot runway when the wheeljack slipped. Instinctively, he grabbed for the wing jack under the wing and his right hand was crushed between the wing and the jack pad.

Cierakowski was described as one of the nicest guys in the 348th and it seemed an unfair mishap for him. He was forced to lie on his stomach on a bed in the Port Moresby base hospital with his right hand stitched to his back for a skin graft operation for several months. The heat and humidity were balanced by the special care and attention of the nurses who responded to the gentleness of the slightly embarrassed mechanic.

For the next four months SSgtr Charlie Fox was assigned to head up O'Neill's crew. Larry O'Neill was a quiet young man from Missouri who left the Army Air Forces in December of 1945 to get a degree in civil engineering. He got a commission in the Navy and retired as a Commander in 1965, returning to his old home town of St. Louis. He would fly an outstanding mission in December 1943 while Fox cared for his P-47.

By the end of 1943 the Fifth Air Force had consolidated its superiority over the eastern end of New Guinea. Only the airstrips in the Wewak area offered any immediate threat and crews of V Fighter Command were whittling away at the threat from that quarter. Cape Gloucester was invaded by Allied forces in December and other Allied air units were able to command the attention of the Japanese air forces to Kenney's northern flank.

Consequently, there was a lessening of aerial combat for fighter pilots in New Guinea in general. Many of the incidental victories were the result of hot or aggressive pilots attacking hapless lone Japanese reconnaissance or random fighter planes. This slack pace would continue well into 1944.

However, there was a period at the end of December which not only brought some new and impressive victories to the 348th, but gave the group its first real test without the direct influence of Neel Kearby. General Krueger's force, codenamed ALAMO, landed in the Arawe sector of New Britain on December 15 and Cape Gloucester on the day after Christmas, 1943. The objective of neutralizing Japanese airfields was quickly realized since the 8,000 defending Japanese troops were virtually cut off from resupply by the rugged terrain between Rabaul and the western end of the island of New Britain.

Mike Dikovisky of the 340th carried a spittoon in his cockpit for the chewing tobacco juice he had to dispose of. Nobody could understand how he negotiated oxygen mask and free flowing tobacco juice during combat maneuvers.

John Moore became a key group leader during the first part of 1944.

On December 26, more than one-hundred V Fighter Command aircraft covered the convoy over the beachhead to beat off determined Japanese air attacks. Sixty-two claims were put in by V Fighter Command pilots including twenty-two by P-38s, eighteen by P-40s and twenty-two more by P-47s, of which seventeen were made by 348th pilots.

The 342nd Squadron took off at 2:55 in the afternoon with a big force of twenty P-47s to patrol the beachhead area while the landing ships withdrew. Nineteen of the planes assembled over the target area at about 13,000 feet when one P-47 turned back early. Remaining planes formed into four flights with an additional trio of P-47s in a modified vee formation. They orbited Umboi Island which experienced heavy, white cumulus clouds up to 30,000 feet.

The 342nd Fighter Squadron was actually the last of the American fighters over Cape Gloucester when its Thunderbolts arrived to cover withdrawal of the convoy at about 5 o'clock in the afternoon. A formation of dark-brown Japanese bombers was sighted coming in from the northwest at 16,000 feet. Most of the 342nd pilots saw them at the same time and couldn't decide whether they were G4m Bettys or Army Ki-49 Helens. But the wind was up and they were the enemy, no matter what the type, and the 342nd attacked quickly.

Captain Ed Roddy was leading Red Flight and opened the attack with a head on pass from beneath on the lead v-formation of bombers. His bullets hit two of the bombers and he observed flames coming from one of them when he streaked past. A 7.7 mm slug from a Japanese gunner ricocheted off the P-47's canopy and cracked the glass, so Roddy could not even identify the type of planes he had just attacked. Wind howled through his cockpit and a sudden explosion told him that his Thunderbolt had been hit in the belly, apparently by one of the tail cannon of the bombers he had just passed.

Lieutenant Marvin Grant was following on Roddy's wing and saw the first target fall in flames. Grant moved to the left side of the enemy formation and made a long 45 degree pass at another bomber. He watched a number of hits flash all over the bomber before it caught fire and fell into the sea. Grant then pulled up and saw Lieutenant Larry O'Neill, who was also flying Roddy's wing, shoot down the second bomber in the formation. O'Neill then went wild and shot down three more bombers to record his fifth victory.

Lieutenant Bob Sutcliffe was leading the 342nd's Blue Flight with Lt. George Orr on his wing at 19,000 feet over Umboi Island when he sighted six green-colored bombers with an escort of three fighters. Circling like sharks Sutcliffe and Orr came in at opposite ends of the bomber formation and dived to the attack. Sutcliffe made a head on pass and set one enemy on fire while another left a telltale stream of smoke. With one more deft strike from the Thunderbolt's guns after Sutcliffe glided in from the rear the Japanese bomber was observed by Orr to go down in flames.

Orr's combat report recorded both his and Sutcliffe's victory: "We dived on the fighters and I fired at one but missed when he dived away. I then made a stern attack on bomber formation. One caught on fire and another started to smoke. Further attacked the smoker from the rear at close range it burst into flames and crashed into the sea. Lt. Sutcliffe destroyed a Betty which I saw explode on his first pass. Lt. Sutcliffe witnessed my destruction of two Bettys and will confirm my claim."

Captain Walter Benz and Lieutenant Bob Gibb immediately climbed for altitude as soon as they spotted the bombers and dived to the attack from the rear. Benz closed to about 500 feet behind one of the bombers and fired a four-second burst from 20 degrees deflection. Both Benz and Gibb watched the Japanese trail fire from its ruptured gas tanks and fall into the water below. Squadron commander Major Gallagher shot down another of the Bombers and Lieutenant Wyroba accounted for yet another Betty (or Helen) to wipe out the entire formation. Lieutenant Winans Frankfort added one of the escorting Tonys when he caught it and shot it into the sea.

Major David Campbell, commander of the 341st until Moore took over in November 1943.

Drent, Wheeler, Nixon, Foulis, Zeine, Anderson of the 341st. Frank Morrison has his back to the camera. (Cronk)

One other Betty was added to the total when 348th commander Colonel Rowland let eight P-47s of Parry Special flight into the battle area. Fighter control told Rowland to "give it the needle" and intercept the incoming raid on shipping in the Cape Gloucester area. Rowland's P-47s were at 15,000 feet over the ships when he noticed what appeared to be a dogfight to the south. He headed his force in that direction when the fighter director called and informed him that an enemy torpedo bomber was starting a run on an American warship in the area. A quick search seaward revealed a dark brown Japanese bomber at 2,000 feet making a left turn in the direction of friendly ships.

Another P-47 below made a half-hearted attempt to shoot the bomber down and then climbed away from the area. Rowland shook his head, noticed that no other friendly fighters were around, then grinned before he dropped his own external tank and rolled over to make a screaming dive on the enemy.

With his wingman following and the rest of the flight heading toward the dogfight above, Rowland made one pass on the Japanese, which he now identified as a Betty, and was surprised to see that it was pressing its attack even though it appeared badly damaged with heavy gray smoke trailing behind. Rowland drove home another attack to within 200 yards from the rear and the Betty exploded, losing its entire left wing and falling the last few feet a ball of flames into the sea.

There was not much of an inkling back at Finschhafen that the 342nd had such a big show until the first seven P-47s returned between five-thirty and six o'clock. Ten more came right in on the first group's tail and treated the groundcrews to a royal beat up of the field.

A great whooping commotion erupted from the men on the ground when the wild victory rolls and low passes of their Thunderbolts told them that the 342nd had been in a fight and were coming home with many victories. In singles, pairs and some flights of three the P-47s slowrolled and roared down the field like some debauched giant birds. Marvin Grant celebrated his second air victory by coming in over the trees along one side of the runway to the end of the parking ramp and pulling up in steep climb to at least 4,000 feet.

Lt. Bob Anderson of the 341st. (C.J. Blend)

Ed Roddy was transferred to the 58th Fighter Group, basically for expressing an unpopular opinion. He rose to command the 58th and is remembered as one of the shining stars of the 348th.

Charlie Fox was on the flightline trying to take it all in when he noticed Linechief Joe Baxter shouting encouragement to Grant. "Roll that mother...," he kept exhorting the rampaging pilot until Grant swept into a perfectly graceful maneuver. Normally dignified and relatively restrained, Baxter cheered, jumped into the air and batted his fist like a shadowboxer.

Fox was even more impressed by Bob Sutcliffe's roll. He actually came down below treetop level at the opposite end of the runway, straightened out and drove his screaming P-47 the length of the strip. He was so low that pieces of coral dust were sucked up through the pierced steel matting by his propeller before he pulled up just as he reached the trees and rolled his fighter.

When O'Neill finally came in for a landing, Fox was eager to find out how he had done. The P-47 that O'Neill was flying had been a headache for Fox—the only P-47 that he maintained that ever gave him sustained trouble—and was inordinately troublesome after this auspicious mission. While O'Neill was taxiing, one of the brake cylinders malfunctioned and caused the fighter to make an awkward groundloop.

Fox was dismayed at the final bit of clumsiness shown by his P-47, but did manage to find O'Neill perfectly unharmed. A broad grin cracked the normally waxen countenance of the victorious pilot when he let his groundcrew know that he had claimed four kills. Fox was bursting with pride in the young O'Neill.

Nobody in the 342nd would ever equal the feat of claiming four Japanese aircraft in a single mission—except for "Dinghy" Dunham's four scored after he had left the 342nd to command the new addition to the 348th, the 460th Fighter Squadron. Fox recalls that O'Neill was awarded the Distinguished Service Cross for his performance that day.

Fifteen bombers and two Tonys had been claimed by the 348th for the loss of a single Thunderbolt. Since the first combat of August 16, 1943, the 342nd Fighter Squadron had accounted for over fifty Japanese fighters and bombers with a loss of around four of

Bob Gibb was an original member of the 342nd who scored five kills in a short time. He was killed in action in Korea.

their own fighters in combat. The 341st Squadron had claimed twenty-eight victories for the loss of two of their Thunderbolts and the 340th had accounted for ten more victories. There would be more to come for that squadron to close the gap.

At Port Moresby the 348th had been largely spared the burden of Japanese bombing. With the added threat of American air units at Finschhafen the enemy stepped up bombing attacks and sent out at least six night raids between December 18 and the end of the year. Several men were killed by the insidious anti-personnel bombs known as "daisy-cutters" and the 348th groundcrews began to share directly the dangers their pilots faced.

Larry O'Neill after his last victories. P-47D-11 42-22903.

One of the improvised solutions to the night bombing problem was a modified version of the Douglas A-20 Havoc light bomber, known by the designation of P-70. Packed with radar and other necessary equipment, the redoubtable bomber made a slow and ineffective nightfighter. Fewer than a half-dozen claims were made over New Guinea in P-70s.

Charlie Fox was awakened rudely one night in his Finschhafen tent when the sound of an aircraft engine bearing down on camp indicated a sneak bombing attack. There was no alert sounded and no sound of antiaircraft going off, but the men of the camp shot out of their tents and vaulted into the first shelter or slit trench they could find. Fox was sore for days afterward from slamming himself to the ground.

There was no explosion or crash and the aircraft simply dived for the strip again and again. It was concluded later the aircraft was nothing more than a slightly lost P-70. Another nocturnal P-70 reported surprisingly heavy antiaircraft fire over Cape Gloucester at the same time that the guns at Finschhafen were blasting away at an intruder bogey. The controller finally told the P-70 pilot to come down since he was over his own base and not Cape Gloucester.

After December 20, when two Betty bombers dropped six bombs harmlessly into the jungle, there was a week's lull in the

Japanese attacks that gave the 348th groundcrews a short but uneasy breather. The impressive victory of December 26 had generally raised spirits, and the 342nd in particular had a new surge in morale. The end of 1943 had vindicated the group as a top fighter outfit. By December 31, Kearby's twelve victories scored as commander of the 348th was rivaled by seven credited to Rowland, Dunham and Roddy. John Moore had six victories and Larry O'Neill had his five.

There would be no Japanese night attacks until December 27. During the day, however, the 348th repeated its successes of the day before, this time with the 340th and 341st taking the honors.

Field Order 179 directed the 348th to the Cape Gloucester area once again and the 341st arrived over Arawe at about nine in the morning on December 27. Sixteen P-47s of the squadron were roaming at 7,000 feet over the water when about forty single-engine fighters were sighted dead ahead, above and below the American formation. The fast, white wakes of U.S. Navy PT boats in the blue water below turning to escape the attacks of the single-engine fighters above indicated that the bogeys were Japanese. Two P-47s were sent to engage the enemy above and the rest of the 341st dived to the rescue of the PT boats.

Col. Bob Rowland had trouble with his radio, but led two flights down to the attack and picked on a brown-colored Zero which was just climbing away from strafing a patrol boat below. Rowland looked around and saw only the flight led by Captain Arthur Weeks following closely behind, so he chased the fighter at an indicated airspeed of 325 mph at less than one thousand feet off the water. Just west of Arawe the Zero suddenly pulled up into a righthand chandelle, but Rowland was able to follow him long enough to put a burst into his belly and engine. The Zero belched black smoke and fell to explode in the sea below.

Captain John Moore kept hearing cries from the controller at Arawe that he was being attacked. When Moore called and asked the controller's position he heard no answer. He called again and this time the controller responded, "I'm being attacked, give me some cover!"

Jerome J. Fischer early 1944.

Someone in his flight gave Moore a sighting and he was able to see bogeys to his right, far out in the water. The P-47 flight's tanks were dropped and Moore led his fighters into a gaggle of Zeros attacking a PT boat. One Zero broke away to the left and Moore was able to give him an accurate two-second burst.

Two Zeros were above Moore and half-rolled on him and his wingman, Lieutenant Henderson. The P-47s dived for a cloudbank and lost the enemy. When they emerged Moore saw another Zero diving away and followed it into an overcast. Playing hide-and-seek in the fluffy mass, Thunderbolt and Zero ducked in and out of the clouds until Moore got his quarry in his sights and fired a long burst into the cockpit and engine area. The Zero fell off on its left wing and crashed into the woods about ten miles north of Arawe. Arthur Weeks happened to fly into the area just in time to see the Zero crash and burn. Moore's first victory was also confirmed.

Lieutenant John Lolos was flying Weeks's wing and had his big day in combat. He dived to help a P-40 that was chasing two Zeros when one of the enemy turned head on into him. Lolos held the gun button down until the Zero passed very close to the right. During a fast climbing turn he looked back to see his flaming target crash into the water. Another Zero attacked from the front and Lolos repeated the performance, only this time the Japanese pilot managed to bail out. Yet another Zero managed to latch onto his tail and Lolos jinked and skidded until Weeks was able to come to his aid and shoot the Japanese down.

The two P-47s that climbed to engage the Japanese above were flown by Merle Zeine and

348th line sometime early in 1944. (Guy R. Roberts)

William Foulis. They dropped their tanks and zoomed up to engage four Zeros that seemed to be separated from the rest. Foulis pointed the nose of his fighter up steeply and fired on an enemy plane from the rear with slight deflection. Hits were scored on the tail and then on the canopy and engine when the .50 caliber fire was pulled through the Zero's fuselage. Tiny bits of the canopy flew off and smoke and flame poured from the engine.

Foulis flew over his doomed victim and was surprised to see the pilot bail out. Foulis then watched the Zero crash into the ground west of Arawe and saw Lt. Zeine finish off another Zero which fell away smoking badly to crash nearby into the woods east of Arawe. For whatever reason, the rest of the enemy planes disappeared during the fight.

The Japanese encountered by the 341st during this fight were the most skilled and aggressive ever encountered by the squadron. One P-47 was reported missing and its pilot was believed to have parachuted into captivity. Another 341st pilot, Lt. Lynch, had the scare of his life when a really good Zero pilot got behind him at low altitude. 7.7 mm bullets crashed into the P-47 cockpit and wounded the man in the arm. But the big Thunderbolt protected its human cargo long enough for the pilot to ditch and escape into the water

Randall Hilbig and crew chief SSgt Cavit Vinson. (M. Vickers)

off Arawe. A nearby PT boat saw the marker dye in the water and rescued the pilot who was virtually submerged in spite of his Mae West.

Just as the 341st was about to encounter the enemy the 340th Squadron was scrambled on a vector to the same enemy formation. Sixteen P-47s raced through absolutely clear weather and sighted an enemy force of twenty fighters at about 15,000 and twelve divebombers below at about 1,000 feet. While other flights took out the fighters, Captain Meade Brown led Blue Flight down on the Vals. Meade fired and exploded the leading Val with an accurate burst from one-hundred yards behind. His wingman, Lieutenant Richard Fleischer, attacked another group of three Vals and exploded two of them with a single pass.

Lieutenant Mac Hnatio was leading the second element of Blue Flight and witnessed the astoundingly rapid destruction of the three divebombers and recorded the subsequent action in his report: "...I then noticed the second two ships of that flight come in to the attack. I closed in on the last one, fired and turned to the right slightly, firing at the first one. I looked back and saw the first one crash into the sea and the second one right beside it in flames.

"We turned sharply to the right and started to climb. From above and about two o'clock came four fighters. I turned into the fighters and came in on the second man in the formation. He pulled up to the right. I pulled up with him, firing all the time. At that time I was fired on by the other ships of the formation and broke away. Looking behind I saw the fighter I had fired on crash into the sea. I had been hit and not knowing the extent of the damage returned to base."

Other 340th flights mixed it up with the Zeros, Oscars and Tonys above. Lieutenant Richard Lake claimed a Zero and a Tony, Lt. Jerome Fischer got another Zero, Lieutenant Stanley Souders was credited with yet another pair of Zeros and Lts. Frost, Zaage and Pitchford each added single kills. Squadron leader Hervey Carpenter added another Val to cap a sixteen victory day for his unit. The 340th suffered only two damaged P-47s.

The last day of the year saw another ten victories for the 348th to bring its tally above the 120 mark. It was another scramble to Arawe and the 340th and 342nd Squadrons again engaged the Japanese. The 340th caught three Vals and quickly dispatched two of them. Sixteen P-47s of the 342nd found six Vals and five Zeros below them and fell on the enemy. All six Vals and two Zeros were claimed.

Lieutenant Robert Gibb added another degree of luster to the day when he claimed two of the 342nd Vals to gain his fifth victory. He was element leader of White Flight when the enemy was sighted at ten minutes after one o'clock in the afternoon. His flight was at 14,000 feet when Gibb saw three Zeros and five divebombers far below. He followed the flight leader through the Zero formation and fired an ineffective 45° deflection shot at one before he passed through the Japanese fighters and down to the water where he saw three Vals disappear under a 500 foot overcast.

Gibb went right on into the cloud and spotted one Val dead ahead. He fired a single one-second burst from three hundred yards and another two-second burst from one hundred yards. The Val veered off to cross the shoreline and crash into the trees. Gibb then cleared his tail and went down after another Val. Another two-second burst and Gibb was an ace. Lieutenant Bob Knapp flew behind Gibb and witnessed the whole thing.

Finally, the 348th was recognized for its remarkable record by the award of a Distinguished Unit Citation. In spite of the doubt cast on the P-47 as a combat weapon and the general consensus that only the P 38 could effectively engage the Japanese over the long distances of Southwest Pacific operations, Neel Kearby and the 348th proved that the Thunderbolt could be used with devastating effect.

Neel Kearby about the time that he left the 348th Fighter Group.

Two 341st pilots late 1943 - early 1944.

The citation itself is a testament to the record of the 348th:

CITATION

THE 348TH FIGHTER GROUP IS CITED FOR OUTSTANDING PERFORMANCE OF DUTY IN ACTION FROM 16 TO 31 DECEMBER 1943. IN THE MIDDLE OF DECEMBER 1943, THE 348TH FIGHTER GROUP WAS DESIGNATED TO HELP PROVIDE FIGHTER COVER FOR TROOPS ENGAGED IN LANDING OPERATIONS AT ARAWE AND CAPE GLOUCESTER, NEW BRITAIN, AND FOR BOMBERS STRIKING AT ENEMY INSTALLATIONS. THE AIRPLANES OF THE GROUP FLEW THE FIRST MISSION IN THIS IMPORTANT ASSIGNMENT ON 16 DECEMBER 1943, THE DAY OF THE INITIAL LANDINGS, AND THEY WERE CONTINUALLY IN THE AIR OVER ARAWE AND CAPE GLOUCESTER FOR THE REMAINDER OF DECEMBER.

SEEKING OUT AND ATTACKING THE ENEMY AIRCRAFT OF ALL TYPES, OFTEN IN ADVERSE WEATHER, THEY COMPLETELY DISPERSED HOSTILE BOMBERS AND DIVE-BOMBERS ATTEMPTING TO ATTACK OUR GROUND AND NAVAL FORCES, AND ALTHOUGH OFTEN OUTNUMBERED TWO OR THREE TO ONE, FIERCELY OUTFOUGHT PROTECTING ENEMY FIGHTER AIRPLANES. THE GALLANTRY DISPLAYED BY THESE PILOTS, MANY OF THEM HERETOFORE INEXPERIENCED IN COMBAT, IN FLYING THESE HAZARDOUS MISSIONS EVERY DAY, AND THE TIRELESS DEVOTION TO DUTY OF THE GROUND CREWS IN WORKING DAY AND NIGHT TO KEEP THEIR AIRCRAFT IN TOP FIGHTING CONDITION ENABLED THE 348TH FIGHTER GROUP, IN A PERIOD OF 16 DAYS, TO DESTROY 79 ENEMY

AIRCRAFT IN THE AIR WITH A LOSS OF ONLY 2 OF ITS OWN, A RATIO OF ALMOST 40 TO 1. THE COMBAT PROWESS OF THIS ORGANIZATION WAS A FORMIDABLE FACTOR IN THE CAPTURE OF ARAWE AND CAPE GLOUCESTER AND MADE AN IMPORTANT CONTRIBUTION TOWARD THE NEUTRALIZATION OF THE ENEMY IN THE BISMARCK ARCHIPELAGO. THE COURAGE AND DEVOTION TO DUTY DISPLAYED BY THE PERSONNEL OF THE 348TH ARE IN KEEPING WITH THE HIGHEST TRADITIONS OF THE ARMED FORCES OF THE UNITED STATES.

Chapter 9

Combat: January-February 1944

Sometime in the last weeks of 1943 Neel Kearby's FIERY GINGER III was retired and sent to the newly arrived 58th Fighter Group. The 58th and 348th had developed something of a rivalry from the days that they shared quarters at Bradley Field during the spring of 1943.

Actually, the rivalry was reportedly centered between Kearby and the commander of the 58th, Colonel Atkinson. Rumor had it that the 58th was rarely assigned missions that would promise contact with Japanese aircraft because Kearby had the power to delegate operations to the two fighter groups. The allocation of P-47s was also apparently in Kearby's hands for many of the Thunderbolts acquired by the 58th were handed down from the 348th.

FIERY GINGER III was used on subsequent operations with the 58th and was identifiable to its crews by the markings that were left intact, including the name and twelve victory marks under the cockpit. 58th Fighter Group pilots must have had mixed feelings, to say the least, taking the famous old P-47 out to do the workhorse duty of ground attack.

Kearby's next P-47 was serviced by a crew headed by Ssgt Pankyo in the 341st Squadron. Roscoe "Ace" Slider was as adamant about his job as Kearby was about his, creating some friction between the two men. Kearby had enough respect for the old soldier Slider to simply switch squadrons rather than pull rank on him.

On January 2, 1944, a force of about 7,000 Americans was landed at Saidor, almost halfway between the Huon peninsula and Madang. When the Saidor invasion force was doubled the Japanese to the south were cut off from retreat and had to mount a grueling march through the mountains.

From his end of the projected encirclement of Rabaul, MacArthur had taken control of the Admiralties and Bismarck Islands during March. Almost completely encircled, Rabaul evacuated all of its effective air units during the months of February and

Lt Bernard M. Mahoney and his P-47 "RIDGEWOOD ROWDY."

Lt Bernard M. Mahoney, "RIDGEWOOD ROWDY", and friends.

March. By the end of April both Madang and Hollandia had fallen to the Allies, effectively cutting Wewak off from the war.

Perhaps there was a sense of urgency in Neel Kearby's mind when Saidor was invaded because he could project to the near future and guess that his P-47s would likely be relegated to ground attack missions once Wewak was neutralized. He continued to fly his usual fighter sweeps with the 348th whenever he could get away from the desk as January 1944 entered the scene.

However, Kearby was pressing hard to become leading ace in the theater and by the beginning of the year was within five kills of assuming the front rank. The day after Saidor was invaded he got away from Headquarters, V Fighter Command to fly a series of sweeps with the 341st Fighter Squadron.

He managed to find three pilots to take off on mission number 1-58 at about eight-twenty on the morning of the third of January. The rest of the squadron was covering a bombing attack over Borgen Bay. Thus, Kearby was once again able to get a small force to cover him while he ranged against the Japanese at Wewak.

This time he was fortunate enough to find a Ki-21 Sally just as it was taking off to the west from Wewak strip. Kearby led his wingman down and left the other two up at about 25,000 feet for cover. There were about six other fighters visible in the area, so Kearby was taking something of a large risk to make his attack.

In this case the attack was as swift and uncomplicated as it could be. Kearby simply glided like a falcon onto the tail of the Sally and exploded both engines with a short burst. Flames slipped back from the once sleek and pristine bomber that was now shedding burnt pieces of metal into the dark smoke marking its dive. After the Japanese aircraft fell into the water off Wewak strip the two Thunderbolts climbed back to join their comrades.

Kearby was back in the air by 1:30 in the afternoon with another three P-47s for the 341st on mission 1-60. An hour later they were over Wewak again and within fifteen minutes Kearby had an opportunity to register victory number nineteen.

His combat report for the mission describes what Kearby saw and did when he sighted the enemy aircraft from his vantage point at 27,000 feet:

"At 1445 one enemy Zeke was sighted below proceeding from But to Wewak strip at 4,000 feet. Two of our P-47s had 'SNAFUED' and had returned to Finschhafen, so my wingman and I came in for the attack.

"I opened fire at 1,000 feet from dead astern indicating about 350 mph. I saw strikes on the fuselage and after a three second (burst) the Zeke burst into flames. As I passed him I turned slightly

Mike Hnatio in January 1944.

Ed Roddy's P 47 with crewchief on the wing. "BABS IV" in white and red. February 1944.

to see that he definitely went down. Instead, the fire went out and the Zeke continued on its course. I made a 360° turn and came in from dead astern once more. No evasive action was taken by the enemy airplane.

"I gave him a six-second burst and he again caught on fire, but after I went by him the fire went out again. We were down to 1,000 feet now and then I turned to come in again; the enemy plane crashed into the sea.

"The weather was clear at sea with cumulus inland from 2,000 to 15,000 feet. We proceeded to base and landed at Finschhafen at 1630/L."

Six days later Kearby collared Captain Walter "Jim" Benz and a couple of wingmen for another sweep over Wewak. The four P-47s took off from Finschhafen at about ten minutes after ten in the morning and were over the target area by forty-five minutes after eleven. There were rain squalls and clouds at the P-47 altitude of 20,000 feet, but the Americans could see Wewak harbor clearly enough to observe a large ship covering itself with a smokescreen. Apparently the four Thunderbolts were not entirely unnoticed.

More threatening attention became evident after the American flight had been patrolling for about a half-hour when eighteen Tonys came boring in from the right. Perhaps the Japanese were becoming impatient with Kearby's unwelcome intrusions into their airspace and were finally determined to do something about it.

Kearby obliged them by turning the flight head on into the teeth of the enemy formation and opening fire at the leader when they were about three-hundred yards apart. The Tony took strikes on its fuselage and began smoking when it flashed by Kearby.

Lieutenant Charles Cronk was flying on Kearby's wing and automatically drew himself as much as possible behind the relative protection of the Thunderbolt's engine and forward armor while he followed his leader straight through the Japanese formation. He dared look back long enough to witness Kearby's Tony crash into the sea. He could also see Benz and his wingman in a tangle with the whole formation of angry enemy fighters that had passed only a moment before. The fight was now taking place at the base of the overcast at 20,000 feet.

Since a climb would take him straight into the blinding mist of the clouds above, Kearby decided to make a gentle turn to the left until he saw two Tonys dueling with one of the other P-47s. The Tonys were diving after the P-47 at about the ten o'clock position when Kearby led Cronk to the aid of their American comrade.

Apparently the Tonys thought better of it and broke away, allowing their P-47 quarry to join the pursuit. The Americans were after them with Kearby in the lead, following one of the Japanese into a twisting climb and getting in one good, long burst.

The other Tony was now coming in at Kearby from the left so Kearby could not concentrate on his kill, but turned into the attack. The Japanese pilot was probably only interested in rescuing his comrade because he made a sudden left turn away from a head on confrontation with the Thunderbolt.

Kearby quickly came into range at about 800 feet and calculated about a 4 radii lead at the exposed belly of the Tony in a perfect ninety degree deflection shot. He jammed down on the trigger and the Japanese flew through the tracers which made bright flames erupt in an orange sheet from the right wing root. The Tony fell like a blazing match into the sea.

Jim Benz was in the third P-47 rescued by Kearby's element and he saw the Tony roll over and fall into the water off Wewak. When he had time to look around again, however, there was no sign of the colonel. Kearby was all alone now and noticed that he was down to 6,000 feet with a group of Tonys only about 5,000 feet above him. Discretion was the order of the day even for the usually aggressive Neel Kearby and he dove to the deck and some welcome protection provided by low clouds before he headed for Gusap.

With the destruction of the two fighters confirmed Kearby was now tied with Dick Bong as Top-scoring ace of the SWPA. Bong and Lynch were still back home on temporary duty and leave, but would be back in action within the next few weeks and the race to break Eddie Rickenbacker's WWI record would become intensive. With twenty-one confirmed victories and the claim of one or two Japanese aircraft on each combat Kearby could count on breaking the record within days or weeks at the most. As it was, Kearby was flying much more than Kenney had wanted and Fifth Air Force Headquarters became understandably nervous. Kearby was required to relinquish V Fighter Command to General Paul "Squeeze" Wurtsmith on January 13 and was reassigned to Hq, 308th Bomb Wing where it was hoped his considerable administrative talent would be used to coordinate operations between the command's fighters and bombers.

Meanwhile, the 348th was enjoying one of the best victory-to-loss ratios in the theater. Whenever the group met the Japanese, kills were scored and few Thunderbolts lost. The last P-47s lost were the two that went down on December 27 (no P-47s would be lost the entire month of January), and total group victories over the New Britain operations would exceed eighty Japanese aircraft. January commenced the period of general quiet, but the 348th continued from time to time to add to its record.

One of those times came on January 18, 1944, when a flight of the 340th Squadron flew a successful Kearby-type four plane fighter sweep over Wewak. Lieutenant Mac Hnatio led his flight off the ground a little after seven in the morning through perfectly clear weather between Finschhafen and Wewak.

Hnatio took his P-47s to the usual altitude of advantage; this time to 28,000 feet over the target area. The Thunderbolts were cruising on extreme fuel economy when eight to ten Oscars were sighted below at 20,000 feet approaching Wewak from the south. With a slight course correction to put him in the rays of the sun that was reaching its zenith from the east at that particular time of eleven in the morning, Hnatio prepared to attack.

Unknown to him, as soon as he started his dive on the lead Oscar, the other three P-47s were diverted when they avoided a pass by a flight of nearby P-38s. His own P-47 was committed to the engagement with the Oscars below and he closed the distance with terrific speed.

The Japanese were certainly unaware of his presence since they deviated not a bit while Hnatio quickly slipped into position on the wingman of the lead element. Within a few seconds the range narrowed until the Oscar filled the gunsight. A single burst of fire shot off the Oscar's canopy and shredded the tail so that it detached itself from the rest of the fuselage.

Hnatio was so close to his victim that oil covered his windshield and he had to pull up to avoid colliding with one of the enemy. Far above, Lieutenant Ralph Heiden was flying tailend Charlie in the P-47 formation and saw the Oscar burst into flames and take the long plunge into the jungle below.

There were about fifteen other Japanese fighters now visible in the area and his three P-47s could see Hnatio's fighter struggle in the general direction of home. They formed up on him once more and dived out of the area to outrun the alerted Japanese. Hnatio managed to clear his canopy enough to get home and put in a claim for his fourth victory.

Neel Kearby's hope for a P-47 equipped Fifth Air Force came reasonably close to being realized during January 1944. With the arrival of the 58th Fighter Group that would be operational in February there were now nineteen squadrons of fighters in V Fighter Command and eleven of them were equipped with Thunderbolts.

Lt. Andy Lytle at Finschhafen, January 1944. (G.R. Roberts)

Bob Knapp at Finschhafen, January 1944. Knapp was a pilot before the war. His dad was a violin teacher. (Vickers)

Four other squadrons used P-38s while three flew P-40s and yet one more attached to a bomb group used available P40s or P-39s.

However, this period proved to be the high water mark for the P-47 and the phaseout of the P-40 in the Southwest Pacific. By the end of the year P-51 fighters would largely replace the P47 and the P-40 would be relieved of its yeoman service.

The bombing of Finschhafen by Japanese aircraft that had paused at the end of December was renewed on the night of January 23, 1944, when six Bettys scored a direct hit on a liberty ship, killing five men. The next night two more divebombers dropped their loads without causing much damage.

It must have frustrated the Japanese not to be able to assess the damage they were doing because the next day a single fighter made a pass on an LST and scored a near miss with a 550 pound bomb. Four days later a similar attack by a Zero also scored a near miss on a liberty ship in the afternoon.

One more Japanese fighter-bomber attack in the 348th Group part of Finschhafen came on the last day of January. A Japanese fighter identified as a Zero came over late at night and dropped a heavy bomb. There was a large white splash in the darkened sky over the harbor, but no damage was done.

The 340th Squadron fell victim to a Japanese attack during the early morning hours of February 6 when six Betty bombers came over and dropped their bombs on the dispersal area. Two P-47s were damaged and parts of the airstrip were covered with rocks and mud.

Ssgt Richard Miller was working in the 340th dispersal area during the noon hour on February 17 when he experienced a stroke of mixed luck. An Oscar, probably of the 77th Sentai flying out of Alexishafen, flew low over the base before any alarm could be sounded and dropped a single deadly "Daisy Cutter" bomb. Lethal shards flew in every direction and Miller went down under the barrage.

When he picked himself up again he was surprised to find that everything was still joined together. There was some blood and a little bruise, but no major damage was done by the shrapnel that struck his head. Apparently, the piece of metal was spent and simply bounced up from the ground to glance off the side of Miller's head.

Relatively few casualties plagued the 348th throughout the beginning of 1944. The group was lucky in that while other units lost personnel to the Japanese air attacks there were no more than one or two fatalities in the 348th. Miller was an example of one person in the 348th who was lucky enough in a potentially dangerous place and time.

One of the more tragic losses for the 340th Squadron occurred on February 18 during a routine local patrol. Four P47s of the squadron were orbiting the Finschhafen area when the flight leader noticed two of his planes passing under him. There was one horrific flash of metal grinding into metal almost silently to the witnesses in the air and on the ground.

Both planes fell like broken toys into the sea about five miles northeast of the Finschhafen strip. Alarms went off and both patrol boats and PBY patrol planes immediately raced out to find possible survivors. Nothing was ever recovered of the remains of Lieutenants David Riley or Walter Monroe. It was one of those sudden accidents that seemed to take more of a toll than enemy action.

348th records claim that the group suffered 162 actual combat losses during the entire operational period. Only eight of those losses are definitely attributed to combat while forty seven others are listed as killed or missing due to operational accidents. Presumably, the others were claimed by Japanese antiaircraft except for one that was shot down by friendly antiaircraft fire and another that was shot down by a P-38 in error.

The most fruitful mission the 348th had between the end of 1943 and the middle of March 1944 came on February 3, 1944. The 342nd Squadron was just leaving the Wewak area after a B-24 strike at about 11:40 when three Oscars and four Tonys attacked from behind and above. Sixteen P-47s of the escort turned into the attack and engaged in individual attacks. With P-47s of the 342nd on all sides, the Japanese went on the defensive and fought briefly but bravely. For the next ten minutes dogfights twisted and snarled at the 22,000 foot level about five miles west of Wewak while the B-24s droned undisturbed toward home.

Lt. Malcolm Rand got on the tail of one Tony that was trying to dive away from the area and fired until the pilot jumped and opened his silvery-white parachute. Lieutenant Bill Wallace approached another Tony from the rear and the Japanese pilot tried to escape by diving. Wallace fired a few bursts and convinced this Tony pilot to also abandon his fighter and take to his parachute.

Rand had followed Bill Dunham into the midst of the dogfight when he first sighted his Tony on Dunham's tail. Dunham was firing at an Oscar that he later claimed only as probably destroyed because he was forced to break away with the enemy snapping at his heels. The P-47 pilot rolled and dived his big fighter with the Tony following and shooting all the time.

Rand had joined the chase and fell in behind the Tony. "I closed range and fired a burst," he later recounted, "striking him in the fuselage and wings. He burst into flames and broke off. I gave him another burst and saw pieces fly off him. The plane started down in a spiral and the enemy pilot bailed out."

Dunham just before the move to Saidor in March 1944. Natural metal must be a recent application. P-47D-21, 42-25414. Crew Chief SSgt R.W. Neal, Armorer Sgt W.E. Way.

Banks's Crewchief SSgt Giometti on the right and Marion "Red" Iddings on the left. Finschhafen, February 1944.

After Wallace had pulled up from his combat with the other Tony he looked around to clear his tail. He could see Lieutenant George Davis on the tail of yet a third Tony.

Davis had watched one of the other planes of his flight damage an Oscar when he sighted the Tony above and to the right, on the tail of another P-47. The P-47 dodged the enemy bullets as well as it could before Davis got behind the Tony and forced it to dive away to the right. It was not difficult for the Thunderbolt under Davis's hand to catch the Tony, but he had to chase the enemy fighter down to 10,000 feet before he could draw into range. When he did, Davis fired a long burst from 300 yards and twenty-five degrees deflection and the Tony went into a violent spin with heavy smoke pouring back from the engine and cockpit. Besides Wallace, Bill Dunham witnessed the Tony go down when Davis pulled up to join his flight which had regrouped at 17,000 feet.

Eight enemy fighters had been claimed in the ten minute battle. Dunham flew the only casualty on the American side when his P-47 suffered minor hits in the wing and engine cowling.

On February 4 Ed Roddy led another four plane sweep over Wewak in the afternoon. He arrived over the target area at 26,000 feet just in time to miss a Japanese fighter that had landed at Boram.

A few minutes later he saw the silvery shape of a Helen bomber almost directly below over the water heading for Borum. Belly tanks were ordered dropped and the four P-47s went straight down in a stern attack on the enemy plane. Roddy noticed that there was no tail cannon firing when he pressed his attack and quickly decided that the bomber was some sort of converted transport.

The Japanese was just about 500 feet off the end of the peninsula when Roddy opened fire and saw his bullets strike all over the left wing and fuselage. There was a wicked hail of antiaircraft fire when the P-47 overshot its target, but Roddy noticed one of the other P-47s firing at the unfortunate Helen. In spite of the heavy blanket of antiaircraft bursts around him, Roddy made a 360 turn and shot at the bomber once again, this time right over Borum strip.

Roddy noticed many more strikes flashing all over the enemy plane. The steel core of each bullet struck the metal of the plane

Beaming Lt. George Davis of the 342nd Fighter Group.

and made a small marking burst of light while ripping devastatingly through the airframe. Roddy passed the target once again and weaved his P-47 to throw off the aim of the gunners on the ground below. A glance to the rear told him that he was successful when a black pall of smoke signalled the destruction of the Helen.

Lieutenant George Dougherty was leading the second element behind Roddy and saw everything. The Helen caught fire, rolled over and crashed into the small hill near Borum strip. It was the eighth and last victory for Ed Roddy.

By now the 348th was officially credited with well over 150 air victories. It had been nothing short of astounding that a unit equipped with a fighter type that was virtually written off before it even entered combat should gain so many victories at such minimal loss in a very short space of time. Just as astounding was the fact that Kearby's dream seemed to be coming true, even if only for the moment. The P-47 would continue to dominate V Fighter Command into the first half of 1944 until the P-38 equipped nine squadrons, the P-47 six with several other due for conversion at the end of the year.

March saw the end of the 348th at Finschhafen. On March 13 the 340th Squadron aircraft and air echelon arrived at Saidor where work on the camp area was progressing. The squadron mess hall and showers were already constructed, with the proposed clubs and administration buildings scheduled due to be built.

The 341st Squadron began arriving at Saidor by March 27 and the 342nd was settling in by the end of the month. First patrols by the 340th began as soon as the squadron was capable of launching missions on March 14. For a short time the group would be in range of the Japanese, but couldn't capitalize on the advantage until the end of May or beginning of June.

However, if the immediate days ahead took the 348th Fighter Group out of the forefront of the New Guinea air war they also caused it to fight the less glorious but nonetheless vital battles in the ground attack role. There would be a good deal of divebombing and strafing in support of ground troops. The first missions out of Saidor would include patrol, convoy cover and other missions tha didn't include the prerequisite of long range. Only when the grou moved its base to Insoemanai Island off Wakde in May would have another opportunity for aerial combat.

Chapter 10

Transitions: March-April 1944

By the end of February 1944 when the action around the Wewak area promised to abate and the 348th was looking forward to the confusion and delay of another station move Kearby was getting understandably restless. Bong and Lynch had both returned to combat and were scoring victories while flying on any mission they chose as freelance pilots of the V Fighter Command.

Ted Wood of the 342nd between the beginning of 1944 and April 1944.

Randall Hilbig of the 342nd between the beginning of 1944 and April 1944.

Time was pressing on Neel Kearby and he cut every corner of his safety margin to beat all comers in the ace race. No matter how he may have tried to deny it, the magic number twenty-six was driving him as surely as if it were a hypnotic spell. Bong was slightly ahead with twenty-two confirmed kills and Lynch had seventeen while Kearby still had twenty-one on February 27.

Charlie Fox remembers a typical mission involving Kearby during the Finschhafen period. The 342nd Squadron had been scrambled for another mission to New Britain. Colonel Kearby had flown in for another four plane sweep and simply waited patiently for the sixteen planes to take off so he could join them as an extra man.

He sat in his P-47 with the engine ticking over while the other planes got into the air. Something came over the radio and he grinned as he glanced back to the flight line. With a little circular motion of his hand he indicated that he could hear the 342nd was broadcasting that it was in combat already and he immediately took off to join the fight.

On February 27 Kearby was in the air again, this time flying a P-47 of the 340th Fighter Squadron in the company of Colonel Bob Rowland. Late in the afternoon they were patrolling Cape Hoskins at 22,000 feet when a Mitsubishi Ki-21 Sally appeared below. Rowland positioned on the wing of Kearby's Thunderbolt while they dropped tanks. The two Americans then dived more than 20,000 feet to end up behind the quarry.

It was nearing dusk and the ground below was already dissolving into shadows which would momentarily hide the Sally. Kearby slipped into range and opened fire from about 300 yards behind. Strikes blossomed on the blue-gray hull of the Japanese bomber.

Rowland saw the hits on the wing and fuselage before Kearby pulled up and broke away to the left. There seemed to be fire emitting from the Sally, so Rowland flicked on his gun camera to record Kearby's victory. When the fire seemed to go out and the smoke trail behind the bomber faded, Rowland automatically pressed his own gun trigger from dead astern at 250 yards and saw the usual bright flashes all over the bomber's wings, engines and fuselage. The Sally rolled to the left and both wings erupted into flame before it crashed into the water northeast of Cape Hoskins strip.

Some months after this combat of February 27 Colonel Rowland's film was reviewed by Colonel James Guthrie and Lt.

Colonel Floyd F. Volk of Headquarters, V Fighter Command Intelligence who decided that the Sally should be awarded to Rowland. He submitted a new individual combat report and the victory was confirmed.

Apparently, Rowland never realized that the Sally had crashed until the camera film was analyzed. But, there it was on film. It seems likely that this was the same Sally awarded to Kearby as a probable on February 9, 1944, for whatever reason that date was determined. Thus, it is likely that Kearby's probable of February 9 and Rowland's victory of February 27 were in fact the same Sally destroyed on the same day.

Such as it was, mounting impatience must have been intolerable for Kearby. Neither could his nerves have been put at ease by the fact that Bong and Lynch were now flying together and that they had each scored on March 3. Bong's score now stood at the gateway since he needed only three more kills to break Rickenbacker's record. There was no doubt that he would top the twenty-six mark within perhaps a few days and Kearby was faced with dwindling opportunities offered by retreating Japanese air forces.

The war was a closing window of opportunity for P-47 pilots to claim air victories in New Guinea and the urgency mounted to do something quickly. The ultimate toll of the pressure on Kearby would be exacted within a few days.

March 5 was a day of general quiet for fighters of V Fighter Command. The only claim registered by early afternoon was made during another sweep by Bong and Lynch. Tom Lynch attacked another Oscar at about 1:30 in the afternoon and scored his twentieth victory. Bong had covered Lynch and had no real opportunity to score himself, but the sense of urgency that Kearby must have felt would have been enough to drive him beyond all reasonable bounds.

Lynch scored his victory near Dagua, southeast of Wewak. Perhaps this bit of information itself encouraged Kearby to schedule a sweep to those familiar hunting grounds. Whatever the incentive he managed to collect Bill Dunham and Sam Blair and takeoff from Saidor by four o'clock in the afternoon. By 6:30 Blair and Dunham returned alone to file their report.

It seems that Colonel Kearby would have flown his mission of March 5, 1944, out of Finschhafen where the 348th was yet based while waiting for the move to Saidor, but the collective memory of group veterans dictates that he took off from Saidor. Apparently it was at Saidor that FIERY GINGER IV developed some sort of problem and Kearby got another P-47. He also managed to find Captain Sam Blair and his old friend Dinghy Dunham who agreed to go along as his enthusiastic wingmen.

Kearby had intended to take his three-ship flight as far as Tadji, just up the coast from Wewak, where Bong and Lynch had so much luck recently. Dunham and Blair realized that their old leader was itching for a kill and fell in dutifully on either wing—until Kearby had his first shot. It was anybody's game after the first crack.

At about ten minutes after five the three Thunderbolts arrived over the Wewak area and began patrolling up and down the coast. Kearby was the first to see a Tony approaching the Dagua strip at about twenty minutes after five o'clock, but he eased his fighter back into an orbit at 22,000 feet when it became evident that the enemy would land long before the Americans could reach it.

Japanese Sally bomber of the 14th Bomber Sentai in the sights of a Fifth Air Force Fighter. (USAF)

341st Squadron presentation P-47 from Republic employees. 2/10/44. "WELLLLL" on nose.

Not more than five minutes later all three American pilots saw a vic of Japanese bombers, glistening green with unmistakable red national markings, coming in from the sea at about 500 feet. There were three of them coming in over the bright blue water in a perfect formation that matched the P-47 flight exactly. It must have seemed like the ideal setup to Kearby.

In point of fact, what the P-47 pilots identified as G3m Nell bombers were probably a trio of Ki-48 Lily bombers of the 75th Sentai, since the Nell had not operated over the area for some time. The 75th Sentai dispatched a total of twelve Lilys from Hollandia to the Wewak area on or about the March 5, 1944, date.

As it was, no time was lost in ordering Dunham and Blair to drop their tanks and, by the time they did, Kearby was already on the way down. Blair fell in behind Dunham and watched while the Japanese bombers started circling Dagua strip to the right. When the P-47s had dropped to 1,000 feet they saw that they had been discovered since the quarry now began a gradual let-down to head up the coast to the west. Ahead, Kearby's P-47 was firing away at the lead bomber which was down to no more that 200 feet.

Blair saw what he took to be two separate bombers rear up in flames and crash to the ground. In truth, it must have been the Japanese aircraft at which Dunham fired only a second or two after Kearby's attack.

No more than a moment later Blair closed to two-hundred yards behind the aircraft on the right and fired a two-second, almost no-deflection burst. Flames poured back from the fuselage of the doomed bomber before it fell off on its left wing and exploded when it crashed into the ground below. Blair brought the P-47 smartly into a turning zoom climb to the left and looked around for Dunham and Kearby.

The next thing that he saw was Kearby reversing his turn to the left and break to the right with an Oscar on his tail. Dunham streaked in from the front and fired a head on burst that caused volumes of flames to erupt from the Oscar.

There were other Oscars diving on Blair from behind, so he went down into the protection of some clouds in a valley. To his relief, Blair found Dunham a few minutes later and the two headed for home after vainly trying to reach Kearby by radio. Blair was troubled by the fact that he saw a radial engine airplane crash into the ground at Dagua strip.

Dunham was even more worried than Blair from what he had seen a few minutes before. He, too, believed that Kearby had shot

341st P-47s on Saidor, April 1944.

down his victim on the first pass. Following closely on Kearby's tail he had shot at the left hand bomber and sent it down in flames. Even at the terrific speed at which the P-47s were flying there was time for Dunham to take a split-second and skid onto the tail of Kearby's target, firing an ineffective burst before he wisely zoomed upward to the left.

During his zoom, Dunham had time to witness Blair's victory over the third Japanese plane. When he reached 180 degrees of the turn, however, he saw Kearby's P-47 climbing directly toward him with the Oscar following closely behind. Reacting quickly, Dunham pushed the nose of the Thunderbolt over and raced to meet the Oscar in a head on pass before it could claim Kearby.

His aim was good and the first burst hit the Oscar's engine and fuselage. The Japanese pilot broke off the attack on Kearby's Thunderbolt and turned to meet Dunham, but the P-47's second burst seemed to be fatal as the Oscar turned into a giant fireball. Dunham passed very close to Kearby and looked around to see what he believed to be the P-47's canopy flying off. By the time he was able to level his own fighter again there was no sign of Kearby's plane.

In retrospect, it seems that Kearby and Dunham had fired at the lead bomber and the aircraft to its left within the space of about three seconds. Perhaps Kearby was a little too eager and fired an ineffective burst. The fact that Dunham thought Kearby's target needed another pass suggests that it was not destroyed right away.

What seems certain now is that Kearby lost the momentum of his dive by making a 360 degree turn to shoot at his bomber again. Both Dunham and Blair believed that Kearby had destroyed his target on his first pass and was attacking one of the other bombers.

It may have taken as much as five to ten seconds for the complete circle, but Kearby made a second attack on his first intended victim and destroyed the bomber with a dangerous sacrifice of speed and altitude.

The pilot of one of the Oscars above must have thought that he would never get an opportunity like this again. In a perfect position for a bounce was a P-47 below, climbing slowly to regain precious lost speed and altitude. If he hadn't done it yet, the Japanese pilot probably dropped his tanks if he carried them and primed the two 12.7 mm Type 1 machine guns that fired through the propeller just ahead of the Oscar's cockpit.

Kearby was certainly aware of the angry little Peregrine Falcon, as the Oscar was dubbed by the Japanese, descending on him with its heavy caliber talons extended and its engine screaming like its bird of prey namesake. Even with his options limited the supreme airfighter Kearby must have estimated his chances within the scant moment allowed him. He may have seen Dunham's P-47 and angled his own fighter toward that possible means of rescue. There was little chance of outrunning the Oscar and Kearby was still too low to dive away.

It was standard practice for Japanese Army Air Force pilots to draw into close range of the target before firing a burst at the enemy. This practice was probably the case now when the enemy fighter zoomed close enough to fire a burst from within one-hundred yards of the Thunderbolt's cockpit and engine.

Most likely the Oscar was from the veteran 77th Sentai which was still very active in the area. This Japanese pilot had no more than time enough for one or two chances to fire before Dunham came down like judgment day to divert his attention. Japanese records for the date mention only that an Oscar was engaged by enemy fighters and heavily damaged, but managed to crashland at one of the Japanese strips. It seems to matter little in view of the fact that the great Thunderbolt ace was lost forever.

Bill Dunham was beside himself when he landed back at Saidor. He demanded that a fighter be prepared so he could go back and look for Kearby. His fellow pilots tried to calm him, but in the end he had to be restrained from going back alone to look for his friend who moment by moment became more certain to have crashed into the endless New Guinea jungle.

The reaction to Dunham's and Blair's reports was mixed. There were those who could not believe that he was really gone and retained the hope that the indomitable Kearby would return. Others were simply shocked and tried to sort out their own feelings—and recomputed the chances for their own survival.

Yet others, especially those in the ground crews, shook their heads in confirmation of their own conviction that Kearby was just taking too many chances. More than once he would charge his Thunderbolt into the center of the combat like a bullfighter with utter disregard for the deadliness of the bull. This time he had taken one chance beyond the number allotted to him.

Colonel Neel Kearby was a polished military pilot. He had been responsible for training and leading the 348th Fighter Group into outstanding success. He also wanted personal glory and realized that his life had to be the stake for the prize. In the end he had crossed the hair's breadth distance between glory and catastrophe and had paid the ultimate price.

341st maintenance at Finschhafen or Saidor.

341st camp area probably at Saidor. (Cronk)

The last air action fought by the 348th before the group moved to Saidor came on March 11, 1944. Thirteen Japanese fighters were claimed by the 340th Squadron during a late morning sweep of the Wewak area by eighteen P-47s. Only three squadron P-47s were damaged in a landmark mission for the 340th.

1st Lieutenant Lyle Dowsett was leading the second element of White Flight at 22,000 feet over Wewak when he sighted about fifteen Japanese fighters from 25,000 feet to the very tops of the trees below. Lieutenant Andy Lytle was flying Dowsett's wing and saw six of the Oscars flashing their silver bellies and green/brown sprayed camouflage about 2,000 feet below. The two P-47s dropped their tanks and the chase was on.

For the next fifteen minutes the P-47s flew a twisting and savage engagement in which thirty to thirty-five Oscars, Tonys and perhaps one or more of the new Ki-44 Tojos maneuvered to escape. They used steep turns, half rolls, split-esses, dives and climbs, fast chandelles and slow rolls to either escape the wrath of the P-47s or aggressively try to wrest the offensive.

Dowsett and Lytle drew first blood when they each downed an Oscar. Lytle saw the wing of Dowsett's target literally crumple off in flames. The two of them then attacked a pair of Tonys and Lytle shot one of them down into the water. Lt. Tom Barber came along in time to shoot down another Oscar closing on Dowsett's tail.

Mac Hnatio was leading the second element of Blue Flight and downed another Oscar for his fifth victory. He saw six Oscars in the marking style of the 77th Sentai—stylized sevens resembling birds or feathers on the tail—coming in from the west and circling north.

Immediately the P-47 element dropped its tanks and turned to face the Japanese fighters. After the first pass Hnatio turned madly to get on the tail of one of the enemy.

Surprisingly, the P-47 pilot managed to get a thirty degree deflection lead on one Oscar and watched his tracers arc just below the greenish/gray fuselage. Pulling his fighter into a tighter turn, Hnatio managed to move the line of tracers into the engine of his victim. Lieutenant William Carter was on Hnatio's wing and saw the Oscar fall into the sea two miles off But airdrome.

The leader of Blue Flight was Lieutenant Richard Fleischer who sailed into the same group of Oscars and shot two of them down. The pilot of one of them bailed out, but his parachute failed to open. The other Oscar victory crashed into the water west of Kairiru Island. Fleischer also observed Mike Dikovitsky shoot another Oscar into the water. It was Fleischer's fifth air victory and Dikovitsky's third of five.

Lieutenant Bill Bennett saw what he at first believed to be two P-47s before they started an attack on 340th leader Major Hervey Carpenter. While one enemy plane began getting strikes on Carpenter's P-47 Bennett quickly identified it as a Tojo and fired at it to get it off his leader's tail.

Carpenter was relieved to look back and see the Tojo go into a wild zoom and fall off into the depths below. Lieutenant Lloyd Zaage had already downed one Oscar when he noticed Carpenter dive on another and send it smoking into the jungle. Dikovitsky saw another Oscar hit by Carpenter explode and crash into the water.

Another P-47 was being hit by an Oscar at close range when Carpenter made a desperate shot from a bad angle to drive off the Japanese fighter. Captain Yoshiro Kuwabara of the 77th Sentai was involved in this engagement and claimed a P-47 during the fight, probably the same one saved by Carpenter. Kuwabara was killed in a fight with another P-47 unit three days later and had more than twelve kills to his credit.

Unknown to him at the time, Carpenter had been flying his most successful combat in a damaged fighter. Two Oscars and a Tony were following Carpenter and the other P-47 damaged by the Oscar and chased them as far as the Sepik River.

The two damaged P-47s were pulling away from their pursuers when Carpenter noticed his left wing was on fire where a 20 mm shell from the Tojo had exploded. With a slight bit of relief he noticed that the hole was just about two feet from the cockpit and that the fire was exhaust being drawn through the hole.

After outdistancing the enemy he throttled back to take stock and was able to see that the left tire was completely burned. The radio, airspeed indicator and hydraulics as well as the water injection system were shot out of commission. He was obliged to make a wheels up landing at Saidor.

Moving to Saidor. (Cronk)

When Lloyd Zaage broke off combat due to his low supply of gas he went down to about 4,000 feet and began to relax. It was a bit too soon, he regretted a short time later when he felt bullets begin to hit his P-47. He sent the P-47 into a diving spiral to the left, but the enemy hits had already made his engine run so rough that he could hardly see the instrument panel for the vibration.

He got down to the water and trimmed the Thunderbolt when the startling specter of a black Tony crept up only a winglength away. The unruffled Japanese fighter slipped behind the obviously damaged P-47 and fired the rest of its ammunition. The P-47 could not maneuver so Zaage simply sat there and took it until the Tony wandered away. Zaage managed to land at Saidor with ten gallons of fuel left.

Carpenter later reported the quality of the Japanese pilots was exceptionally high and they "were very aggressive and determined." Some of the other pilots involved in the combat thought that these were the best Japanese pilots the 340th Squadron had ever met. All three damaged P-47s had either stayed in the combat area long enough to give the enemy a good target or were lured to lower altitudes by the decoy Japanese fighters playing off the treetops.

It was one of the greatest missions flown by the 340th. Fourteen Japanese fighters had been claimed destroyed and three others damaged. One Oscar claimed by Captain Bill Chase was observed to go down smoking and crash in flames on a small island off But strip, one of only two victories in the battle to have crashed on land rather than the sea. Two more 340th pilots were now aces and the squadron's victory total now stood at forty-eight.

Charles Cronk's flight returning to base. (Cronk)

By the end of March the 348th Group was settling into the mud and rain of Saidor. Charlie Fox remembers a few clear days at the base, but the tops of the Owen Stanley Mountains seemed forever obscured under a heavy cloud cover. At least the group personnel had better quarters to deal with the wet conditions since the tents all had wood floors and were raised on stilts to avoid the muddy water.

The rainy days curtailed much of the operational flying and the men of the 342nd Squadron devised some unique diversions. One day Ace Slider came careening into camp in Joe Baxter's jeep, blowing the horn and shouting for everyone to come and see what he had brought back.

Tied to the back of the jeep was a boa constrictor about three times the length of the jeep. The thing didn't move and appeared to be dead. Slider dragged the reptile into the tent he shared with Baxter and the result could be heard all over the camp.

Baxter told Slider to get that thing out of his sight and not to dare ask to borrow his jeep again—ever! The exact language delivered at the top of Baxter's voice was described as extremely "more colorful."

If the 348th couldn't always get to the enemy, it seems that he managed to reach the group at Saidor. The red alerts were usually just "Washing-machine Charlie" slipping in under the radar in a

Mike Hnatio and Armorer Tony Drozd. (Tony Drozd)

Captain Daniel R. Kester, 340th Intelligence Officer, and Mike Dikovitsky.

badly tuned bomber to drop a bomb or two just to harass the sleeping troops.

One night a single phosphorous bomb was dropped which did nothing else than convince the naked personnel lying flat on the ground that foxholes would be a good idea. The next night, however, Tokyo Rose claimed over the radio that Imperial Japanese bombers had bombed a secret underground hangar at Saidor. The men of the 348th had not seen a hangar since they left Australia and enjoyed a good laugh at the claim.

On April 12, 1944, the Fifth Air Force completed a successful series of bombing raids on Hollandia. That day an A-20 of the brand-new 417th Bomb Group had some difficulty finding Saidor in the rough weather on the way home. The pilot managed to land on the downhill end of the runway and slid almost into a groundloop on the rain-slick surface.

Another A-20 was a bit too fast in following that one and missed the u-turn at the end of the strip. The 342nd Squadron P47s were lined up at the very turn and were in the way when the A-20 came barreling through.

Ssgt Bob Firestone let his jaw drop when the bomber slammed into his P-47, "Dirty Old Man", usually flown by Jim Benz. The P-47 spun around and hit another Thunderbolt while the bomber hit a drainage ditch, broke apart and trapped the pilot upside down in his portion of the cockpit. Many 348th hands worked frantically to free the A-20 pilot from his straps while water, gasoline and hydraulic fluid flowed freely in the ditch. He was removed unconscious from the wreckage while several other A-20s were making similar perilous emergency landings.

Another rough day at Saidor came a few days later during the infamous "Black Sunday" of April 16, 1944, when about two-hundred bombers and fighters of the Fifth Air Force were trapped by a sudden weather front while returning from a raid on Hollandia. The most accessible landing place was Saidor and most of the aircraft in distress were trying to reach the strip. Thirty-two aircraft were lost in the process.

Confusion was rampant and there were some fatal errors. One B-25 photo reconnaissance bomber (F-10) and a P-38 reconnaissance (F-5) came in from opposite ends of the runway and collided.

Wreckage of a Ki-61 Tony, Probably at Saidor. (Cronk)

Captain Ed Popek in his P-47 "Little Bess" got three Kates in June 1944 to score his fifth victory. He was with the 348th from the beginning.

342nd P-47 with interim horizontal stripe.

Jim Benz's "Dirty Old Men" cowling on a later P-47.

Captain Weddle managed to get some of the crewmen out of the wreckage and earned his second soldier's medal. Captain Arthur Schrager, the group dentist, also did his bit during the emergency by driving one of the ambulances.

Even though the group was not in the air at the time there was some anxiety over the fact that Colonel Rowland was flying to Saidor during the emergency. However, he managed to skirt danger and eased some minds when he landed at Saidor late in the afternoon.

In spite of the fact that missions were usually routine and sometimes scheduled far apart there were some innovations. Captain Max Wiecks and Lieutenant Andy Lytle took off on the first glidebombing test on April 3. For a few days only small bombs were used in raids on Kar Island. Wiecks and Lytle dropped their loads on a house on the southern end of the island and the test was considered successful.

Major Carpenter received orders at the end of the month to return to the U.S. and Captain Wiecks replaced him as commander of the 340th Fighter Squadron. Andy Lytle replaced Wiecks as Ops officer.

One other note in passing about the turbulent period of March and April 1944 is that brand-new unpainted P-47D-21 fighters began appearing in the group. Silver aircraft had been arriving in V Fighter Command since as early as January and the appearance of the highly visible machines heralded a new period of intensive action for the group.

Chapter 11

Thunderbolt in the Shadow

Hollandia fell late in April 1944. With that Japanese base now in Allied hands the P-47s of the Fifth Air Force were even more handicapped in their chances of meeting the Japanese in the air. The nearest enemy aircraft were based over four-hundred miles away on the Vogelkop peninsula.

From Bunabun Harbor near Kar Island to the north around the mouth of the Sepik River about fifty miles east of Wewak, the 348th Fighter Group was engaged during the beginning of May with glidebombing Japanese installations. Allied ground troops found the going much easier than earlier campaigns because of ground attacks by aircraft which prominently included the 348th. Morale among the personnel of the group was not enhanced by the mundane nature of the missions, but there was satisfaction in doing a worthy job for the ground forces.

The 340th Squadron was doing most of its bombing with a skeleton crew. Most of the squadron embarked on May 9 by LST

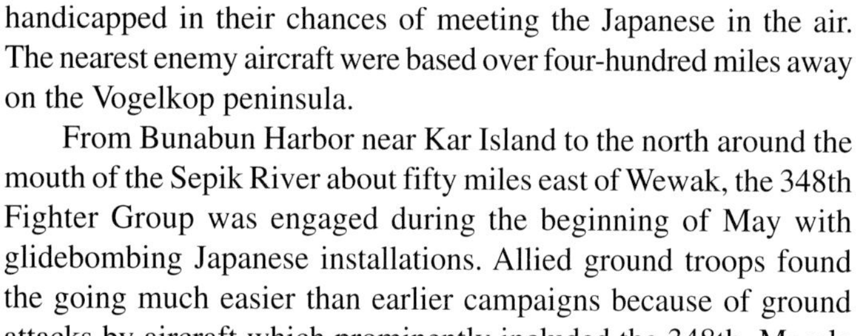

Tony Drozd of the 340th sending a personal greeting to Premier Tojo. Drozd didn't realize it yet, but Tojo had no more than a few months left as Premier when he would be deposed in July 1944.

P-47D-23, 42-27901, of the 340th on Wakde in June 1944. (Roberts)

Bob Sutcliffe on Wakde. (Vickers)

David Eastham on Wakde.

from Saidor to the new base on Wakde Island, northwest of Hollandia. A force of seventy enlisted men with five ground officers and thirty pilots remained behind to carry out the bombing missions. They bombed areas near Hansa Bay, Bogia Harbor, Potsdam Harbor and Nubia until they also moved to the new base by the end of May.

Enroute to Wakde Island the 348th, like every other unit making the move, stopped at Hollandia. The former Japanese base was suitable for some units, but others—especially the P-47 groups—had to use other fields. Range was one factor and the limited length of the runways at Sentani or Cyclops airdromes discouraged use by the heavy Thunderbolts.

Joe Moor was impressed by the beauty of Hollandia Harbor when his LST landed there later in May. The gorgeous scenery was somewhat marred by the clutter of ships in the harbor and the chaos

Interim marking scheme on Wakde.

David Eastham on Wakde.

Ted Wood on Wadke.

of equipment, supplies and ammunition piled on the white coral beach.

Some troops on the beach couldn't direct Joe and his twin brother, who were in the company of Lieutenant Howard Cosyns, a pilot of the 342nd Squadron, to any point in the area. The confusion was so complete that the three men took off on their own in "Muriel", one of the squadron ambulances.

They headed up the road that seemed to lead to the strip at Sentani, having taken a carton of rations from an unloading LST for their day's food. Heading slowly up the mountain grades the three men found an impressive array of Japanese fighters left behind by the fleeing enemy. There were mostly Oscars and Tonys standing stoically about, no longer able to resist the American presence.

It was lucky that someone noticed the ambulance was low on fuel because there were yet some gasoline drums scattered about. After handpumping Japanese aviation fuel into the vehicle the men decided to eat and got their letdown for the day. What they thought was the standard 10-in-1 ration happened to be a case of iron-ration raisins. It was all they had to eat that day.

Later, when they decided to start back down to the beach, U.S. Army engineers were coming up the narrow road with heavy equipment. The only thing for the ambulance to do was back up the treacherous mountain road until a turn could be made (nobody wanted to face bulldozers and graders in a showdown with a Dodge panel truck).

Somehow, the maneuver was negotiated in spite of several near things at the steep edges of the road. The engineers passed at a wide spot in the road and the ambulance made its way down the grade until it joined some other 348th vehicles at the bottom. Within a few days the entire group was on its way north and west to Wakde.

After Stan Cierakowski returned to take back Larry O'Neill's P-47, Charlie Fox returned to his former position as assistant crew chief on another P-47. Joe Baxter decided to send Fox with about twelve other mechanics to Port Moresby for the training and orientation of new P-47 pilots.

Fox was impressed with the quality of the pilots he met at Port Moresby. He also thought they were very young. He was only twenty-four at the time, but a year of service in New Guinea had aged him considerably.

Popek and Knapp in June 1944.

Howard Lorenz of the 341st by his #44.

Even though it was only mid-1944 the first examples of the P-51 Mustang had arrived at Moresby, according to Fox. He was privileged to taxi one of the fighters around the parking area and found the steerable tailwheel quite simple to operate. Other than that, his normal prejudice for the P-47 led him to conclude that the coolant system on the Mustang would make it quite vulnerable to engine damage.

Sometime in July 1944 Fox returned to Wakde Island via Hollandia and he got a chance to see the same wrecked Japanese aircraft that had impressed Moor. Fox was not quite so taken with them, however, and considered the Oscar a rather smallish copy of American trainers.

With his C-47 refueled Fox made the final leg of the trip to Wakde. The island was about a mile wide by two miles long and had gone through several bombings by the desperate Japanese on Biak Island to the north. None of the 348th planes were seriously damaged even though the B-24s had taken hits on the crowded little island. the men of the 348th were actually bivouacked in foxholes on another strip of land nearby and traveled by LCP boats to the airstrip on Wakde.

When Fox landed on the island he was told by Joe Baxter that he was a crew chief again, this time on squadron number 73, which had been Slider's old number and the one used by Kearby when his P-47 was maintained by the 342nd. The pilot assigned to Fox's was Lieutenant Edward Wade, who flew 167 missions with the 348th. He was a good pilot, in Fox's view, easy on his airplanes, but unlucky in not being able to find any enemy aircraft.

Shortly after Wakde had been secured the LCP ferry began running between the campsite and the main island airstrip. Marion Iddings was waiting on the beach with Captain Ted Wood to catch the boat when they noticed a pair of MP guards waiting with a Japanese prisoner. Iddings eyed the man and noticed that he was no more than five feet and three inches tall and weighed about 120 pounds.

He turned to Wood and casually commented, "Scrawny little shit, isn't he?"

Circumstances of collision between C-47 and 341st P-47. RIGHT: Taken approximately the same time as the collision.

Immediately afterward.

Another #44, probably prior to collision.

Lt. Andy Lytle's P-47D-21, 43-25623 about the middle of 1944.

Both men were surprised when the Japanese prisoner replied in perfect English, "I can beat hell out of you, any day."

Captain Wood never let Iddings forget the day or the look of absolute astonishment on his face.

While the 348th was biding its time at Hollandia it endured some precarious exposure on the beach. Several times the Japanese carried out bombing attacks on the tempting targets lying prone in the open. One attack apparently caused big fires among the group's stocks lying in the coral sand. One of the 348th executive officers, Major Lloyd Johnson, got the Bronze Medal for organizing and directing carrying parties to save antiaircraft equipment and other supplies before he was ordered out of danger by the beach commander.

During the harried transition between Hollandia and Wakde there was still time for 348th Group business to go on as usual. On May 24 John Moore became the Deputy Group Commander while Bill Dunham took over command of the 342nd Squadron from Bill Banks on the same date. Banks moved up to group headquarters and eventually commanded the group late in the war.

The 348th finally did get back into aerial combat during the invasion of Biak on May 27, 1944. Somehow, the Japanese man-

340th groundcrewmen by Mike Dikovitsky's P-47D-23, 42-27899. (Roberts)

Ed Popek and crew by "LITTLE BESS." Left to right: Linden Kipps, Popek and R.H. Franzen. (M. Vickers)

Guy Roberts, Jerome Fischer and Mike Dikovitsky on Wakde, June or July 1944.

aged to surprise the Allied planners with a vigorous response both on the ground and in the air around Biak. The original Allied plan was simple enough, but the operation became stalled and developed into a bitter and prolonged fight.

The 348th Group was able to cover the Biak invasion beaches and encountered the Japanese in the air for the first time in a number of weeks. In three engagements the group accounted for more than twelve Japanese aircraft for the loss of one P-47 and its pilot.

On May 27 the 342nd Squadron was patrolling over the beachhead in the afternoon between ten and fifteen thousand feet when seven Oscars and a Tony were sighted below at a few hundred feet. The low-flying Japanese were apparently intent on strafing the invasion convoy.

Lieutenant Marvin Grant was leading the second element of White Flight when he took his wingman down on the Tony which was being followed by three Oscars in an odd formation. Grant was indicating 475 mph when he passed the lead Oscar which made a violent turn to the left to avoid the screaming Thunderbolt on its tail. The P-47 slowed to about 400 mph while Grant drove right up the tail of the Tony and gave the enemy plane a short burst from about seventy-five yards away. The Tony rolled over and burst into flames before it crashed below.

George Burgess in Green Flight had dropped his external tank at the same moment as Grant and followed him in the attack on the apparently oblivious Japanese formation. "Grant overshot the first Oscar," Burgess recalled later, "and I went up his tail giving him a long burst. Grant saw him crash into the trees and explode. I made a climbing turn then and pulled in behind another Oscar and gave him a long burst and when I pulled up and looked I saw him go into the trees and blow up."

Lieutenant Bob Sutcliffe got another of the Oscars which is reflected in his terse combat report: "10 miles east of Bosneck I saw a flight of four Oscars at approximately 1,000 feet. My flight

Richard Fleischer's P-47 "SOLID CITIZEN THE 2ND" (340th Squadron) at Saidor April-May 1944. (Guy Roberts)

dove down from 6,000 feet. For an instant I lost sight of the enemy. I next saw one coming straight at me. I doubt if he saw me because no evasive action was taken. I fired a long burst from 300 yards and saw said plane burst into flames, roll over and split 'S' into the trees. This action occurred about 1645K."

His victory happened to be Sutcliffe's fifth, making him the twelfth ace of the 348th Fighter Group. Lieutenant Charles Nickell also gained confirmation for one of the Oscars to give the 342nd Squadron a total of five victories for V Fighter Command's only claims that day.

Grant's P-47D-4 42-22694 "RACINE BELLE" Finschhafen, March 1944.

Two days later the 342nd Squadron was over Biak again and repeated the performance. Sixteen P-47s were over the southern part of the beachhead covering the fighter director ship when cries for help were heard over the radio at about 8:30 in the morning.

Lieutenant Bob Knapp listened with some apprehension to several A-20s calling for help over the radio. They were being attacked at the same time that ground control reported Zeros strafing the beachhead.

"I spotted the A-20s going east on the deck followed by one unidentified Jap fighter," Knapp stated in his combat report.

"I chased him off, but lost him in the sun. I turned the flight west and spotted a Zeke heading due west along the beach. After a three-mile chase I caught him and fired about a 4-second burst starting at 300 yards and closing to 100 yards from dead astern. The plane burst into flames and hit the water. It was a Navy type Zeke and painted brown."

Marvin Grant was leading an element of White Flight once again when he sighted three Zeros flying near the ground and heading southwest. He called them in to the rest of the 342nd and made a diving turn to get on their tails. Two of the Zeros changed direction, letting Grant get on the tail of the third. Somehow, after four minutes of pursuit, Grant lost sight of his intended victim.

Grant's wingman, Lieutenant Albert Newman, passed his leader in the chase and saw the dark blue-gray Zero in time to call out his position. Grant saw the enemy fighter dead ahead and fired a long 400-yard burst which startled the Japanese pilot into making a steep lefthand climb. Newman and Grant began to shoot at the same moment—Newman from 50 degrees deflection and Grant from head on—and the Zero plunged straight down into the sea, trailed by flame and smoke.

Captain George Orr found another Japanese fighter which he was able to identify as a Mark 1 Oscar attacking an American destroyer. Orr quickly let down from his altitude of 8,000 feet and dropped tanks to take after the Oscar which was now evidently alerted and trying to escape. The Thunderbolt drew to within 200 yards before Orr fired forty-four rounds from each of his eight guns to flame the Oscar which then crashed about 20 miles southwest of Mokmer strip.

Grant and Newman had to wait until their gun-camera film was developed before Newman was officially credited with the destruction of the Zero. Orr and Knapp were given credit for their claims. For Knapp it was the third of his eventual five victories.

348th line at Saidor, April 1944.

Second from left Lt. Knellinger and 2nd from right Lt. Craddock, both of the 341st Squadron chat with sailors on ferry trip, probably on Wakde. (Cronk)

Lt. Marion L. Burt and crewman of the 340th on Wakde, June 1944. "CHRIS" P-47D-23, 42-27905. (G.R. Roberts)

On June 3, the 340th Squadron joined the scoring over Biak when sixteen of its P-47s were in the air during the morning over the beachhead. About fifteen Japanese single-engine fighters were observed attacking American barges below and the 340th dropped tanks to come to the defense of their charges. The time was about 11:20 in the morning.

Major Max Wiecks and his wingman, Lieutenant William Daley, had been chasing a Hamp through cloud just a few minutes before when they heard the fighter controller calling out bogeys to the southwest. They disposed of the Hamp and headed for Mokmer strip on the channel coast between Biak and Dutch New Guinea.

Just south of the Mokmer area Wiecks looked behind him and saw what he thought were two P-47s coming down. He noticed that the two silhouettes coming out of the sun had nonretractable tailwheels and frantically called to Daley to break to the left as the Oscars drew into firing position!

At about the same time Captain Dick Fleischer and his wingman, Flight Officer Roy Martin, saw four dark green Oscars strafing the barges and attacking a PBY flying boat. Fleischer and Martin got rid of their external tanks and fastened onto the tails of two Oscars. The other two Japanese turned into the attack head on and Fleischer got a burst at both fighters before they sped past. He was able to look back and see them break away and down.

341st camp on Wakde. (Cronk)

Fleischer then continued after his original prey until it pulled into the low overcast. The American was very close at that moment and decided to mush straight into the gray blanket to keep the green tail and red national markings in sight. A few seconds later they broke into the clear sky and Fleischer fired a long burst which brought black smoke pouring from the Oscar's engine. The Japanese fighter slowed and seemed to stop in midair. Another point blank burst form the eight .50s and the dying Japanese falcon spun into the sea.

Wiecks and Daley had been able to outdistance their attacker in a diving turn and straightaway dive and at that very moment came on the scene to witness Martin shoot down the second Oscar. All four P-47s headed for home. Lieutenant Noble Jones also flamed two Japanese fighters during the engagement to give the 340th a total of five kills for no losses.

Not quite so lucky was Marvin Grant of the 342nd on the next day. He was patrolling once again the Biak area northeast of Bosneck at 10,000 feet and had just turned his flight to the south when he felt bullets ripping into his airplane. Frantically, he rolled and dived and tried to squint into the sun at the same time to find the enemy. He was sickened for a moment when he thought he saw his wingman heading down for the sea with black smoke trailing behind. Later, he realized that it was the same Japanese fighter that had attacked him. George Burgess had shot the Oscar off his tail.

Grant then gained altitude to about 14,000 feet and spotted four Oscars several thousand feet below. It was the classic setup for 348th pilots and Grant sent his Thunderbolt into a savage dive. Three of the Oscars chandelled to the left, but Grant fired a 90 degree deflection shot at the leader and it immediately blew up. A short head on burst then sent the Oscar's wingman smoking into the sea.

Lieutenant Bill Overbey had seen the enemy fighters coming down from the sun and was frustrated not to be able to warn Grant because of a malfunctioning transmitter. One of the Japanese was able to get on Overbey's tail and put bullets into his P-47 before the American was able to shake his pursuer with wild skids and rolls.

"I pulled back up, but found I couldn't pull but 45 inches (of manifold pressure)" reported Overbey later, "so I started for home. I saw a plane dead astern and several miles away. I saw he was a Nip so I throttled back so as not to overshoot. At about 100 yards I started firing and he immediately burst into flames and crashed into the sea. I found out later that there were 20 Zekes and a large number of bombers in the area."

ABOVE AND FOLLOWING PAGES: 340th armament crews. Credit-Tony Drozd

Marvin Grant had claimed his fourth and fifth kills in this battle to become the latest ace of the 348th Fighter Group. A week later he downed two B5n Kate bombers to round out his scoring and Ed Popek scored three more times to tally his fifth kill.

In the period from May 27 to June 12, 1944, V Fighter Command accounted for forty-three Japanese aircraft, of which the 348th claimed twenty-six. The cost had been less than prohibitive, but two 348th people had paid for the successes. Lt. Colonel David Campbell had left the 341st to command the 49th Fighter Group

Dikovitsky on P-47D-23, 42-27899 in mid-1944.

340th armament crew. Credit- Tony Drozd

and was last seen on the tail of an enemy fighter when he simply disappeared into cloud over Babo on the Vogelkop peninsula during the June 3rd mission.

Lieutenant Winans Frankfort had been shot down once before and returned to the 342nd Squadron, but disappeared during the May 27th fight. Around 1990 a construction team working for a logging company stumbled over Frankfort's P-47 in the Biak area and removed the ammunition to avoid the hazard. A few months later, Dutch aircraft archaeologist Max Ammer found the site and investigated not only the P-47 but also a Zero nearby that had .50 caliber bullet holes in what remained of the fuselage.

Ammer concluded that the P-47 was chasing the Japanese fighter in a dive when both aircraft ran into the ground. The remains were in very poor condition suggesting that both had crashed in the pursuit. For Frankfort, it would seem that his final mission had added one more victory, giving him three confirmed and one probable while he gave the ultimate sacrifice for his country.

The fight for Wakde had been short after the invasion of May 17. The 800 Japanese defenders were quickly overwhelmed and American forces were able to use the two-island complex in good order. It was not so easy with the island of Biak which was invaded at the end of May and not secured until late in June with pockets of fanatical Japanese resistance lasting until August.

One of the larger problems with both places was disease, such as scrub typhus. At least one 348th groundcrewman died of pneumonia from sleeping in an exposed foxhole during the first days of

340th armament crew: Drozd, Al Scanlon and Pete Evanoff, 7/24/44.Credit- Tony Drozd

Credit- Tony Drozd

open camping on Wakde. Ssgt Cornelius Gentry, a 342nd crewchief, developed a sinus infection and Captain Weddle sent him back to Australia for a few months—much to Gentry's mixed feelings of misery and appreciation of good living down under.

Many of the casualties of the Biak invasion were victims of disease before the sanitation measures permitted livability in the area. However, the capture of the Biak airstrips not only gave the Allies new bases for air strikes, but also reduced the threat against overcrowded Wakde. A number of aircraft, including P-47s of the 348th, were destroyed or damaged during June before Biak was neutralized.

The Japanese now had to rely on the few remaining aircraft they had left in the Vogelkop peninsula or risk some of their remaining aircraft carriers in the dangerous approach to New Guinea. Time was running short for Japanese air power in the Southwest Pacific.

During June and July Japanese airmen were retreating on foot from the south toward Cape D'Urville and Sarmi between Wakde and Biak. The 348th developed deadly techniques in strafing the beaches early in the morning or late in the afternoon. Four plane flights of the 340th Squadron, for example, would stagger themselves upward in a string formation. When the leader on the low end of the string would sight enemy troops he would chandelle steeply, the rest of the flight would respond to the signal and spray the area with a deadly pattern of fire that the enemy couldn't hope to escape.

Ironically, V Fighter Command pilots probably killed many of the same Japanese pilots who had been reported shot down in the preceding months. Up to forty per cent of the claims made by American pilots in the Pacific were probably not lost in fact to the Japanese. The abundance of abandoned Japanese aircraft on captured airfields and Japanese aircrew lost to the elements or to American attacks during the retreat represented a large portion of enemy losses.

7/18/44. 30: Drozd's tentmates, 6/15/44. 31: Chet and Cathcart, 340th cooks.

Credit- Tony Drozd

Two examples of those incidental losses on the retreat were Captain Mitsuyoshi Tarui of the 68th Sentai and Lt. Shogo Saito of the 78th Sentai. Tarui was a veteran from the earliest days of Japanese operations and scored at least ten victories in New Guinea. Saito was an Oscar pilot with over twenty victories, including a B-24 over New Guinea. Saito was killed during the retreat on July 2 and Tarui on August 18, 1944.

Whatever the case, very few Japanese escaped from New Guinea to tell the story. Whether they were killed in aerial combat or lost trying to get out on foot the Japanese lost at least two air brigades and a number of sentai (approximately squadron) were written off.

During July and August the amenities at Wakde improved considerably. Insoemanai, the smaller island used to quarter the personnel, was quickly cleared of scrub and undergrowth. The 340th had already erected a mess hall and installed the luxury of a water cooler and established a public address system to broadcast news and music. Volleyball and basketball courts were constructed to encourage the hotly contested tournaments that inevitably followed.

After the middle of June the doldrums set in like concrete. From July through October the 348th engaged primarily in neutralizing Japanese airbases on the Vogelkop peninsula, west of Geelvink Bay and striking the Ambon-Ceram and Halmahera Islands area. Biak, Halmahera, Noemfoor and Morotai were being prepared as staging areas to strike at the Dutch East Indies and for the coming invasion of the Philippines.

The combat evaluation report for August 1944, prepared by Headquarters, 348th Fighter Group leads with an interesting observation: "In a recent skip-bombing flight, an experiment was made using 1000 lb. demolition bombs with 8-11 second fuse delay. Excellent results were obtained. On take-off, the ship handled the same as if carrying full wing tanks. In the air, control of the ship was a little better with the bombs than with full tanks. The bombs can either be released singly or from an altitude of 1000 feet. The IAS in the bombing run was between 230-250 M.P.H. The 'Mark 8' gun sight is a great improvement over the old "K-3-A" type, since it gives better lead for moving targets and is mounted higher, thus giving better visibility for strafing. Anti-aircraft fire was not encountered during the period."

In July the 348th also became the only fighter group in the Southwest Pacific with four operational squadrons when the 460th Fighter Squadron was added to its roster. Bill Dunham was selected to command the "Black Rams", as the 460th became known. Dunham brought Captains George Orr and Bob Sutcliffe and Lts. Willis Cooley, Frank Russo and DeWitt Searles from the 342nd. Bill Carter, Wallace Harding and Richard Frost came from the 340th while the 341st sent Charles Cronk, John Lolos, George Della, Frank Morrison and James Curran.

Marion Iddings also agreed to head the list of ground crew personnel staffing the new squadron. With a cadre of experienced pilots and ground crews the 460th was off to a good start for the operations that lay ahead.

However, the squadron was hardly fit for combat duty in the Southwest Pacific and V Fighter Command scratched its collective head in wonder at the job necessary to bring the unit to operational readiness. The 460th had been hustled out of the United States as soon as it was formed to meet the repeated demands of theater commanders for increased air strength. The pilots of the unit were undoubtedly well-trained, but there was no real cohesion that proper experience as a unified organization would have provided.

Training was begun at Nadzab and the problems were initially tackled. There were the usual incipient problems, but, for once, there were enough airplanes to conduct at least a nominal training program. At the end of July it was possible to form the flights and give pilots some orientation in the 348th method of damaging the enemy with reasonable chance of staying alive. Ground crews fresh from the United States were given the initial shock maintenance terms in the theater and then trained to perform with efficiency in spite of the conditions of those terms.

When July drew to a close most of the older pilots had been on combat operations for a year and had been in the heat and discomfort of the Southwest Pacific even longer. The average length of a tour in the theater was about fifteen months, but even cases of combat fatigue were not permitted return to the United States at the time.

Whatever the reason for keeping pilots and groundcrew beyond normal rotation periods is not clear. The war in Europe had passed its crest with the D-Day invasion and no new combat units were being sent there. In fact, since some P-38 units were being converted to P-51s in England, enough of the twin-engine planes and their pilots were being diverted to the Pacific to lessen the strain on V Fighter Command.

The prospect of more P-38s coming to the theater did not especially hearten the P-47 crews, and the immediate situation of no rotation materially helped sap morale. For the 340th pilots, however, there was some cheer in the news that several fresh pilots were scheduled to come into the unit from a batch of replacements assigned to the group. It was hoped that soon some of the old hands could go home.

One of the pilots who came into the 340th during August was Lieutenant Clifford McMillin. The first time he had flown a P-47 was in March 1944 during his initial days as an officer in the USAAF. He had left Iowa State College in the middle of a term in 1943 to accept an appointment as an aviation cadet. It was probably only the mere chance of a slight illness that got his name scratched from P-38 training for Europe and placed instead on the P-47 list for the Pacific.

McMillan ended up in Headquarters Squadron of Fifth Air Force waiting for a squadron assignment. He kept his hand in by flying P-47s out of Port Moresby between July 9 and August 5. By the time he reported to the 340th a few days later, Wakde was like a rear area with movies, swimming in the warm water offshore and bulldozed areas where tents and more permanent structures were sprouting like mushrooms.

If McMillan had been eager to matriculate into the 340th and wondered about the comforts of his first operational base, he would find that the military has a way of spoiling plans. Without warning, the 348th was alerted on August 23 to prepare for movement to Noemfoor. The next day the 340th and the 341st Squadrons were scrambling to pack up for the move. Only the 342nd could take its time since it was scheduled to move in September.

One distinguished guest paid a visit to the 348th on Wakde that the group appreciated more than a little during the long overwater flights it would make in the future. Charles Lindbergh had been in the Southwest Pacific since June to help extend the range of P-38 and P-47 fighters. Before that he had helped the Corsair pilots in the Central Pacific extend the range of their own fighters.

During June and July Lindbergh had visited and flown with the 8th and 475th Fighter Groups. He had not only helped those P-38 units (as well as the venerable 49th Fighter Group) to extend the range of their fighters, but had actually flown combat missions with the 475th.

On August 16, he left the 49th Fighter Group on Biak in a P61 Black Widow nightfighter for Wakde. When he stepped off the LCP ferry from the landing strip to the living quarters in the afternoon many of the 348th groundcrewmen were either just coming or going to lunch. The airminded youngsters as well as older veterans quickly recognized the tall pilot and for a moment forgot the anger of the war and remembered the adventure that had drawn them to aviation in the first place.

Lindbergh found the Headquarters area and Major John Moore's tent. He and Moore discussed fuel economy in the P-47. The men of the 348th had already heard of his nonstop flight in a P-47 from Brisbane, Australia, to Port Moresby, New Guinea—without external fuel tanks. So, there was a guaranteed audience when he spoke to the squadrons the next day.

A few minutes before three in the afternoon on the next day he was off in a borrowed P-47 for more talks with the Thunderbolt pilots of the 58th Fighter Group. Those who were on the airstrip that day remember Lindbergh's textbook walk around the airplane, strapping himself in the cockpit and calling the clear signal from both sides before switching on the propeller energizer.

His takeoff was also textbook. Brakes set on before takeoff power was reached, then the brakes off and a long straight roll down the runway with the stick in neutral. Within a moment the P-47 was off the ground and disappearing into the sky. The proven veterans of the 348th marveled at the skill of a real pilot.

Credit- Tony Drozd

Chapter 12

Return to the Philippines

Lieutenant Clifford McMillin flew his first combat mission with the 340th Fighter Squadron on August 17, 1944. It was a strafing mission to Ceram Island off the southwestern coast of the Vogelkop peninsula. When McMillin returned from the mission he and all the other new pilots were given a critique by Major Wiecks and began to appreciate the complexity of teamwork required in an American squadron like the 340th.

Fortunately, the rest of the missions from Wakde were uncomplicated glidebombing affairs around the general area where nothing exciting was likely to happen. General MacArthur was in the Hollandia area at the time, signifying that the hottest missions were going to be well to the north.

Since McMillin was a new pilot in the squadron he went by ship to Noemfoor while the older pilots flew the P-47s. The island had been bulldozed clear of vegetation by the time McMillin got there and the living area had been built up with dining hall, latrine, showers and even a radio shack in the process of being erected. The cleared area was crawling with insects, lizards and birds trying to find new cover. There was even some discovered Japanese equipment that the enemy had hastily tried to hide when they were forced to abandon the island.

Dunham about the time he took command of the 460th in July 1944.

342nd aircraft on Wakde about September 1944.

A priority item for all arrivals at Noemfoor was the treatment of all clothes and bedding in barrels of disinfectant to guard against the Dengue Fever carrying insect. The solution was so repulsive that the joke was the fever ticks would stay away just to avoid the smell. The foul odor would stay with the clothes at least for a few washings, anyway.

Some of the animals with which the tent-dwelling 348th personnel had to live were decidedly exotic. There was one insect that was about three inches long and known as the stick because that is exactly what it resembled. When it was disturbed it would jump about a foot in the air with a clattering wooden noise.

McMillin remembered the little four inch green lizard that "would scoot up the tent ropes and sometimes up the center pole right in front of you." One afternoon he was rounding a jungle trail corner and there was a three-foot long lizard standing on its hind legs staring at him. Before McMillin could blink, the beast disappeared into the jungle. The jungle was incredibly dense and probably concealed many animals that the American pilot did not care to track down.

Mosquitoes were also plentiful and threatened any pilot or crewman who was without mosquito netting or atabrine. Sometimes the little atabrine tablets would turn the eyes or skin yellow, but it was

Dunham's P-47D-21, 42-25414.

Bob Sutcliffe in August 1944.

believed back then that they would protect the user from getting malaria.

By September 1, 1944, the 460th Squadron was in training in the backwater of the war and was quickly becoming combat ready. On September 20, Bill Dunham put on his Major's leaves and could look up with pride at the formations of the 460th Fighter Squadron which flew with the indelible mark of the 348th Fighter Group.

Also during September the lessons that Lindbergh had passed on regarding cruise control took effect and extended the range of group ground strike missions. Targets as far as Kaoe Bay in the Halmahera Islands were being attacked. The 340th began consistently breaking its own records for distance and on September 6 flew a mission to Kaoe Bay that totaled one-thousand miles.

Sixteen P-47s made the trip and dropped fifteen 500 pound bombs on the strip at Kaoe. Unfortunately the flak was heavy and Second Lieutenant Miles McDougal's P-47 was hit by a heavy burst. His plane was seen to crash into Wasile Bay, near the mouth of Kaoe Bay.

Morotai Island was invaded on September 15 and 348th P-47s assumed the duty of covering the landing convoys. The invasion went along smoothly and within a few days the Allies had another base; this time in the Halmaheras themselves and well within striking distance of Mindanao in the Philippines.

September saw a change of equipment for the 348th. The older P-47D-16 and D-21 models began to be phased out of squadron service and were replaced by the newer D-23 model. The main difference in the D-23 compared to the older models was the strengthened shackles for greater facility of required bomb loads. The 341st Squadron improvised its own bomb truck that simplified the entire bomb loading procedure.

Increased bombing missions made the 348th more expert in that type of attack. The 340th Squadron would, for example, begin a bombing dive from 14,000 feet and dive at a 70 degree angle to about 7,000 feet, using gunsight to pinpoint the target. Deadly results, especially against airstrips, were the rule.

The 342nd Squadron issued a memorandum on August 18, 1944, that contained some interesting notes on obtaining maximum range. For the flight to the target the P-47 pilot was advised to hold altitude and avoid climbing unless he can easily reach an advantageous tailwind. On the return from the target, drop tanks should be jettisoned and all ammunition fired. The power setting should be at 36 inches of mercury with sufficient rpms to hold 185 to 190 mph at 200 feet minimum descent until reaching 3,000 to 5,000 feet.

It would seem that the talks given by Lindbergh on August 17 had some immediate results. P-47s of the Fifth Air Force would benefit in general during the 1,000 mile missions to Balikpapan in October.

Five missions were flown to Balikpapan oil fields between September 30 and October 18, 1944. The first missions were unescorted and generally costly to the Fifth and Thirteenth Air Force B-24 groups that flew them. On October 10 and 14 there was an escort of V Fighter Command P-38s and P-47s of the 35th Fighter Group with elements of Thirteenth Air Force P-38s augmenting the force. Weather was as much of an obstacle as the enemy defenses, but the results were determined to be crippling for Japanese oil production.

Charlie Fox remembers the period as one of logistical support for the Thirteenth Air Force B-24s by the 348th. The 5th Bomb Group B-24s that staged through Kornasoren Airdrome on Noemfoor required all the fuel available and Fox, among other groundcrew personnel, had to drain all the fuel from their 348th Group P-47s so the big bombers would have sufficient gas for the trip.

After thirteen hours in a B-24 to Borneo and back the Thirteenth Air Force bomber crews were understandably stiff. Fox appreciated his own status as a fighter groundcrewman after "Watching those air crews pry themselves out of those B-24s after returning from the mission..."

The first Japanese raid on Noemfoor was experienced on the night of 8/9 October. One Japanese bomber came over at about 2:35 in the morning and made a south to north pass over Kornasoren. It dropped three phosphorus bombs in the 341st camp area and was reported shot down by antiaircraft fire. It was well that the Japanese crew, whatever their fate, did not know that their sacrifice had netted only a damaged shower for the 341st.

Clifford McMillin had, by chance, been admitted to the hospital with a urinary tract infection on October 8. The excessive humidity on Noemfoor had dehydrated him to the point that he developed an internal colic that caused severe pain. In his misery he had to lie on a hospital cot and listen to the peculiar whoosh of the Japanese bombs while they landed and exploded only 300 yards away.

The 340th Squadron paid the Japanese a return visit on October 9 when fourteen of its P-47s attacked Boela and Liang airdromes in the Ambon-Ceram area. Three P-47s dropped 500 pound bombs on Boela and started a fire with smoke rising to five-hundred feet southwest of airstrip number two. The eleven other P-47s cratered Liang strip and its dispersal areas.

One P-47 and its pilot were missing after the raid. Lieutenant Warren Howland was last seen early in the outward leg of the mission returning home. Even though he was only about ten miles from base he and his P-47 simply disappeared without a trace.

Bombing missions for the 341st Squadron in October were typical of 348th operations during the period. The squadron attacked Boela and Lahai on Ceram, Liang on Ambon, and Babo and Sagan on Dutch New Guinea. 199 bombs were dropped by the squadron with 177 falling in the target area for a nearly ninety per cent accuracy rate.

There were no missions for the 341st in November, and presumably none for the rest of the group, in anticipation for and execution of the move to the Philippines. On October 20, 1944, General MacArthur kept his promise when forces under his command landed on Leyte Island in the southern Philippines.

The subsequent Battle of Leyte Gulf must have been equally gratifying to the Navy as well as MacArthur when virtually all of Japan's seapower capability was crushed and the invasion was in all probability secured. V Fighter Command aircraft landed on Tacloban, Leyte on October 27 and soon made themselves operational in Philippine airspace.

Popek with groundcrew Franzen and Kipps.

Group shot of 341st pilots late in 1944.

The 460th Fighter Squadron was fully equipped and trained in time to be chosen the first 348th Group squadron to land in the Philippines. On November 4, 1944, sixteen P-47s were lined up on the sulphur yellow flight line of Morotai with their crews waiting eagerly for the takeoff. Bill Dunham mounted his P-47 when the word was passed to him and the Thunderbolts took off in record time, circled the field in a parade ground perfect formation and headed for the Philippines.

Dunham landed his squadron at Anguar Island and was delayed when the 460th was ordered to cover a B-25 shipping strike on November 10. It was the first action ordered for the new P-47 squadron and Dunham made the most of it.

The B-25s struck the Japanese convoy in Leyte's Ormoc Bay while it was attempting to counter the invasion that was now just under three weeks old. Dunham led his Thunderbolts down aggressively on a Japanese destroyer that attempted to defend its convoy against the American bombers. There is no record of the eventual fate of the destroyer, but it was at least heavily damaged as were several other ships in the badly scattered convoy.

There was one casualty in the 460th, albeit not from enemy sources. On the flight inbound to Leyte, Second Lieutenant Andrew McLendon lagged behind the rest of the squadron by about three miles. Some aggressive P-38s whose pilots were apparently not familiar with the shape of the P-47 or did not expect to see it so soon in Philippine skies attacked McLendon and shot him down into the Mindanao Sea.

Other losses during the period robbed the 348th of some old hands—well-liked hands at that. John Moore was flying a routine divebombing mission over Ceram when he dived through cloud to find a target. There was some sign of antiaircraft fire and Moore may have fallen victim, but no sign of him was seen after he entered the cloud.

Another pilot was lost when the 342nd Squadron flew a bombing mission to the Vogelkop peninsula on October 24. Four P47s took off at 10 o'clock in the morning for a mission to Laha airdrome. Weather deteriorated during the flight and the four bomb-laden Thunderbolts headed for Babo airfield. The base had been bombed earlier in the day by fourteen Thunderbolts of the 342nd and at least one twin-engine Japanese plane was sighted near the south end of the strip. Thus, the four P-47s were sent to strafe whatever they could find on the damaged base.

At 10:45 the P-47s roared over the field in the face of very light antiaircraft fire and destroyed a Dinah while damaging another Val in the revetment area. The pickings seemed pretty good, the weather was clear and the return fire seemed accurate but too light to worry about. The four P-47s reformed and turned back for another pass. How many times they decided to strafe the place is not known, but one was too many for Lieutenant Malcolm Rand who pulled up into a right turn off the strip, started smoking from the engine and dived straight into the ocean to explode immediately.

Rand disappeared after the explosion. The other three P-47s circled the area but could not find their squadronmate. It was probably nothing more than small arms fire or, at the most, a 20 mm cannon that got Rand. Several other flights were made in the area to search for him, but one of the elements of ground attack missions had claimed the unfortunate pilot; the chance stray bullet that could down the most seasoned and skillful pilot.

On November 12 the 460th Fighter Squadron went out on a glidebombing mission to Linao. The sixteen P-47s hit several buildings in the area, one of which exploded, and strafed a seaplane on the water near Linao until it was destroyed.

Seventeen barges and what appeared to be a minelayer were sighted on a beach near Ormoc Bay, three of the barges being strafed into uselessness. A patrol boat that was determined to be American was also sighted and a destroyer was seen burning in the bay. The pilots also got what could have been their first view of flying enemy aircraft when they observed two unidentified planes at 10,000 feet over the north coast of Leyte.

Later in the day the 460th bombed objectives at Ormoc and flew an uneventful fighter sweep to Negros Island before it experienced its first aerial combat and victory. A flight of squadron P-47s was patrolling the Tacloban area at 9,000 feet in broken cloud conditions when a single Hamp was sighted about a thousand feet below flying across the area.

Captain Richard Frost, a flight leader originally from the 340th Squadron, was leading the formation and turned to dive at the enemy fighter which reacted with gentle turns to the left and right, as if to hold its general course while watching the attacking Americans. Eager in his first chance to score, Frost overshot the Hamp which belatedly tried something of a split-S maneuver. The P-47 recovered the initiative and fired a 30 degree deflection shot which hit the Japanese fighter in the wings and fuselage. The Hamp's left wing caught fire and the plane splashed into the water off San Jose.

Bombing and strafing missions continued until the 460th ran into another air battle on November 18. Major Dunham was leading a patrol of four P-47s in the Buri area when two unidentified Japanese planes were observed diving on a P-61 Black Widow night fighter. The P-47s were able to chase the fighters away, but never

P-47 of the 342nd in late interim markings, circa October 1944.

LST moving the 348th on one of its moves later in 1944. (Schubert)

got close enough to tell what kind of fighters they were before they disappeared into cloud.

Five minutes later an impudent pair of Japanese fighters jumped the American P-47s and Dunham turned his flight into the attack. The Japanese apparently lost their daring and turned off toward the west in the direction of Cebu.

Dunham was not to be denied, however, and closed on one fighter which he identified as a "Zero 32". He closed to within thirty yards and fired until the enemy dived into the water west of the Camotes Islands. Dunham's wingman fired at the other plane, but lost sight of it while it dove vertically to an altitude of about 2,000 feet.

Lt. William Thompson was leading the second element of P-47s and was trying to catch up with Dunham when he noticed that the combat was well in hand. However, there was a Tony flying below at about 2,500 feet and Thompson led his wingman down into a dive to attack the enemy from astern. The Thunderbolt fired one long burst and the Tony began to trail white smoke before it rolled over and crashed into the sea about one-hundred yards off the coast of Cebu.

The first Japanese fighters were silver in color with red Hinomaru national markings in the standard positions. They were probably both Oscars and the Tony was a very dark green color which suggests that it came from the 17th Sentai which camouflaged its fighters in a similar manner. Whatever the unit it came from, the Oscar or Hamp that Dunham claimed was his tenth confirmed victory, making him the only other pilot in the 348th besides Kearby to score in double figures.

The next day another patrol was up in the afternoon when four P-47s took off on a local scramble. George Della was leading the flight in an orbit over Ormoc Bay when he saw what he took to be a Hamp above him at 19,000 feet.

His report describes the action in which Della claimed his second kill: "...I pulled almost straight up for a head on pass, firing a long burst at the enemy plane. There were hits in his engine and left wing. As he dove down past my left wing, between my wingman and myself, I split S's and observed the ZEKE 32 still diving and smoking badly. My wingman had followed me through and we both circled and saw the enemy plane crash into the water midway between the CAMOTES ISLANDS and CEBU."

While Della was returning after his latest victory another flight of four P-47s was scrambled to 18,000 feet just south of Ormoc Bay. Another Hamp was identified flying west about one thousand feet above the 460th flight. The P-47s pulled up into an almost vertical climb when the Hamp suddenly turned and fired in a head on dive. Lieutenant Paul McGuire watched his fire hit the enemy's engine and left wing while the tracers crossed menacingly above his canopy. When the Hamp zoomed past McGuire he rolled the P-47 and watched the Japanese fall and glide with heavy smoke streaming back, finally crashing into the sea between the Camotes Islands and Cebu.

November continued to be a month of hot and heavy action around the Leyte area. The Japanese were hardpressed to contain the American advance and became even more desperate in view of the obvious impending new landings on Leyte and elsewhere. November 24 was an example of the kind of rough action the 460th faced. Fifteen P-47s took off at 9:15 in the morning for a bombing mission to Masbate Island airdrome. After dispensing more than twenty bombs on the runway and adjacent buildings the P-47s strafed other installations including one antiaircraft position whose crew decided the situation was hopeless and took to cover.

On the way back from the mission some of the Thunderbolt pilots noticed shipping in the Port Cataingan area. When they reported the presence of enemy shipping the result was that eight more P-47s were bombed up and dispatched on a skipbombing mission. At about 2:15 in the afternoon two P-47s bore in on a large freighter in the north part of Port Cataingan and scored four direct hits. Large dirty yellow explosions resulted and the freighter was visibly listing while the two eager Thunderbolts further punished it with a thorough strafing. Another freighter was hit in the stern by a bomb and it was run aground to avoid sinking. A third vessel, probably a barge was hit by another bomb and all three ships were strafed by the P-47s after they had spent their bombs.

George Della and Lieutenant Edgar Stoudt took off on a patrol of Nagaha Bay about the time that the P-47s were returning from Port Cataingan. After patrolling for half an hour at 15,000 feet, Della saw a flight of P-38s from the 475th Fighter Group below at 8,000 feet in combat with what appeared to be four Mitsubishi J1m "Jacks". Della and Stoudt immediately dove into the fray and, while Stoudt was able to shoot down one of the jacks with his initial burst, Della missed with a deflection shot.

The chase was on when they went into a turn to the left and Della overshot, pulled up into a zoom climb for altitude and dived on the Japanese fighter's tail again. Della fired one more short burst and the Jack slow-rolled into a vertical dive and burst into flame before it crashed on the south coast of Pacijan Island. Then everybody participated in the chase on the one remaining enemy fighter that was heading for Cebu. Della and Stoudt were short of gas and grudgingly left the quarry to the P-38s.

On November 25 the 460th returned to Port Cataingan to mop up anything left of the shipping after the previous day's attack. The beached freighter was attacked and blew up. Later in the day four P-47s bombed Bitoon Harbor and eight others attacked Valencia airdrome. Later in the afternoon four other P-47s patrolled Valencia and called in strikes until low fuel forced them to return to base. Yet another flight of four Thunderbolts returned to bomb shipping in Bitoon Harbor before returning to base just before dusk.

Moving into the camp at Tanuan. The ground was finally drying up. (Schubert)

Between the twenty-sixth and twenty-ninth of November the 460th was engaged in strikes on enemy airdromes and coastal shipping and in escorts such as cover for a TBM Avenger strike on Legaspi airdrome in the afternoon of the twenty-sixth. Other bombing and strafing missions were also flown with varying results. One twin-engine Betty was claimed on the ground at San Jose, but the strafing P-47 was damaged by flying rocks from its own gunfire.

Such heavy flying could not go forever without some losses and they came on November 29. Sixteen P-47s were prepared for takeoff at 8 o'clock in the morning and were off twelve minutes later. Trouble began early when one Thunderbolt balked and required its pilot to abort the takeoff and land in the water. The rest of the formation carried on at 6,500 feet toward their target, a convoy north of the Camotes Islands, when the lead wingman, Lieutenant Thomas Sheets, noticed a single Oscar behind and to the left.

The rest of the P-47 formation was just completing the bomb run and Sheets jettisoned the one remaining bomb under his wing to climb in the direction of the Japanese fighter. The Oscar apparently sighted the P-47 coming toward him and started to dive away to the west. There was little chance of diving away from a P-47 and Sheets drew into range and fired several short bursts.

Strikes flashed all over the enemy plane and it went into a steep dive to crash and explode in the water east of Cebu. One other P-47 was hit by antiaircraft fire and went down, but the pilot was picked up unhurt by a PBY after the fighter crashed.

On the next day the 340th and 341st Squadrons landed on Tacloban and ended the 460th's monopoly in the Philippines. But there was one big action left for the latest addition to the 348th Fighter Group before it joined the rest of the unit. As it was, the 460th had practically equaled the record of the 348th's last six months and brought the total air victories to over 250.

The mission began at 2:30 in the afternoon when sixteen P47s took off to bomb shipping in Port Carmen. Half an hour later the P-47s started on the bomb runs and there was a sense of routine encouraged by many such missions during the past few days. So, there was a great surprise when six Oscars dived through the third flight and shot down Perry Tubre who was seen to crash into the sea with his P-47. The lead flight of P-47s saw six more Oscars above and cried out the warning, a bit late for Tubre.

All P-47s jettisoned their bombs and reacted quickly. Lt. DeWitt Searles was leading the first flight and turned to climb after the Oscars above and ahead. For some reason the Oscars did not vary from their course and, as the 460th flight reached their altitude, only attempted a shallow dive to the left. Searles may have been puzzled by the Japanese tactics but drove right up on the leader's tail and fired a 45 degree deflection shot. There were many hits on the canopy and fuselage. Searles watched while the Oscar dove straight down trailing smoke and fire, disappearing into a cumulus layer at 3,000 feet.

"HELL'ZA POPPIN" in late 1944 342nd fuselage stripe marking.

Lieutenant Sam Denmark was in the last flight and noticed another Oscar to his right and five-hundred feet below after the initial attack. Both P-47 and Oscar were headed in the same direction and Denmark was able to close to within one-hundred yards. The two aircraft were only about two-hundred feet off the water when the P-47 opened fire and bits of cowling came flying back from the doomed Japanese fighter. The trapped fighter began to burn before it rolled over and crashed straight into Bohol Strait. All other enemy aircraft disappeared and the P-47s returned to base.

It was the first time since its arrival on Leyte that the Japanese had been able to deter the 460th from accomplishing an assigned mission. What was worse, a squadron member had been lost in combat and only the halfhearted resolve of the enemy had prevented a major disaster.

The rest of the 348th began preparations for the move to Leyte around the end of the first week of November. Thirty enlisted men and thirty officers of the 341st Squadron stayed behind with the aircraft while the rest of the personnel boarded LST 569 bound for Dulag, Leyte. They landed on November 15 and endured unloading vehicles and equipment through a downpour of rain and deep, sticky mud. With no little effort they made it through to the campsite near Durauen.

Most of the enlisted men of the 342nd had heard of the famous Navy food and Joe Baxter decided to rotate the personnel traveling by air and sea to allow as many men as possible to appreciate the nautical fare. The first morning out the 342nd breakfasted on real eggs prepared to order, and hot biscuits—at least the sea echelon did.

The LST transporting the 342nd broke down that first day and returned to Biak where a new ship was boarded. Within a few days they caught up to the convoy in time to land in the drenching rain and the arduous unloading.

Charlie Fox helped rush the 342nd equipment off the LST to facilitate getting the ship out of what was certainly a target area for Japanese attacks. There was nothing to do but get the vehicles on the muddy shore since the roads were impassable in the mire and rain. At about ten o'clock that night Fox realized that he and his buddies were sitting under the shelter of a 90 mm antiaircraft gun.

When three red alerts convinced him that he didn't want to get caught under the gun when it went into action, Fox wandered with several other men into Tacloban. The townspeople had converted a small schoolhouse into a hostel for the Americans and the 342nd people enjoyed some local native food and had a warm, dry night's sleep on the prepared bunks.

Clifford McMillin was still a junior pilot in the 340th and did not rate flying a P-47 from Morotai. He, too, relished the Navy food on the LST, but was not as lucky as the 342nd people in finding agreeable quarters at Tacloban. He stood out in the relentless rain after some sort of camp had been established and held a steel mess kit that held a porridge of dried potatoes, meat and other food covered by a peach sauce that soon was mixed with rain water collecting in the kit.

The 341st war diary for November 17 notes what must have been a break in the endless showers of the rainy season. One passage notes that, "The sky over the camp area was alive with dogfights between P-47s, P-38s, P-61s and Japanese fighters."

With the increased presence of American fighters the constant alerts and disheartening possibility of enemy air raids must have been gradually diminishing. On November 14 a particularly bad Japanese attack caused some damage to the airstrip that housed the 460th Squadron and gave a groundcrewmen an opportunity for some display of heroism.

Staff Sergeants Richard McClennon, William Miller, Francis P. Qualles and Corporal Ray Cope ran out to the flight line before the all clear was sounded and warned landing pilots to get clear of their planes and later helped with wounded personnel. Corporals James McClain and Ira Merriman noticed a P-38 hit by a bomb and also ran out while the raid was still in progress to help the wounded of the ground crew caught by surprise.

What the Japanese could not do, the weather could and the 348th was forced to abandon the strip at Bayug. Most of the personnel moved to Tacloban strip #2 by the end of the month and waited for the airplanes due around the first of December.

One of the last formations to take off for Tacloban from Morotai was a twenty-eight plane flight of the 342nd Squadron led by Bill Banks. Bob Knapp took Table Blue Flight and three others were led by Captains David Eastham, Charles Whistler and George Davis. The last leg of the flight was off by 9:45 in the morning.

Around the northern part of Mindanao the weather became so intense that the 342nd flight was forced to divert to the northwest. The P-47s crossed Mindanao and tried to find a passage through

342nd #77 late in 1944. P-38 drop tanks were highly successful on P-47s.

Bohol Island and the Camotes Sea to the west coast of Leyte. There was no luck in finding a way through the murk which ranged from the sea to the highest apparent altitudes.

With gas running low and no visible route forthcoming to Leyte, Knapp asked Major Banks for permission to return to Morotai with his flight and everyone else who had sufficient gas. Permission was granted and Whistler, Eastham and Davis followed Knapp with their flights.

Second Lieutenant Charles Hartman was in one of the flights short of fuel and he went ahead on course for Leyte. His flight crossed the south end of Bohol and flew on the deck up the coast of Cebu, then out below Camotes Island to the west coast of Leyte. They crossed Leyte south of Baybay and continued to follow the east coast. Somewhere southeast of Bugho Point the P-47s began to run out of gas and Hartman saw one of them ditch into the sea. It was Lt. Rumpf who was picked up by a native boat after his P-47 sank within thirty seconds.

Briefly, Hartman was relieved to see the downed P-47 with its canopy open and the pilot moving out of the cockpit. A few minutes later Hartman's own fuel light came on and he began gliding over the beach in search of a landing spot. His motor cut out once and he switched to auxiliary gas which lasted long enough for a single gentle turn before the engine stopped again.

Hartman immediately opened his canopy, leveled the plane, dropped flaps, cut switches and settled in for the crashlanding with only the rush of wind past his head to break the feeling of utter loneliness. Just before the water came up in a final rush, he noticed that his airspeed was about 100 miles an hour.

The tail broke water first, as it should have done in a proper water crashlanding. Twice the tail skipped on the gray waves of the sea and the nose came down into the water, stopping the P-47 completely. Hartman quickly unbuckled his parachute, inflated the Mae West around his neck and dove over the side. He was fortunate in that a motor launch rescued him within a few minutes. Not so lucky was the group that headed back for Morotai. Lt. Sam Kilgore ran low on gas and radioed that he was bailing out near Palmas Island, about 100 miles south of Mindanao. He was never found. The same was true of Lt. Albert Newman who flew back in Whistler's flight and was later heard to radio that he, too, was out of gas. Captain Eastham informed every responsible party as soon as he landed at Morotai and even went out on search flights himself, but neither man was ever found.

One other 342nd pilot, Lt. Douglas Matthews, was reported missing in a flight off Leyte on December 1, and it is probable that he was in the formation of twenty-eight P-47s. As it was, the 342nd was on Leyte by December 2, 1944, but the loss of three pilots in a single non-combat flight must have been a difficult blow.

341st scoreboard on Leyte.

Chapter 13

348th Resurgent: December 1944-January 1945

V Fighter Command had one of its best days of the war during the landings at Ormoc Bay on December 7, 1944. In day long engagements the P-38s and P-47s accounted for over fifty Japanese aircraft at the cost of a single P-38. The 348th alone claimed fifteen kills in combats between 9:50 in the morning and four o'clock in the afternoon.

Dunham at Tanuan, Leyte, in December 1944.

The 460th Squadron was the first in combat when sixteen of its fighters escorted other P-47s on a bombing strike against a Japanese convoy headed for the west coast of Leyte. Takeoff was at 9:20 through generally clear and beautiful weather and the P47s assembled at 18,000 feet to head for Ormoc Bay. The formation was over Jaro on Leyte when aerial combat was sighted over the bay.

Quickly the formation split into flights and elements to cover the dive bombers and to attack any enemy in the area. Several P-38s were sighted at first, then a formation of nine Sallys appeared. Lieutenant Tom Sheets and Flight Officer William Aswell dived on the tails of the Japanese bombers which were just starting a bomb run on an American warship below. Sheets and Aswell slipped in astern of the bombers which were at 5,000 feet and fired virtually at the same time to flame two of the Sallys. The victims spun into the water below and the bomb run was effectively disrupted.

Lieutenant George Grace found a Ki-45 Nick flying over Poro Island and heading for Ormoc Bay at an altitude of 3,000 feet. Grace's element leader attacked first and overshot the Nick which managed to drop a bomb before Grace was able to get behind the twin-engine Japanese fighter. After Grace fired a single long burst the Nick caught fire in both wings and crashed into the sea north of Poro Island. Two more P-47s engaged no fewer than seven Hamps which apparently thought better of the situation and jettisoned their bombs to race for safety.

Dunham, again in December 1944.

The 460th accounted for eleven more enemy aircraft on its next mission, a fighter sweep over San Isidro Bay between two and three o'clock in the afternoon. It was also the greatest day of his combat career for Major Bill Dunham who accounted for four more kills before he landed at Tacloban. He was leading nine P47s over the target area at 18,000 feet when thirteen Hamps were sighted over Arevalo Bay about 6,000 feet below.

Dunham immediately ordered his formation to dive in line abreast and descended on the enemy. He could see the leader of the Japanese formation ahead. The P-47 came up swiftly from the rear and Dunham fired a short burst which lit up the Hamp with accurate strikes. Dunham looked back while he flew over his victim and watched the Japanese pilot bail out. After turning to the left, Dunham noticed another Hamp on the tail of a P-47 and closed in from dead astern to save the P-47 by firing at the Japanese until it burst into flames and crashed into the water off the north tip of Cebu Island.

Fifteen minutes later Dunham had picked up a wingman and was circling the target area waiting for the P-47 formation to reassemble when four Oscars were sighted above. Dunham motioned to his wingman and stalked the Japanese flight in a gentle climb from behind. One of the Oscars apparently detected Dunham's presence and broke to the left. The American quickly moved his gunsights to the remaining three and concentrated on the right hand Oscar. A single burst of .50 caliber fire caused the Japanese fighter to burn fiercely and fall to crash into the water off Palompon. A slight leftward adjustment in his aim and Dunham sent yet another enemy fighter into the water.

The 341st Fighter Squadron was off on a glidebombing mission to the same Japanese convoy at about 2:45 in the afternoon. Bill Foulis was leading White Flight back from the mission about an hour later when he spotted a Dinah coming in from the northwest. The Dinah was about a thousand feet above and Foulis could

Benz at Tanuan, Leyte, in December 1944.

Banks at Tanuan, Leyte, in December 1944.

see that it was camouflaged in green and brown with the usual angry red roundels on the wings.

Foulis ordered his flight to climb in pursuit and his combat report takes up the narrative: "The DINAH attempted to outrun us but I caught up with him and when about 50 yards away and slightly above him, I fired a one second just as he started to turn to the right. Both engines immediately burst into flames and the Dinah made a diving turn and crashed into the water. I pulled up into a high wingover and then proceeded to base. Captain Robert A. DuCharme, leader of Red Flight, observed me making my pass and saw the Dinah, with both engines ablaze, crash into the sea."

With the Dinah confirmed by DuCharme and Foulis's impromptu victory roll, the 348th ended its scoring for the day. It was the first scoring in double figures that the 348th had since March eleventh, and it was the best day the group had in a year. Sixteen pilots were aces by the beginning of December and the total of aerial kills was over 250. More was to come, but time was also running out for Kearby's Thunderbolts to make their record.

It was the best hunting of the war for the Fifth Air Force in the Philippine skies of November and December 1944. For the P-38 fighters as well as the P-47s it would be the crowning moment in the Pacific war. Never again would they have such opportunities or score such impressive numbers of victories before Japan collapsed just a few months later.

Not that the Japanese were ready to capitulate at the end of 1944. Even though Premier Tojo had been replaced earlier in the year and Imperial peace feelers were being extended through Russia, the desperate kamikaze attacks were initiated in the Philippines to somehow change the swelling Allied tide.

One desperate tactic involved the landing of Japanese paratroopers on San Pablo Airdrome during the night of December 6. An estimated twenty to thirty Japanese transport planes flew over and dropped a force of paratroopers in the San Pablo area during the evening of the sixth. Fortunately, most of the 348th had already moved to Tanuan, but those crews remaining at the strip were handed rifles and told to defend their positions against seasoned, tough Japanese elite troops.

341st maintenance, late 1944.

San Pablo was about one-half mile from the 348th camps and the 348th guard posts were understandably edgy and prone to shoot at anything that moved in the night. During the first night at least one Japanese was able to infiltrate close enough to leave a grenade by the 340th mess hall.

On the night of December 7/8 an estimated fifteen man Japanese patrol breached the perimeter in the 341st guard area. Two communications corporals—one a switchboard operator and the other a teletype operator—were found in their foxhole on the morning of the eighth bayoneted and slashed to death. None of the 348th groundcrew relished the thought of hand-to-hand combat with a well-trained and remorseless enemy. The remainder of the camp personnel formed a perimeter that night with the 342nd being the core of the defense on a small knoll running through the area.

The same day one luckless Japanese soldier was spotted running for cover and every American within range opened fire, killing the man almost instantly. By the ninth the 348th guards were tired, dirty and thoroughly soaked with rain. Their trucks came during the day and a grateful group of men left for the relative security of Tanuan. Even a Japanese bombing raid would not seem quite so terrifying now.

On December 12, the P-47s of the 340th arrived at Tacloban from Morotai. One pilot was reported to have bailed out enroute, but was probably picked up by a Catalina since no report of a 348th fatality was submitted.

The 341st and 342nd Squadrons scored some of their first kills in Philippine skies during fighter sweeps on December 10. Lieutenant George Davis barely missed ramming the wreckage of a Tony which blew up practically in his face over Cebu Island. Another Tony was confirmed when Davis chased the damaged fighter into a cloud and a parachute was seen to emerge from the base of the white billows.

In was the fourth confirmed victory for Davis, who, like Neel Kearby was a slow-drawling Texan. If Davis scored moderately during his sixteen months in combat it was not because he lacked aggressiveness or ability. He was a good pilot who followed the rules of teamwork until the opportunities presented themselves for him to make a personal score. He would get seven confirmed victories in the Pacific and fourteen more during the Korean war.

Davis perhaps matured as a fighter pilot during the Korean war and took his chances to the point of recklessness. On his last mission over Korea, flown on February 10, 1952, he had downed

460th Squadron, Leyte. Left to right: Unknown, Della, Frost, Searles, unknown, Bill Carter, Turner, Dunham, Frank Russo. Sitting: Harding. (Parsons)

Front row: SSgt Alfred R. Plechaty, Dikovitsky. Back row: SSgt Edward S. Seegart, SSgt Robert A. O'Boyle, Sgt Robert F. Kavenaugh.

one MiG-15 and reportedly slowed his F-86 to the point of stalling to shoot down his fourteenth victory. The Chinese Communists have claimed ever since that one of their aces, Chang Chi-wei, shot down Davis much the same way Kearby had fallen in World War II.

For his courage and daring Davis was the second 348th pilot to win the Medal of Honor. Albeit the award was granted in another war with another unit, the honor reflects on the character of the 348th Fighter Group.

The 340th Squadron scored its first victories in the Philippines on December 11 during a cover mission over the Ormoc beachhead on western Leyte. Lt. Mike Dikovitsky was leading White Flight when he saw the reflection of a completely unpainted Zero with three other green camouflaged Japanese fighters in some sort of scattered formation. He led his wingman, Lt. Charles Murray, down on the two closest enemy fighters and Dikovitsky shot down the unpainted Zero while Murray got another.

Missions were beginning to come more frequently and Clifford McMillin started flying combat on the next day. It was a generally routine flight, but McMillin shared the general feeling of 340th pilots who were glad to be in the air and able to shoot back at the enemy.

Japanese raiders were still coming over to bomb at night. Twice enemy planes had tried to sneak into the traffic pattern over the Tacloban strip at dusk to strafe aircraft in the landing pattern. American pilots retracted their wheels as soon as their fighters left the ground to be ready for combat. The 90 mm antiaircraft guns seemed to go off every night, signaling the weary crewmen of the 348th to head for the trenches.

If all the headaches of just surviving from day to day weren't enough, there was the added tension of operational crashes on take-off or landing. There were several crashes and a few fatalities during the early weeks of Philippine operations.

McMillin was almost one of the flying accident casualties during one of the Tacloban missions. He had just started down the runway with two 250 gallon external fuel tanks slung under his wings when he realized that he wasn't getting enough revolutions from his propeller. He remained calm and contacted the tower to let them know he was going to cut the throttle and try to get stopped.

He put on as much of the brakes as he dared, but the end of the strip—and the beach and ocean just beyond—was coming up with alarming speed. The most frightening thought was the wheels going off the steel mat runway and catching the sand, flipping this seven-ton gas tank on its back.

Fortunately, the Thunderbolt slowed enough for him to skid the big plane from side to side through the sand and into the water. When he stopped and looked around he was fifteen feet out into the water and could hear the firetrucks and ambulance wailing to the rescue. The P-47 was dredged out and repaired and McMillin flew another mission the same day.

The end of December proved to be the end of the great air battles for the Fifth Air Force. More than fifty Japanese aircraft had been claimed on December 7 for the high-water mark of V Fighter Command victories. The back of Japanese airpower in the Philippines had been broken and action would diminish by January 1945.

There were three good fighter battles left for the 348th at the end of December which would net more than fifty kills. By the end

ABOVE & FOLLOWING: Various of Mike Dikovitsky late in 1944.

of 1944 the group would have scored more than 330 of its approximately 360 kills in the Pacific war.

The first of those battles came during the beachhead patrols of the Mindoro invasion on December 20. Twelve P-47s of the 342nd were on an hour long patrol over San Jose strip when formation leader Jim Benz looked around to find eight Japanese fighters attacking his second element. They were part of about twenty Zeros that hovered above the P-47s that were climbing from 9,000 feet.

Benz quickly ordered tanks dropped and the flights to dive away from the enemy, but his order was not fast enough for Lieutenant John Pate. Pate noticed heavy smoke and thick streams of oil around his cockpit after his evasive diving maneuver had caused the Zeros to break off their attack. He promptly decided to leave the badly damaged P-47 and parachuted to the beachhead below. Within a few hours a C-47 picked him up and he was lucky to suffer no more than a wrenched shoulder and knee.

George Davis had also moved smartly and maneuvered onto the tail of a Zero which took hits in the cockpit. The pilot was certainly either killed or badly wounded when the Zero jerked around wildly and spun crazily into the ground. Two other Zeros were about to get the same treatment from Davis when another Japanese attacked from above and head on. Bullets flew into the P-47's engine and prop and one shell plowed into the left wing, blowing the retracted tire and puncturing the oxygen cylinder. Davis broke away in understandable haste.

Bob Knapp was leading the second flight at 5,000 feet over the beach when he heard the warning over the radio that the other two flights were under attack above. Climbing to 11,000 feet, Knapp and his wingman observed one Hamp pulling up from the fight.

The chase began and Knapp fired a two-second burst which sent the Japanese fighter crashing in flames about five miles north of the airstrip. Knapp shot down another Zero that crashed about a mile inland, emitting an oily black trail of smoke to mark its destruction.

Shortly afterward Knapp saw another Zero jump four P-38s. The audacious Japanese pilot gave the P-38 formation a long burst, then apparently changed his mind and climbed away. It was a bit too late, however, for Knapp was able to fire a short burst before he pulled up to avoid overrunning the Zero. Lt. Bill Krueger was able to stay close on Knapp's wing throughout the combat and his diligence paid off when he slipped in behind the Zero to shoot it down with an accurate burst.

Knapp was astonished when he saw another Zero attacking no fewer than six P-38s singlehandedly. The Thunderbolt dived and fired a two-second 60 degree deflection shot which scored hits all around the Zero's canopy. Unfortunately, the P-47s had to pull up to avoid hitting the P-38s and neither Knapp nor Krueger saw what happened to the incredibly brave enemy.

George Davis of the 342nd and Mike Dikovitsky of the 340th.

As it happened, the P-38 pilots were able to confirm Knapp's second victory and he became the latest ace of the 348th. George Davis's kill also happened to be his fifth and the two pilots brought the group's ace roster up to seventeen.

Clark Field near Manila had special strategic and symbolic meaning for the Americans. It was the key base in the Philippines and was responsible for most of the air raids on Leyte and Mindoro. It was also the scene of one of the great moments of humiliation for American airpower when virtually the entire Far East Air Force was caught on the ground and destroyed in the first days of the war. The initial shock that Allied airmen felt in meeting the redoubtable Zero was also experienced in the Philippines.

To the 348th went the honor of first meeting the Japanese in combat over Clark Field after returning to the Philippines. Thirty-one P-47s took off between 7:30 and 8:15 on the morning of December 22, 1944, to escort the B-24s. The weather was clear at the escort altitude of approximately 10,000 feet and the bombers were herded toward Clark from the southeast. The objective was sighted at about twenty minutes past ten o'clock.

A P-47 was damaged by a 20 mm cannon shell in the initial contact with the Japanese at 10:25 when the 341st Fighter Squadron was jumped by a single fighter from above. The P-47 pilot immediately rolled into a dive and the Japanese fighter followed, allowing Lieutenant David Mumpers in a following flight to get a stern shot. The Japanese fighter, which was later believed to be the first Ki-84 "Frank" encountered by the 348th, went down in flames.

Lieutenant Bill Foulis, who was leading the 341st Blue Flight, saw a pair of Tonys about two-thousand feet above his formation. Foulis led his wingman up to attack the enemy fighter and they responded by separating, one Tony diving down to the left. The entire Blue Flight went down after him and Foulis noticed that the quarry was painted black and was using flaps to make very tight turns. He was able to avoid the fire coming from the pursuing P-47 and even forced Foulis to break sharply to the right. It was fortunate for Foulis that his flight was with him when the Tony slipped easily behind him and was about to open fire when he was shot down by Captain Louis Rekers.

He reformed the flight at 16,000 feet and was surprised to find another black Tony virtually flying alongside the American formation. Foulis could even make out a prominent orange stripe behind the cockpit and circling the fuselage before the Tony pilot realized his danger and went into a dive. Foulis followed and drew to within two-hundred yards at about 6,000 feet a few miles northeast of Clark and shot the Tony straight down into the ground.

At the same time the 340th began to run into the enemy. The B-24s had dropped their bombs and were

P-47s of the 348th, probably being transferred to the 58th FG during the period of conversion to P-51s.

coming off the target when Japanese fighters appeared directly over Clark. Lieutenant Mike Dikovitsky noticed one radial-engine fighter diving on his White Flight from the rear. he called to his wingman to turn sharply to the left and turned in that direction himself for a head on pass. The Zero, as Dikovitsky now identified the fighter, turned away into a climb and the two Americans pushed throttles through the wire gate on the aquadront to inject water into the engine cylinders for war emergency power.

The other element had climbed above the speeding P-47s to trap the Zero between four American fighters. Dikovitsky and his wingman flew widely apart to further frustrate any maneuver by the Zero and the Japanese managed to just barely escape the deadly fire from the P-47s. During one desperate turn Dikovitsky drew to within thirty yards and fired a burst which shot off the Zero's canopy and set the fighter aflame. His wingman watched the Zero crash and confirmed the victory for Dikovitsky.

Lyle Dowsett was leading 341st's Blue Flight away from the target when he saw an olive drab Oscar about a thousand feet above, heading for the bombers. His subsequent combat report describes the action: "...I started to climb up to catch the Oscar but he started to make a pass at the last formation of bombers. I started after him but could not catch up until after he had finished his pass. I gave him about a five second burst and he started burning. Then I gave him a second short burst and I saw pieces fall off and the landing gear drop. The pilot then bailed out and the combat was finished."

There was a momentary respite for Clark Field on December 23. That day saw five P-47s of the 341st Squadron make a fire bomb raid on Palombon. It was also the first recorded use of napalm by a V Fighter Command unit.

Whatever rest the Japanese at Clark may have had was completely erased by wild-flying 348th pilots on the attack of December 24. Sixty-six P-47s took off by 8:30 in the morning and by the time all but four of them had landed at about 4 o'clock in the afternoon the 348th had experienced its best day of the war with thirty-three confirmed victories sorted out by the harried intelligence officers.

Once again the 348th was escorting B-24s and the Japanese were forced to either defend the base in the air or lose their airpower on the ground just as the Americans had done in the first moments of the war. Major Bill Banks and Captain Gerald Excell flew ahead of the main U.S. formation and were able to radio positions and altitudes to the remainder of the escort. Banks and his wingman sighted six bogeys, including at least two Zeros, flying northeast from Floridablanca Airdrome at 18,000 feet. The two Thunderbolts immediately dropped tanks and climbed to 25,000 feet to position themselves above and behind the enemy.

When Banks and Excell started their dive they were discovered by their intended victims who turned directly into the attack. Both Japanese fighters concentrated their fire on Banks who responded with fire of his own. The tracers crossed until Banks noticed at very close range that his bullets were striking the righthand Zero in the wing and fuselage. Banks passed his adversary and looked back to see him roll and tumble to crash north of Floridablanca.

Banks and his wingman then climbed to the right and found two more Zeros below them heading toward the west. The Thun-

Wallace Montague by his early P-47 and by the wing of a wrecked Japanese plane.

341st P-51s acquired from the 3rd Air Commando Group (Blue spinner, blue tail).

derbolts attacked and the Zeros responded by making flat turns to the left. Banks fired at one of them and watched it fall with smoke streaming from the left wing from hits on the wing and fuselage around the cockpit. The Zero was observed to recover about 500 feet from the ground and Banks had to be content with a probable.

At the same time Excell had fired a short head on burst at the other Zero and watched the flashes of his bullets around the enemy cockpit. The Zero spiraled downward to crash northwest of Floridablanca. Banks watched the plane crash and looked around to notice that the main American formation was about forty miles from the target. He quickly radioed additional data about the Japanese formations.

Banks had lost sight of Excell but noticed another P-47 on the tail of a Zero which was neatly turning inside of the American's fire. When the opportunity presented itself Banks made a thirty degree deflection shot from the rear. Smoke and pieces of the cockpit structure drifted back toward Banks's P-47 before the Zero fell and crashed.

Meade Brown was leading the 340th's Red Flight when the Japanese tried to attack his formation with phosphorus bombs. One Zero dropped a bomb that exploded far to the right of Red Flight and Brown took after the retreating enemy. With a 20 degree deflection shot from the rear the Zero blew up just as Brown broke off at point blank range. Brown attacked another Zero with a vertical deflection shot in which he did not even see the enemy. He was surprised when the film in his gun camera was reviewed and depicted the demise of his sixth victory.

Lieutenant Jack Quinlan was leading the second element of Red Flight and watched the smoke of the phosphorus burst spread like an octopus. Brown had already taken after the first of the four Zeros and Quinlan turned into the other three. The fighter that Quinlan selected for a head on attack was identified by him as an Oscar before he fired and saw hits and smoke around the Japanese engine cowling. The other two Japanese fighters were attacking Quinlan's wingman, forcing the two Thunderbolts into a hard right turn. Somehow, during their hard turning Quinlan was able to see his Oscar crash in flames. The P-47s were able to dive away from their pursuers and at 5,000 feet Quinlan found a single Tony flying along and convinced its pilot to bail out with an accurate short 60 degree deflection shot from close range.

Bill Foulis was leading Blue Flight again for the 341st and became the 348th's high scorer of the day. He sighted a gaggle of about fifteen Oscars coming from the west, immediately dropped tanks and climbed above the enemy. With a single 30 degree deflection shot he saw smoke and pieces of metal come from his first target. Then he made a head on attack at another Oscar and saw hits all over the engine and smoke following after the two planes passed.

Airplanes were coming from every direction and it was several minutes before Foulis could get another deflection shot and watch his tracers going into the Oscar. Then another head on pass and the Oscar went by with smoke pouring from its engine. A few minutes later he was able to dive at yet another Oscar from the rear and watched his bullets strike the wings and fuselage of the enemy until the fighter burned. William Anahu of the 342nd had just claimed an Oscar himself and watched the last Oscar that Foulis attacked go down in flames.

George Davis also scored for the 342nd when he led the second flight over Clark. He was flying on the left flank of the B-24s just before the bomb run when two Zeros attempted to drop more of the phosphorus bombs on the American bombers. Davis went after one of the Zeros and he and his wingman dived to 10,000 feet where the wingman fired and scored enough hits to encourage the Zero pilot to bail out.

A few minutes later Davis came to the rescue of some other P-47s under attack by more Zeros. Davis fired to drive off one Zero from the tail of a P-47 and the Japanese turned head on into him. Three short bursts from 90 degrees deflection caused the Zero to catch fire and crash into the mountains northwest of Clark Field. Davis then attacked another Zero above the bomber formation and shot him down with a two-hundred yard burst from directly astern.

George Della was leading the third flight of 460th Squadron when he sighted some of the Zeros perhaps one to two thousand feet below his altitude of 20,000 feet. Della ordered tanks dropped and led his flight into the melee. His first burst at a fast-turning Zero was ineffective, but his second was on the mark and one Zero lost a wingman who fell burning into the hills north of the target. Another Zero went down from a no deflection shot and Della was an ace.

Lieutenant Bob Smith was following Della as leader of the fourth flight and saw single Zeros flying everywhere with no apparent purpose. Smith climbed to 22,000 feet and ordered tanks dropped and selected a Zero 32 heading south for a stern attack. The Zero turned around and Smith was able to follow him and fire from 300 yards, causing the right landing gear to come down. The Zero went into an uncontrolled flaming spin.

The Japanese were quick to attack Smith and his wingman with a pair of Zeros. The Americans dived and lost one Zero at about 6,000 feet. Smith broke to the left and his wingman to the right, trapping the remaining Japanese between them. The Zero pilot decided to attack Smith's wingman and Smith was able to complete

Capt. George Orr and his 340th FS P-51.

his turn and fire an out of range burst to divert the Japanese as he was beginning to fire. Smith drew to within 300 yards and shot the Zero down with a no deflection burst.

Most of the 460th pilots sweat out the return to base since they were the last over the target and so many of their combats were protracted affairs against single milling enemy fighters. George Davis, for example, landed back at base with no more than thirty gallons of gasoline in his tanks. Kenneth Saunders was the only casualty for the squadron when his P-47 was observed to crash into the water. The 341st lost two pilots, Lieutenants James Morris and August Svancarek. Svancarek had had a close call on December 14 when he collided with another P-47 and was obliged to crashland back at his base. The 342nd got off lightly with just one P-47 bellied in with damage from enemy fire. The pilot, Lieutenant Gerald Sheely, was uninjured.

The victories were impressive. Seventeen Zeros, eight Oscars, four Tonys and three fighters believed to be Tojos were claimed as definitely destroyed with at least six other Japanese fighters probably destroyed. Meade Brown, George Della and Bill Foulis became the last aces of the 348th and all pilots were jubilant at the intelligence debriefing.

It was the greatest day the group would ever know and one of the best single day performances by any V Fighter Command group. Whatever happened now would seem bland in comparison with this moment for the 348th Fighter Group, which also won its second Distinguished Unit Citation for this performance.

Escort missions continued on through the first part of January to Clark Field until the base was thoroughly hammered by bombs. Some of the later raids were so unchallenged that the escort dropped down to strafe vehicles and installations in the area. On the way back from Clark Field during an escort on January 9, the 340th P-47s strafed a truck and roadblock and killed ten Japanese troops at Los Banos, south of Leguna de Bay.

The only aerial victory scored by the 348th during January 1945 was during a convoy cover and reconnaissance around Negros Island. Eight P-47s of the 460th Squadron had reached their patrol area northeast of the convoy when the controller vectored two of them to investigate a plot southwest of the convoy.

Flight Officer John Smith of Winfield, Kansas, had one previous air claim and was quick to add the Zero 32 to his tally when he sighted the enemy about 5,000 feet above. He had time to notice the fresh green finish of his target's fuselage and the usual angry red roundels on the wings before he fired and got hits all over the engine and canopy. There was no evasive move on the part of the Zero; just a fiery glide into the water about forty miles north of the convoy.

During January 1945 there were fourteen operational accidents in the group. Nine planes received damages that destroyed them while six others received major but repairable damage. There were six takeoff accidents, four landing and four others of various causes.

Perhaps the most unusual accident happened to 342nd pilot 1st Lieutenant Wallace G. Montague. He would undoubtedly describe

Lt. Wally Montague of the 342nd Sq. had an astounding experience in January 1945. Credit: W. Montague

it also as one of the luckiest accidents to happen to any fighter pilot.

At a few minutes before five o'clock in the afternoon of January 7, 1945, Montague was forming up with a flight of four P-47s on a convoy cover mission over Negros. The mission was uneventful and he started home with the rest of his flight around six o'clock. A few minutes later he began to smell gas fumes in the cockpit and settled back to an uneasy homeward trip.

He was over San Pedro Bay at 6:45 when the fumes became worse. The beach was about a half-mile away and the altitude was 2,000 feet. The alternatives were rushing through his mind when a cylinder blew out of the cowling and the engine burst into flame. He applied full throttle in a futile attempt to extinguish the flames before he flew away from the other P-47s and decided to bail out of the potential flaming coffin.

Whether he lost too much altitude or the parachute simply failed to open, Montague landed in the water at full velocity, just a moment after the P-47 crashed about sixty yards away in a ball of fire. He was amazed to surface in the water still alive and was rescued shortly afterward. There were only a few bruises and possible internal injuries.

One particularly successful ground attack mission was flown by fourteen group P-47s to Paridel Bridge, thirty miles northwest of Manila, on January 11. A Japanese convoy of thirty-three trucks was discovered on the highway south of Paridel and the Thunderbolts had a field day. Twenty-five trucks were destroyed and left burning and a number of troops were cut down by .50 caliber fire.

A locomotive on the Manila railroad was also strafed and left spewing steam. Other damage was prevented because of large numbers of civilians on the highways, but four light tanks were attacked and one of them exploded. Lt. Paul McMath was struck by return fire, probably from light guns on the tanks, and crashed ten miles northeast of Paridel. 460th Squadron records list his loss as occurring on January 12, probably due to the outside chance that he could have survived and was making his way back to the American lines.

From the beginning of January the 341st was the first of the 348th squadrons to start conversion to the P-51 Mustang. The heavy mission load and the lack of spare parts forced the squadron to commit its pilots to Mustang operations with minimum training in the type. As a consequence, of the fourteen operational accidents during January, four were in the 340th, six in the 341st, two in the 342nd and two in the 460th.

There were, however, no P-51 non-combat fatalities in the 341st during January. Five Mustangs were totally destroyed, but none of the pilots were lost.

The first 341st Mustang mission was flown on January 6, 1945. Training was hampered by more than just lack of spare parts. Each squadron had a planned training period of twenty to thirty days, but the 341st was practically forced to condition its pilots on the way to operational targets. Compounding the problem was the fact that rotation of pilots back to the U.S. had begun again and the backlog was draining the squadrons of seasoned veterans. As soon as an older pilot became proficient on the Mustang he was on his way home again.

At one point the situation was so bad that green pilots were training other green pilots on an aircraft that demanded precise instruction. On the more positive side, pilots trained in the Mustang at stateside bases learned to love the spirited fighter with as much devotion as the old P-47 pilots loved their Thunderbolts. It would be an arduous process, but the venerable P-47 unit of the Fifth Air Force would be a Mustang outfit by the end of March 1945.

Chapter 14

Mustangs Over Japan

Luzon was invaded by the Americans via the Lingayen Gulf on January 9, 1945. By the middle of February Manila had fallen back into Allied hands and the inevitable march through the Cagayan Valley on northern Luzon that would end in June 1945 and the complete neutralization of Japanese forces began at the same time. Japanese forces opposing the drive were insufficient to take the offensive, but managed to fight an impressive delaying action, anyway.

The 348th Group moved from Tanuan to San Marcelino just north of Manila Bay and southwest of the Cabusilian mountains early in February. Lt. Clifford McMillin again went by boat and was eager to get back into action. He had seen his first Japanese plane over Clark Field on December 24, but was stunned to discover that the enemy was above and behind him in a most advantageous position. Luckily, the Japanese pilot was apparently also a bit inexperienced and flew away without firing a shot.

McMillin had expected to stay longer on Leyte and had a hut with bamboo walls and floors and thatched roof built—just in time for the move. He was determined to improve the living conditions for himself and his three tentmates and requisitioned a new tent that wouldn't leak for the new airstrip living quarters.

The airstrip at San Marcelino was a dirt strip with many wrecked Japanese aircraft scattered on either side. American engineers lengthened and improved the runways, but McMillin thought he guessed

Clifford McMillin in his plane "Bouncing Betty" showing 500 pound bomb under the wing.

Clifford McMillin and his plane P-51D-20 44-64061.

Clifford McMillin, "In front of my tent at San Marcellino."

Clifford McMillin: "Our sign in front of operations tent at Ie Shima." (Arlene McMillin)

the reason for all the wrecked aircraft when he observed that the takeoff direction pointed straight into the mountains.

Charlie Fox had been perfectly content at the Tanuan base on Leyte. He had the best P-47 he ever crewed, a D-23 model named "No, No, Alfred", that ran like a jewel. Life was as pleasant as it could be for a hard-working mechanic of the 342nd Fighter Squadron when a new pilot came out to fly Fox's prized airplane. The P-47 started as easily as it always did and there was no hint of a mechanical glitch in the faultless airplane as it started its takeoff roll. Apparently the young pilot wanted to emulate the style of the older hotshots and gave the plane full throttle to get the nose down to see the runway better.

Fox loved that airplane and decided that this was going to be the saddest day of the war for him when the pilot lost control and began veering all over the runway. A silent admonition to use rudder pedals instead of brakes went unheeded and the thing did a full throttle ground loop into a dirt bank and wiped out the landing gear, prop, engine and most of the wings. The pilot was unhurt, but Fox was glad that he never saw him again.

Around the end of the first week of February 1945, Fox was just as happy to leave Tanuan for San Marcelino by C-46 Curtiss Commando transport aircraft. Even the leaking flap hydraulic cylinders on the C-46 did not entirely discourage him. However, when the hydraulic fluid leaked completely away and the transport had no flaps, brakes or power for the landing gear, he reconsidered the advantages of the Leyte base.

The transport pilot flew around San Marcelino until every other aircraft had landed. Luckily, even though he had no flaps or brakes, the pilot was able to drop the landing gear and have it lock in place. Fox considered that sufficient welcome to Luzon.

Joe Baxter gave Fox one of his first jobs at San Marcelino when he told him to change the engine on his brand-new reconditioned veteran P-47. Barrett Evans, Lou Patzli, Mike Bender and the crews from Maintenance and Engineering pitched in to change the big Pratt and Whitney R-2800 engine. Everybody took a turn ground checking the new powerplants and the P-47 was ready for a slow time flight.

Lieutenant Earl Loucks took the plane up on February 20 and began the test when something went wrong over the coast. He tried to ditch, but the open canopy slammed shut on his head and the P-47 overturned in landing on the water. His body and parts of the P-47 were recovered within a few hours.

348th boneyard, probably at Ie Shima.

San Marcelino strip, taken without a struggle from the Japanese. (Schubert)

The war had to go on and Fox got a new plane—his first P51—and a new pilot in Lt. Robert Dow on February 21. Fox came to appreciate the speed, rate of turn and climb of the new airplane as well as its long range. Sometimes, after missions of ten hours or more, Dow had to be helped out of the cockpit, even though he was a young and vigorous pilot.

The 340th Squadron found some plump targets on February 11 while patrolling off Bataan peninsula. Four Japanese barges were sighted heading from the direction of Manila and were destroyed by strafing. Lieutenant David Standiford was forced to ditch during the attack and inflated his dinghy uncomfortably close to the Japanese survivors. Six Japanese were making for the little rubber boat when Standiford's vigilant strafed and killed them.

Standiford had sighted about thirteen more barges and, after he was picked up, reassembled another flight back at base and led it to the barges which were just approaching Bataan. After the strafing was done, the Japanese on Bataan relived the American experience of watching their reinforcement and supplies consumed by the enemy's airpower. Another thirty barges trying the same route were claimed destroyed during the day.

Twenty-six P-51s were received by the 340th Squadron during February 21 and February 22. On the next day twelve of the P-51s escorted B-25s along the Indo-China coast on a shipping strike. This mission lasted over eight hours and was followed on the twenty-fifth by a similar long range effort to the same area. On February 27, another twelve 340th Mustangs escorted B-25s to Hong Kong

Bob Knapp and his crewchief sometime in 1945. (Schubert)

342nd pilots Charles Hartman, Kyle Greever, Lt. Ross, Bill Krueger and Dick Richard Watrous. (Krane files)

where three Ki-84 Franks were sighted and pursued into a heavy overcast.

On February 28 the 340th returned to ground attack missions with two napalm strikes on the Fort Stotsenburg area. The missions had all been rated as successful and the pilots of the 340th felt a growing confidence in their new P-51 Mustangs.

Missions for March, April and May resumed their ground attack character. The 348th flew 118 missions in March, more than 180 in April and just over thirty in May. The most attacked targets were the Metropolitan road over which they had to go in order to reorganize for a last ditch stand in the Cagayan Valley at the end of May 1945.

Also attacked were the Ipo Dam areas, the island of Corregidor and the formidable Fort Drum. This fort was a battleship-shaped artificial island of concrete and steel that was not destroyed until combat engineers landed on the thing and blew it apart with fire and explosives.

Some of the praise lavished on the 348th Fighter Group during the period March through May 1945 was quite impressive. The routine nature of ground attack may have hampered the group's record in the air, but the ground forces came to know and deeply appreciate the efforts of the 348th.

A 342nd P-51, Langford's MOMMEY.

ABOVE & BOTTOM: Another 342nd P-51 named COLD TURKEY.

A few of the comments by diverse sources indicate the range of action observed of the 348th:

15 April 1945, Report from Lt. Stuckey, 309th Bomb Wing: "Pass the word to 342nd Squadron that the Commanding General, Baldy Force, was highly impressed with their manner of carrying out a difficult job in the face of enemy action."

16 April 1945, From Alamo Scouts: "Results of air strike (12 miles SSW Infanta) 15 April. It is believed that Japs evacuated area...as result of strike. Approximately 60 percent of enemy replacements were destroyed by bombs."

23 April 1945, From 6th Division: "...approximately one hundred Nips killed in last weeks period by air strikes."

May 1945, From XI Corps: "12 P-51s of the 460th Squadron strike in Mt. Purro area, 26 May 1945. Very Good. Many dead Japs were found..."

The one verbal commendation that seems to be valued most highly by 348th veterans is a Fifth Air Force news release dated June 1, 1945:

"FIFTH AIR FORCE, PHILIPPINES...FOR THE FIRST TIME IN THIS WAR A FIGHTER GROUP HAS DROPPED A GREATER TONNAGE OF BOMBS DURING A SINGLE MONTH THAN ANY SINGLE HEAVY BOMB GROUP.

Squadron pilots at San Marcelino.

"THE RECORD-SHATTERING OUTFIT IS THE FIFTH AIR FORCE FIGHTER COMMAND'S 348TH FIGHTER GROUP. DURING THE PAST MONTH (APRIL, 1945) P-51 MUSTANGS OF THIS JAP BLASTING FIGHTER GROUP DROPPED 2,091 TONS OF BOMBS, OF WHICH 2,068 TONS WERE CHECKED OFF AS DIRECT HITS ON PIN-POINT TARGETS.

"THE 348TH, WHICH DURING ONE PERIOD SHOT DOWN 251 JAP AIRCRAFT FOR A COMBAT LOSS OF ONE PILOT, HAS BEEN CREDITED BY GROUND FORCES INTELLIGENCE WITH THE DESTRUCTION OF 10,000 JAPANESE BY BOMBING AND STRAFING DURING THE PAST MONTH.

"DOING THEIR BOMBING "ON THE DECK" IN CLOSE SUPPORT OF INFANTRY DIGGING THE JAPS OUT OF LUZON, THE 348TH PILOTS DID SUCH OUTSTANDING WORK, OFTEN AS CLOSE AS 50 YARDS IN FRONT OF AMERICAN LINES, THAT THE GROUP HAS BEEN OFFICIALLY COMMENDED BY THE COMMANDING GENERALS OF THE 38TH INFANTRY DIVISION AND THE 112TH CAVALRY.

"FLYING AS MANY AS 200 SORTIES A DAY, THE MUSTANG PILOTS FIRED NEARLY 2,000,000 ROUNDS OF FIFTY CALIBER AMMUNITION DURING THE PAST MONTH. THEY STRUCK EVERY CONCEIVABLE TYPE OF TARGET: CAVES, ENTRENCHMENTS, GUN EMPLACEMENTS, TROOPS, VEHICLES, FACTORIES, WAREHOUSES, BARGES, SHIPPING AND ANYTHING ELSE THAT WAS JAP. THEY DID THE JOB WITH THE LOSS OF A SINGLE PLANE, AND THE PILOT OF THAT ONE WAS RESCUED.

"THE 348TH FIRST ESTABLISHED ITS REPUTATION AS A "GO DOWN AND BLAST 'EM" SCOURGE OF JAP SHIPPING. IT RAN UP A RECORD TOTAL DURING THE LEYTE CAMPAIGN AND, DURING ONE THREE WEEK PERIOD THIS YEAR, ITS PILOTS SANK ONE TENTH OF THE JAP SHIPPING CREDITED TO THE ENTIRE FIFTH AIR FORCE."

Squadron pilots at San Marcelino.

Squadron pilots at San Marcelino.

If the ground action took first place during the first few months of 1945 some of the group's pilots found opportunity to make their scores in the air. The first air victories of 1945 for the 342nd Squadron were gained during a fighter sweep over Hainan Island off the coast of China on March 13. Twelve P-51s made it almost to the target when the flight leader was forced to abort for some reason.

Charlie Fox's new pilot, Lt. Robert Dow, and Lt. Clark Kooper were in the last element and lost the rest of the formation in the clouds when the signal to abort was given. In spite of their being separated from the rest of the P-51s and having a low fuel supply, Kooper called out a Japanese transport with its wheels down for landing on an airfield below. Dow followed Kooper down in a steep dive to catch the Japanese—now about to land nearly 12,000 feet below—while they could still claim it in the air.

At about 7,000 feet the two Mustang pilots noticed five black single-engined shapes above them. If they were Japanese fighters it would have been more than foolish to continue down after the transport. The dive was broken off and the bogeys were faced head on.

When the two forces whizzed by each other, Dow and Kooper recognized the fighters as Japanese Franks. Three of the enemy broke to the right and the other two to the left. The two Americans broke to the left and outturned the group of three for an immediate advantage. However, the other two Franks slipped in behind them to turn the engagement into an individual dogfight.

Sometime during the fight one of the Franks overshot Dow and pulled up at very close range. The Mustang pilot could not have missed and began to fire at the underside of the Japanese fighter. Flames poured back from the engine where Dow's bullets were hitting and the Frank burned all the way down to the water.

Dow couldn't look very long to see if a parachute opened because two more Franks had easily glided in on his tail. He was impressed with the ability of the Mustang to turn inside the Frank, but was just as pleased to see Kooper come along and divert one of the pursuers. Dow managed to get away from the remaining Frank and caught sight of Kooper firing at one of the Japanese that fell out of control and crashed.

Squadron pilots at Ie Shima.

Squadron pilots at Ie Shima.

When the opportunity came, the Americans decided to exercise discretion and broke off the engagement to race for home. They did not get off without some damage, however, when smoke was seen slipping back from Kooper's Mustang. His engine quit about twenty miles southeast of Hainan Island and he bailed out. Dow circled long enough to watch Kooper get in his dinghy and then radioed his position before racing home with a critically low fuel supply.

Unfortunately, Kooper was never found. He just became one of those missing in action until he was declared officially dead six months after the war. Dow himself became a casualty just three months later when he was killed in a takeoff accident on another mission.

Two days later the 341st Squadron scored some of its own initial victories of the year. Ten P-51s were scheduled for a fighter sweep to the Hong Kong area and arrived over the target a few minutes before eleven o'clock in the morning. By the time they returned to base two more Japanese fighters were chalked up on their scoreboard with no losses to themselves.

It was cloudy over the patrol area, but not so obscured that the flight of P-51s could not see the dark-colored Ki-44 Tojo three thousand feet below its level of ten thousand feet. Lieutenant Albert Gould had never closed with the enemy before, but when his element was given permission to attack the Japanese fighter he went in like an ace. Closing in to two hundred yards he fired just one short accurate burst that set the Tojo on fire.

When the wing of the enemy fighter crumpled off, Gould watched his target fall and the pilot bail out. It was a gratifying moment for a young fighter pilot. Fifteen minutes later the same formation attacked a pair of J1m "Jack" fighters and shot down one of them before heading home.

342nd P-51 No. 72, serial 44-12706 come to grief.

George Davis late 1944 or early 1945.

About the middle of May 1945 the 348th made an unusually leisurely move from San Marcelino across the foothills of the Cabusilian Mountains to Floridablanca. Floridablanca was part of the Clark Field complex and the runways were being lengthened to accommodate the new B-32 heavy bombers. The Mustang pilots loved the super-long runways that allowed them to breeze their fighters along on the takeoff run for about a mile-and-a-half.

Lt. Kyle Greever at Ie Shima in August 1945, P-51D-20, serial 44-64113.

It was at Floridablanca that some of the 348th ordnance personnel were caught running a brothel using G.I. tents and cots. When it came time to press court martial charges, there were no articles of

Full view of 342nd P-51, probably in the Philippines.

Lt. Al Gould in his cockpit after his March 1945 victory.

war to cover such a situation. The malefactors had to be tried under misuse of government property.

When Marion Iddings heard of it he shook his head and became convinced of another conclusion he drew from Army service. In all, those conclusions totaled four:

1. Australian canned mutton with gravy has to be the worst food in the world.
2. There is such a thing as being sun-kissed and jungle happy.
3. Regardless how you washed olive drab underwear, it still looks dirty and a dead giveaway that you are part of a military unit.
4. You could run a whorehouse with government equipment.

Regarding the "sun-kissed and jungle happy" conclusion, after Iddings had helped form the 460th Squadron a technical sergeant from the U.S. joined the unit. After about six months Iddings asked the man what he thought of the 460th crew when he first arrived. He replied, "You were the wildest looking bunch of people I had ever seen; but you look okay now."

Another example of the phenomenon was an obviously overexposed first sergeant who called another first sergeant and demanded that he get his outfit's flies out of their latrine.

Yet another young guard on the flightline spent all night cutting holes in a pile of drop tanks to make himself an invasion fleet.

341st P-51s in the Philippines. Lt. Schlegel's WEE WILLIE'S WAGON was turned over to the 8th FG at war's end.

The P-51 fighter was another type that did not win easy acceptance in V Fighter Command. Although the Mustang was highly esteemed in the European theater, it simply caused mental reservations in pilots familiar with the P-47 and P-38.

Both the P-38 and the P-47 had proven themselves over many months of combat with the Japanese. The P-47 was especially rugged and famed for its ability to return, even with heavy battle damage. The eight .50 caliber guns that comprised the P-47's armament were considered especially devastating to lightly constructed Japanese aircraft and Thunderbolt pilots had learned to use the terrific dive and roll rate of the P-47 to spectacular advantage. The P-38 was also trusted on long range missions because of the safety factor provided by its second engine.

However, it was easier to train pilots on the P-51 and the youngsters that were used to the fighter were extremely enthusiastic about it. The older pilots had problems breaking well-nurtured habits suited to the P-47. Lieutenant Truman Ragsdale of the 342nd Squadron crashed in April 1945 during a checkout flight and it was conjectured that he unwittingly set the P-51 rudder trim for the P-47 takeoff position.

The 460th Squadron was going through transition to the P-51 during March on Mokmer strip, Biak, and learned some hard lessons about the care needed to land the Mustang. Second Lieutenant Thomas Stenger was making a landing on March 6 when his P-51 stalled on flareout approach. He crashed and sustained serious head injuries. However, later in the month Ops Officer Captain Wallace

Harding led seventeen transitioned pilots to Morotai and flew to the Philippines around March 21.

Authoritative rumor promised that the 348th would be involved in the invasion of Okinawa at the beginning of April. Unfortunately, the group was already committed to the Floridablanca move when Okinawa was invaded on April 1. Consequently, while the battle for Okinawa was being fought during April and May the 348th was settling in to the mop-up war on northern Luzon.

June was a month of limited air action as the 348th no sooner became settled at Floridablanca when it was alerted for another move; this time to the Okinawa area, which puzzled group members that expected it to happen in April. Operations for the 340th Squadron began on June 1 when eight of its P-51s bombed and strafed several buildings in the Bontoc area. During a June 12 mission to areas well north of the Balete Pass Lieutenant Wayne E. Black developed a coolant leak in his P-51 and bailed out near Solano and was picked up by friendly troops.

The missions became utterly routine during the final drive to the northern Luzon port of Aparri. By the end of June there were only isolated pockets of Japanese troops, desperate and starving, in remote areas of Luzon; a remarkable mirror image of the fighting on Luzon early in 1942. An entry in the June history of the 342nd Squadron expresses the feeling of routine combat: "The procedure for these strikes was uniform—detailed briefing, close cooperation with the ground controller, and satisfactory results. The situation was so well in hand that ground troops advanced days before schedule..."

During June the 348th was awarded its two Distinguished Unit Awards. Around June 20, all operations for the 348th in the Philippines had ceased. General Yamashita's forces in the Philippines were isolated and ravaged by disease as well as battle attrition. The campaign was over and there was literally nothing for the tactical air forces to do.

For a few days the personnel of the group were treated to a life of relative luxury compared to previous camps. The weather was unpredictably mild and efforts to brace Floridablanca against an expected typhoon were diverted to improving the living conditions. Three day passes were also issued for the luckiest men and natives ignored the camp restriction's ban to sell fruit and war souvenirs to the receptive Yank market.

Cliff McMillian decided to satisfy his curiosity and visited Manila. He was amazed by the openness of prostitution in the city when he and his companions were approached by little boys as young as six years old trying to introduce their sisters. The Americans wondered if the Japanese allowed this sort of thing when they were in charge or if the Yanks presented a special case.

Even though they had been expecting it for some time, the personnel of the group were again suddenly whipped into action

341st formation being led by Colonel Banks.

CLOCKWISE FROM TOP LEFT: 348th P-51s on Ie Shima.

for the move to Okinawa. On June 30 the 342nd Squadron struck its tents at dawn and loaded equipment aboard squadron vehicles to form a convoy down to Subic Bay. About noon the squadron was loaded aboard LST 651 and was ready to leave by nightfall. After so many moves in the past few months the men were not so eager to establish a new base so late in the war.

The 340th was loaded aboard LST 660 while some of its excess personnel and equipment were put on the 460th Squadron's LST. By the Fourth of July a convoy of some twenty-odd LSTs and four destroyers was ready to embark from Subic Bay. A special 4th of July celebration was presented while the ships left the bay during the afternoon. Two Grumman TBM Avenger torpedo bombers towed target sleeves along both sides of the convoy while 20mm and 40mm antiaircraft guns rumbled their practice shots like rolling thunder.

There was no little apprehension about the move to Ie Shima, as the destination was revealed once the ships were at sea. Japanese resistance to the Philippine landings had been spirited, to say the least, and reports of the Okinawa invasion suggested that the enemy was going to be decidedly fanatical about this first intrusion on his home islands.

If the thought of landing no more than three-hundred miles from the Japanese mainland caused some consternation it also caused excitement. The end of the war was in sight, and until the end came there was at least one more opportunity for the kind of aerial combat glory that had been won by the 348th in the past.

340th P-51s, probably on Ie Sima.

Whatever the prospects to come, the first dark line of land was sighted on July 9 and the 348th had its introduction to Ie Shima. More than one of the men on the LSTs had their expectations dashed when they got a good look at the place. The 348th historian recorded the impression of Ie Shima as "six square miles of mud, coral and monotony...some 200 feet above the ocean..." "(It was) singularly uninviting when we looked at it."

Cliff McMillin made this trip by air and was not any more impressed by the place. His description of Ie Shima observed that, "It was connected to Okinawa by shallow reefs that looked from the air as though you could almost wade across. This island was just wide enough for an airstrip, and there were four of them on the island, ending on the north at the edge of a high bluff that dropped straight down into the ocean."

Rain made its usual appearance during the unloading of equipment and personnel. The urgency of dispersing the various squadrons from the grouping aboard the tempting targets presented by the ships necessitated the hurried landings. Every man landed with

342nd P-51 being loaded with napalm.

342nd P-51 BEEF INJECTION.

a blanket and shelter half by the afternoon of July 10. Squadron camps began to spring up and several mines and unexploded bombs were removed to acknowledge the final welcome to Japan.

The P-51s arrived on July 12 and the air echelon in C-46s came soon afterward. Operations and alert shacks were immediately set up and anticipation rose for the first scheduled missions. The first mission was an abort when more than twenty group P-51s ran into foul weather on a fighter sweep to Kyushu.

348th fighters made their first offensive appearance over the home islands on July 16. Carrying one wing fuel tank and 500 pound bomb, fifteen P-51s of the 340th Squadron escorted B-25s to Miyakojono on central Kyushu. While the bombers hit their target the P-51s bombed a strategic bridge nearby, scoring two direct hits.

Two days later the 342nd made its tactical debut over Japan with a strike at the same area of Kyushu. Sixteen planes dropped thirty 500 pound bombs on worker's quarters at a factory in Miyakojono. On the way back from the mission Lt. Fred Babcock ran out of gas and had to bail out into the sea. He was picked up two hours later by a PBM flying boat with nothing more than a cut on his forehead.

Heavy wind and rain grounded the P-51s for the next three days. On the 22nd a series of strikes on the China coast was begun. 348th Mustangs ranged over Shanghai during the day and mauled the docks as well as shipping in the area, claiming several Japanese ships sunk or damaged, exact damage being difficult to pinpoint because of the clouds obscuring results.

Again the high wind and threat of severe weather stopped operations for two days on the 25th and 26th. On the 27th the group had its first escort of heavy bombers over Japan when B-24s struck at railroad marshaling yards at Kagoshima, Kyushu. Eight P-51s of the 340th together with six other fighters of the 341st provided cover for B-25s and divebombed shipping in Japan's inland sea on the 28th.

Cliff McMillin was getting a full dose of operational flying in spite of the frequent lulls caused by weather. He was over Shanghai on the July 22 mission and sweat out some of the worst antiaircraft fire imaginable. The clouds that made it difficult to assess the damage done to shipping below made comforting refuge from the visually sighted Japanese guns. The P-51s would swoop out of the clouds like hawks to attack a target and retreat again to the fluffy haven before the enemy gunners could do much about it.

Many of the old veterans of the 348th were finally going home and younger pilots like McMillin found themselves the ranking top hands in the momentarily understaffed squadrons. The traffic pressure on Ie Shima made it even more of a headache for the seasoned pilots who had to lead off the flights and squadrons from the crowded strips two at a time and return in a tight formation to get the masses

LEFT & ABOVE: 460th Squadron P-51s: George Della's NADINE and No. 1281 serial 44-64064.

of airplanes out of the traffic pattern in the shortest possible time.

On July 30 the 340th finished operations for the month with a six plane sweep to Honshu. For all the dangers he had faced simply taking off and landing from Ie Shima, McMillin came closest to becoming a victim of an operational accident on this flight due to the simplest of oversights.

The mission had ended up on the north side of the Sea of Japan strafing targets of opportunity. McMillin's P-51 was out of service at the time and he borrowed Captain George Orr's (the 340th commanding officer at the time) plane. Orr had installed some new radio equipment behind the seat of the fighter that increased weight by a total of about twenty-four pounds. The difference in weight made no difference in the feel of the P-51 on takeoff or cruising, and thus made no impression on McMillin.

When P-51s arrived over the area and selected the target for bombing they would go down in a high-speed dive and bore right in on the object under attack. McMillin went into his dive and immediately experienced what is termed a "high-speed stall" when he tried to pull out. The phenomenon is like a huge hand that held the P-51 down and refused to let it change direction from the dive to recovery.

The P-51 was shuddering along with its nose pointing almost horizontally, but still sliding ever closer to the deadly surface of the sea. McMillin trusted his reflexes developed in training and pushed the stick forward to get the nose down again. The sea was coming up with a rush and the shaken Mustang pilot thought for a split-second that he would join his plane in a horrifying plunge into the gray-blue mass of the sea.

Fellow pilots on the mission gasped when the controls of the Mustang took hold only a few feet above the sea and dragged a slight wake in the water before McMillin could haul back on the stick and climb for altitude. If the sea had not been perfectly calm that day, McMillin reasoned, the P-51 would surely have been dragged into its depths by a stray wave. It was amazing what a difference only twenty-four pounds could have on the performance of even a powerful P-51 Mustang.

On the last day of the month 348th P-51s divebombed positions on the northern coast of Kyushu. The 342nd almost got into an aerial scrap when twelve to sixteen Ki-84 Franks jumped the tailend P-51 and forced it away from the rest of the formation. The Mustang pilot was able to dive away from the enemy, but earned the disgust of the squadron when he reported that he lost the enemy all by himself without giving the rest a chance at engaging the Franks.

Red alerts sounded on Ie Shima in July—the first the 348th had heard in about six months. Most of the raids were ineffective single plane sorties, but one night raid dropped a phosphorus bomb on the crowded parked aircraft and destroyed or damaged about a dozen of them.

From just before dusk until after dawn, there were waves of black P-61 night fighters cruising overhead in the second half of July. Many of the 348th veterans were used to the danger imposed by raiding Japanese intruders and went on with life as usual. Many of the comforts they had learned to improvise for themselves during the past two years began to appear on the bleak Ie Shima landscape and they settled down to the inevitable assault on Japan.

342nd officer's club in the Philippines was dedicated to the memory of Colonel Kearby.

Chapter 15

Fading Away: August-October 1945

It didn't take long for the group to begin scoring aerial victories once August arrived. Bill Dunham was leading a four plane fighter sweep off Kyushu on August 1 when he ran into sixteen Franks and got involved in a vigorous dogfight.

Dunham was leading the flight with Tom Sheets of the 460th Squadron as his wingman and Ed Popek with Captain Bill Rumpf as his wingman in the other element. The weather was rough with rain squalls everywhere below and thunderheads up to 8,000 feet. There were some stratus clouds all the way up to the flight's altitude of 10,000 feet.

At about fifteen minutes after ten in the morning Dunham sighted a formation of B-24s heading over Take Island off the coast of Kyushu. The Americans were close enough to the bombers almost directly below to make out the dark green fuselages and surprisingly dull red insignia of Frank fighters making attacks on them from their altitude of 9,000 feet to almost the altitude of the Mustangs themselves.

The Franks were obviously occupied with the B-24s and didn't even notice the four P-51s coming down to break up their attack. Dunham had led his pilots down in no particular planned attack to make the most of surprise. He picked out one unwary Frank and got flashes on its fuselage with his first shots. The alarmed Japanese tried to roll away, but a second volley smashed the cockpit and disintegrated the glass canopy. The pilot must have been killed right off because the Frank fluttered like a broken toy all the way to the water below.

342nd personnel on Ie Shima in August 1945: Carl Peterson, William Krueger, Irvin Kunselman, Jim Doty. (Les Draayers)

342nd C Flight. Front row: Stanley E. Michalowski, Eugene Henry, Vincent Ross, Bill Rumpf, Bob Roark, McChord and Masterson. Back row: Nugent, Manitt, Siddorn, Eastman, Smith, Thomas and Barnes

Tom Sheets had shot down another Frank that was only about a hundred yards off Dunham's left wing. Popek fired at a Frank that went into a very tight turn. Apparently the Japanese pilot never even guessed that he was being attacked for he held his turn while Popek adjusted his fire from a near miss to the left directly into the cockpit. Smoke and flame licked back from the Frank's engine until it crashed below.

Captain Rumpf chased one Frank off Popek's tail and the battle became a confused affair. Somewhere in the melee Popek lost Rumpf and picked up Sheets on his wing. They attacked one Frank that managed to get away into the clouds, then took turns with brief bursts at any scrambling Frank that happened within range while it tried to get away from the pugnacious Americans.

The Japanese tactics were to divide their formation from the beginning of the battle, which led the Americans to speculate later that the unit was relatively inexperienced. If the Japanese had coordinated their attacks, Dunham's pilots would probably not have been able to make firing passes so freely. It is most likely that the Franks were from either the 47th or 102nd Sentai, which were operating in the Kyushu area by the beginning of August.

Both Popek and Sheets took after one hapless Frank that managed to turn inside their combined fire more than once. Popek would take a shot, overshoot and circle for another pass while Sheets did the same thing several times.

Finally, Popek got a few hits on the Frank's wing and was forced to break away. Sheets got in one more ineffective burst, but set the Frank up for Popek who came boring in

Bob Knapp on his P-51. Before becoming a 348th luminary he was a pilot before the war and was the son of a father who taught violin.

from a forty-five degree angle and practically blew the target cockpit apart with his .50 caliber bullets. According to after-action reports the Frank fell two-thousand feet into the water twenty miles southwest of a place identified as Kaimandakw, Kyushu.

The 342nd may have opened the scoring for August, but the last month of combat in the Pacific proved to be quite eventful for the entire 348th Fighter Group. The 340th Squadron flew mission C-1387, a cover flight for PBY rescue planes codenamed, capriciously enough, Playmate 46 and Jukebox 36, on August 4. Eight P-51s laden with external fuel tanks took off twenty minutes before eight in the morning to meet their charges north of Honshu between the Chosen Strait off North Korea in the Sea of Japan and the East China Sea.

Cliff McMillin had selected this mission for himself and found that he was leading a seven plane flight when one P-51 aborted with voltmeter trouble. Somewhere around the southwest coast of Korea McMillin looked down and saw four Zero model 32 fighters in a precise formation at 2,000 feet. The crisply painted green fighters were probably from the strip on Saishu Island and seemed to have no clue of the American fighters above them.

The situation presented a dilemma for McMillin; drop tanks and risk not having enough fuel to complete the rendezvous with the PBYs or keep them and the added restrictions they presented. In the end he decided that the altitude and surprise advantages outweighed those gained by dropping the tanks and went down with

Colonel Rowland in his P-51. Note F4U Corsairs in background. (Marshall Vickers)

Dinghy Dunham by his 460th Squadron P-51 with its final score.

Ed Popek in his P-51 at the end of the war.

his seven fighters to attack the unwary enemy, encumbered by the external tanks.

With the added weight of the fuel McMillin fell like a stone on the first of the Zeros. His sights were centered on the dark green fuselage of the lead plane that did not flinch from its course while American guns drew quickly into range. Pieces of the Zero's sides flew off with the first burst of gunfire and flames quickly started to erupt. The startled Japanese pilot had just enough time to open his canopy and bail out when McMillin passed overhead.

Lieutenant Charles McDonald exploded another of the Zeros on that first pass before he was also obliged to break away. One of the surviving Japanese turned quickly toward the relative safety of the Korean coast, but the fourth was able to get on the tail of McMillin's overloaded Mustang. McDonald was in position to cover McMillin and took only a few precious seconds to get the Zero in his sights and shoot it down. Another Mustang caught the fourth Zero around the Korean coast and made the bounce a clean sweep.

The decision to keep the drop tanks was the right one and the Mustangs were able to meet the PBYs and cover them in a search for the crew of a downed American bomber. The mission took about seven hours and gratified McMillin with the thought that he had led such a successful operation.

When Ie Shima came into sight, an exuberant Mustang pilot called the tower for permission to let three victorious fighter pilots perform their victory rolls. V Fighter Command was unusually lenient in letting returning pilots demonstrate their kills with low level rolls right over the often crowded home strips. Most commands frowned on the practice for the dangers of crashes were especially high. Some squadrons restricted the tradition, but the 348th group was famous for the practice from the days of its first combat.

Radio silence had been observed during the mission, so the first indication the commanders on the ground had of the combat was the graceful sweep of McMillin's P-51 into a slow roll right over the landing strip. Three more rolls brought grins to the faces of the men on the ground and the Mustangs circled to land. McMillin recounted later that his commanding officer was more delighted about the decision to keep the fuel than the four Zeros claimed!

The last aerial victory credited to a 348th pilot was claimed by Lieutenant Kermit Allen of the 460th Squadron on August 12, 1945. He encountered a Kawanishi NlK Shiden, known as George to the Allies, while he was part of White Flight on a railroad strafing mission to the northern part of the Japanese coast. It took less than a minute for Allen to close with the George and shoot its belly tank off. Another burst and the George went in from low altitude.

A few days before this aerial combat one of the last acts of murderous foolishness in a war of mounting brutality was witnessed by a flight of 348th P-51s. 348th commander Colonel Bill Banks was leading the flight on a sweep to the Fukuoka area during the morning of August 9, 1945. He had received a message from higher headquarters restricting all friendly aircraft from flying within forty-

342nd scoreboard at the end of the war. Note the optimistic itinerary to Tokyo.

Jim Benz and Ed Popek by the same board. Note that the scoreboard totals 176, more than fifty over the official score for the 342nd.

five miles of the city of Nagasaki, which was an identical message to the one he received the day of the Hiroshima atomic bombing.

Coincidentally, the planned sweep area fell exactly forty-five miles to the east of Nagasaki at one point. Again by chance, Banks was leading his flight to that very point at eleven o'clock. The Mustangs were at 20,000 feet and "the weather was excellent," according to Banks.

Visibility was unlimited and the 348th Mustangs had a grand vantage point from which to observe the entire northwest coast of Kyushu. At eleven o'clock there was a brilliant flash of light followed by a high column of clouds expanding almost to the P-51 altitude. Below, the valleys and low ground areas were filling with the gray smoke of history's second operational atomic bomb blast.

Banks was startled by the event, but nevertheless wanted to fly over the area. He was discouraged by rumors of the Hiroshima blast on August 6 and his own lack of data about what was really happening. The Mustangs circled cautiously around the burgeoning mushroom cloud.

After a few minutes Banks led his flight toward home. He was disturbed by what he saw and hoped that it was the portent of the end of all wars. He also shuddered a brief thanks that the weapon was not in the hands of the other side during the war.

Jim Benz was also on the flight and reacted similarly to the event. On the way back to the base he could only reflect in awe that it was "The biggest damn explosion we had ever seen."

John Cook was following behind in another part of the flight formation and thought at first that a number of ammunition dumps, perhaps in the Sasebo area, had gone off simultaneously. The explosion looked to him like the orange sun through a dusty sky before some of the radio conversation he heard convinced him it was an atomic explosion that heralded the war's end.

Historians everywhere except in the United States believe that the Japanese sent an offer of peace the next day not because of the

Closeup of 342nd P-51 THE BALTI-MORON, serial 44-12085 on Ie Shima.

atomic bombings, but because of a series of events of which the bombings were simply a part. The reason Japan had gone to war with the West in the first place was to secure sources of petroleum and rubber. The Fifth and Thirteenth Air Forces had played their part in denying Japan the spoils of conquest in the Southwest Pacific.

While the U.S. Navy had destroyed the bulk of Japan's merchant fleet with submarine and air attack, the Fifth Air Force had also taken a fair toll through the innovation of skipbombing. The Japanese fleet was virtually nonexistent after April 1945 due to U.S. Navy efforts. The Fifth and Thirteenth Air Forces were also largely responsible for the severe shortage of destroyers in the Imperial Japanese Fleet.

Faced with starvation and freezing during the upcoming winter of 1945/46 the Japanese would have been under heavy pressure to surrender if the Americans had not promised to invade and give them the face-saving opportunity to inflict unacceptable casualties to extract more palatable peace terms. The decision of Russia to declare war on Japan and immediately invade Manchuria, Korea and the Kurile Islands had more to do with prompting the surrender than any other single factor at the end of the war.

Not that any of these political considerations had any effect on the fighting attitude of the 348th Fighter Group. The pilots and groundcrews of the group wanted dearly to return home alive, but were just as committed to fighting the war to the bitter end if it came to that. With the atomic bombings there was a change in expectations. "Golden Gate in '48" had become "Home alive in '45." More pessimistic group members added "Bread line in '49?"

Operations continued after August 12 in the hope of an imminent peace but with the realization of the grim fact of war. The last recorded combat mission of the 340th Fighter Squadron was an antishipping sweep by fifteen P-51s to northern Kyushu and southern Honshu on August 14, 1945. Around the noon hour the Mustangs rocketed and strafed two luggers and a sailboat. One of the luggers was left smoking while the other had its stern blown off by a rocket. The sailboat was sunk.

A patrol boat was encountered by the flight some time later and was left burning after it was strafed. A pair of barges that were converted into flak boats, each carrying a number of 20mm flak guns, were also attacked and the guns silenced. Eight small luggers were then attacked near the coast of Kura Shima and the day was ended with the strafing of a small fishing boat.

By the end of the day the order had come to cease all operations against the Japanese enemy. Within the next few days the Japanese surrender delegation landed on Ie Shima on its way to confer with the victors of the Pacific war in the Philippines. The official signing of the peace document would take place in Tokyo Bay on the deck of the U.S.S Missouri at eight o'clock in the morning on September 2, 1945—almost precisely six years after the beginning of World War II.

The war in the Pacific had gone on for almost four years and the 348th Fighter Group had been involved in that war for more than two years. With the end of hostilities those severe terms of overseas tour length that had characterized the Southwest Pacific were lifted. At nine o'clock in the evening on August 25, 1945, the 348th public address system crackled and an announcement was made that all personnel with eighty-five more rotation points would turn in their equipment and report to the orderly room immediately.

Near riot conditions prevailed for the rest of the night. Men who had been overseas for the better part of two years were now aware that they would be going home within the next few days and celebrated to the edge of being arrested and losing that ticket. On August 27, 1945, more than a hundred 348th Fighter Group veterans departed for processing and the trip home.

In terms of Japanese aircraft shot down the 348th stood in fifth place among the six fighter groups of the Fifth Air Force. That rank-

Captain Leslie Draayers, CO of the 342nd FS at Itami, Japan.

Colonel Dunham wearing full battle honors at the end of the war. (Dunham via Tabatt)

ing has to take into account the fact that the 348th was in the final group of fighters assigned to the Southwest Pacific. Also, much of its combat was restricted to the ground attack variety with little or no contact with Japanese aircraft.

On the other hand, the 348th claimed more than half of V Fighter Command P-47 victories. Of the approximately 650 Japanese aircraft credited to Command P-47s, between 330 and 340 were attributed to the group. All Fifth Air Force P-40 victories credited during the Pacific war hardly equaled the 348th's final tally.

It is not practical to try and tabulate the effect that the 348th had on ground targets since there is no reliable measure of the ships, trains, tanks and other vehicles, troops, buildings and various emplacements that fell victim to the angry guns and ordnance of the group.

The comments already cited in the text give a fair indication of how destructive the 348th had been on ground targets.

Only a few of the 348th oldtimers remained on Ie Shima beyond the end of September 1945. By November the group had lost its distinctive aircraft identification colors and was quickly becoming a peacetime unit with all the boredom of spit and polish. Flying slowed down to the point that pilots would look for any excuse to get into the air. Groundcrewmen who could not keep busy enough were subjected to endless G.I. cleanup parties and inspections.

On October 8, 1945, a huge tropical storm, described by the 348th historian as being the "Grandaddy" of typhoons, hit Ie Shima with 170 mph winds that caused among other serious damage; "Flying latrines and typhoon flattened tents." Many ships were destroyed in the harbor and a large number of casualties resulted. Fortunately, most of the aircraft had already departed for Japan and were not the cause of further death and destruction.

Segments of the 340th and 341st had already settled in what was termed as air conditioned Kanoya, and the 342nd followed in a convoy of LCMs a few days after the typhoon. The convoy arrived at a harbor just outside Osaka and the 342nd followed the route of its sister squadrons to Kanoya.

Usual quarters were Japanese barracks near the little town of Itami. The 342nd was stationed on Itami Airfield by October 20 and was joined by the other squadrons from Kanoya. C-47s from Kanoya and LSMs from Ie Shima converged on the port of Osaka where the 348th men were surprised to find a modern city with lights and stores and an exceptionally polite Japanese population that must have harbored some suspicions about the intentions of the gigantic Yankee barbarians.

One of the tasks of the 348th was the mass destruction of collected Japanese warplanes. It must have seemed the most ironic of duties to routinely crush, burn or drive into the sea those warplanes that would have been the object of glorious dogfights only a few months before.

Cliff McMillin had been given the choice of going home from Ie Shima or staying with the 348th for at least six months and receiving his captaincy. Homesickness, calculations of his chances on beating the law of averages in surviving flights in war weary P-51s and a general surfeit of the military persuaded him to go home. He came to regret the decision later when he realized that he would have a golden chance to see a part of the world that he may never see in any other way. As it was, he didn't get home much before the end of the year anyway.

Jim Benz was the commander of the 348th at the end of November 1945 and oversaw the last days of the group. Records indicate that Merle Zeine came back by the end of the year to join Benz in taking the 348th to the culmination of its illustrious career. The former 341st commander must have requested the return to his old unit, perhaps for the sentimental duty of seeing the old outfit home.

In February 1946 Joel Catron of the 342nd Squadron led a group of five officers and 164 enlisted men aboard a transport ship for the trip back home. Leslie Draayers became the last acting commander of the 342nd for the last three months before deactivation. The prevailing view was that any American who spent time in Japan at the end of hostilities was fortunate enough to be part of a watershed moment of history. Of course, the Japanese would not have been so eager to share that particular moment. They certainly could be excused for wanting to forget the entire era.

Throughout March and April 1946 the 348th Group gradually lost its identity as a famous fighter unit and melted into the fabric

WEE WILLIE'S WAGON in service with the 8th Fighter Group at the end of the war.

of postwar military life. By May 10, 1946, the 348th had ceased to exist. Like a reincarnated child it began life again as a P-47 Air National Guard unit, the 108th Fighter Group of the New Jersey ANG, just a few weeks later.

Les Draayers oversaw the demise of the 342nd and commented on the fact in August 1980: "As the last acting squadron commander of the 342nd, deactivation was a very sad occasion."

"...Flying time in the P-51 was down to about two hours per week. We had cannibalized some of our planes to keep others flying and we had quite a time getting them back in order. In the (pro cess) we managed to lose one aircraft. The engineering and ground crew section did a fantastic job in bailing me out of that one. Every week we were sending more people home. I always expected somebody to take a truck or jeep along.

"...I took one of the last planes over to Ashiya Air Base on Kyushu and joined the 35th Fighter Group. I was assigned to the 8th Fighter Squadron as Operations Officer. My flight log shows the cross country from Itami to Ashiya and the transfer papers for the P-51 I was flying as May 15, 1946."

Charlie Fox went home at the end of September 1945 and never got to set foot in Japan. He had been there when the 348th set up shop in New Guinea and was not at all sorry to be heading home before the 348th took its final bow on the Imperial homeland.

After all the arduous movement of the war, things speeded up for Fox. First there was the truck on Ie Shima that went past the Ernie Pyle memorial. The famed correspondent and acknowledged friend of the common soldier had been killed on the island during the April invasion. Then Fox put a nervous toe back on a C-46 for the short flight from Ie Shima to Okinawa. There he saw for the first time a line of hundreds of B-29s on Naha Airfield.

Within days he had flown to Manila and was on the troop ship, ADMIRAL EBERLE, first to Leyte to pick up stretcher patients, then across the Pacific to Tacoma, Washington, when San Francisco was clogged with ships. Another truck took him to McChord Air Force Base and twenty-four hours later he was on a Great Northern Railroad troop train for a six day trip to Fort Dix.

It took just two days at Fort Dix for Fox to get his discharge. After all the training, waiting, boredom, terror and anxiety of his military career he picked up the piece of paper that said he was a full-fledged civilian again.

While he was in the taxi reflecting on the sweat of working to keep the 348th in the fight and the tears of losing friends and pilots to the demands of operations, not to mention the blood that all too many people had shed, Fox ordered the car to stop short of home. It was a moment of heavy emotion, but the veteran crew chief was able to handle the situation. "Let me out at the corner," he told the driver, "I can walk from here!"

Another worn 348th P-51 in service with the 8th FG after the war.

Color Section

1. P-47D-2-RA, serial 42-28072, 340th Squadron number 20, FAIR DINKUM. The pilot is unknown, but the P-47 is indicative of how quickly the 348th became accustomed to the Australian influence. This P-47 was one of the early ones in the Port Moresby area and was named for the Aussie term of approval.

2. P-47D-21-RA, serial 43-25623, 340th Squadron number 18, flown by Lt. Andy Lytle, MY TEXAS GAL. The scheme is intermediate around the period late 1943 to early 1944. Aircraft served at Finschhafen early in 1944.

3. P-47D-4, serial 42-22684, 341st Squadron number 31, flown by Bob Rowland. MISS MUTT II/PRIDE OF LODI OHIO. Rowland acquired this P-47 around November 1943 and flew it through the beginning of 1944.

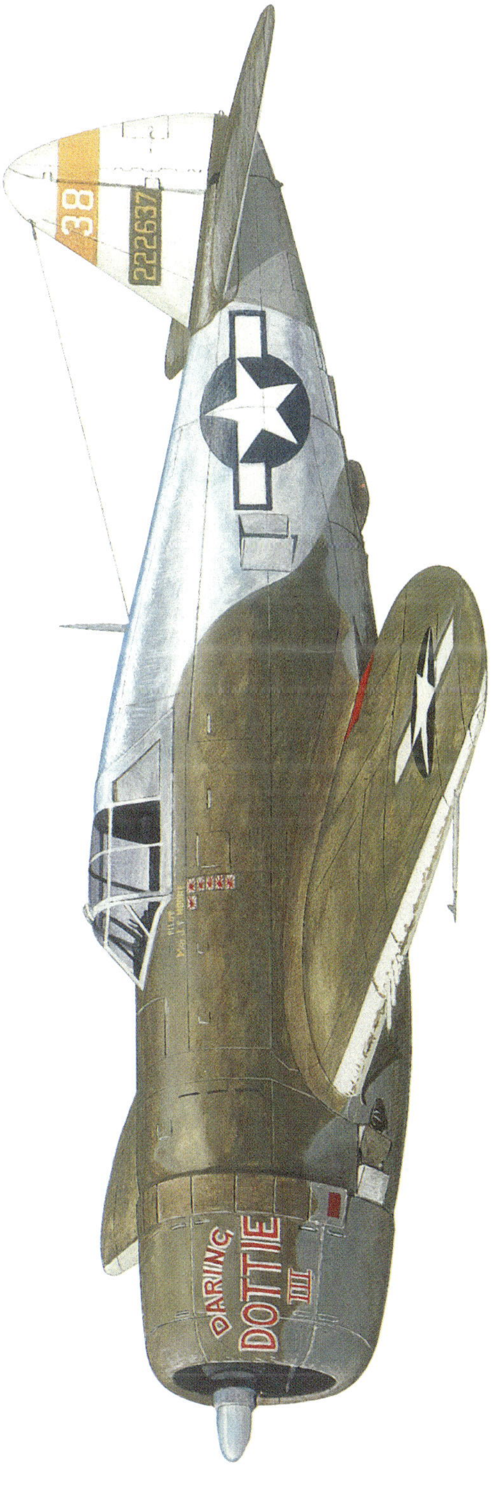

4. P-47D-4, serial 42-22637, 341st Squadron number 38, flown by John Moore. DARING DOTTIE III. The reason for the part camouflage and natural metal scheme was perhaps an effort to determine the effectiveness of natural metal scheme at the beginning of 1944. Moore used this P-47 at Finschhafen.

5. P-47D-4, serial 42-22532, 342nd Squadron number 63, flown by LtCol William Banks. SUNSHINE III. This P-47 was flown during the Port Moresby era and was probably used at Finschhafen. Banks named his aircraft SUNSHINE until he took command of the 348th and used his P-51 named SUNSHINE VII.

6. P-47D-4, serial 42-22532, 342nd Squadron number 99, flown by Lt. Lawrence O'Neill. KATHY/VENI! VIDI! VICI! O'Neill used this P-47 on his big day in December 1943 when he claimed four Japanese bombers in a single mission. His crewchief never liked this troublesome airplane and was glad to get a new P-47.

7. P-47D-23, serial 42-27886, 342nd Squadron number 84, flown by Capt. Marvin Grant. SYLVIA. Used by Grant from the middle of 1944 until late in the year.

8. P-47D-23, serial 42-27899, 340th Squadron number 3, flown by Mike Dikovitsky. JOSE Dikovitsky probably used this P-47 until the 340th converted to the P-51 early in 1945.

9. P-5ID-20, serial 44-12816, 340th Squadron number 1, flown by Capt George Orr until late in the war. The 340th decided to use a mixed swirl of white and red on its P-51 spinners and the tail stripes were added to some P-51s around the spring of 1945.

10. P-51D 341st Number 44, flown by Lt. Albert Gould from the time that the squadron converted to the P-51.

11. P-5lD-20, serial 44-64030, 460th Squadron number 111, flown by Lt. Tom Sheets. DORIS MARIE. Sheets got his last victory in August 1945 using this P-51. The 460th was distinctive in its use of black and white on natural metal.

12. P-51 used by Dunham and was undoubtedly the Mustang he used to get his 16th and last victory in August 1945. All 348th command Mustangs had the multi-colored spinners with each section devoted to one of the 348th squadrons. This was the final P-51, "MRS. BONNIE," used by Dunham.

Appendix A

Commanders/Aircraft

348TH GROUP COMMANDERS

Col. Neel E. Kearby	October 1942
Col. Robert Rowland	17 Nov 1943
Lt. Col. William Banks	8 Jun 1945
Maj.William Benz	26 Nov 1945

340th Squadron Commanders

Lt.LeRoy V. Sutter	30 Sep 42
Lt.Leighton H. Stevens	27 Oct 42
Capt. Francis Oksala	6 Nov 42
Capt. Charles H. MacDonald	17 Nov 42
Maj. Hervey B. Carpenter	1 Oct 43
Capt.Max R. Wiecks	30 Apr 44
Capt.Meade M. Brown	? 44
Capt.George W. Orr	Aug 45 — ?

341st Squadron Commanders

Maj.David A, Campbell	15 Nov 42
Maj.John T. Moore	15 Nov 43
Maj.Samuel V. Blair	18 Jul 44
Capt.Merle M. Zeine	6 Oct 44
Maj.George M. Barnes	Mar 45
Maj.Phillip Meyer	Aug 45

342nd Fighter Squadron

Lt.William T. Storts	10 Oct 42
Capt.William M. Banks	2 Nov 42
MajRaymond K. Gallagher	26 Nov 42
Maj.William M. Banks	18 Nov 43
Maj.William D. Dunham	24 May 43
Maj.Walter G. Benz	26 Jul 44
Maj.Edward Popek	Mar 45

460th Fighter Squadron Commanders

Maj. William Dunham	26 Jul 44
Capt. DeWitt R. Searles	Dec 44
Maj.Clay Albright	Apr 45

AIRCRAFT OF THE 348TH FIGHTER GROUP

340TH FIGHTER SQUADRON

Type	Serial	Pilot	Remarks
P-47D2	42-8077		Squadron #12, Ward's Drome Late 1943
P-47D4	42-22669		Sq. #29, MID 1944
P-47D15	42-23181	Pressly	Sq. #10, Saidor, early 1944
P-47D11	43-23023	Lytle	"My Texas Gal"
P-47D16	42-75905		Feb.-March(?) 1944
P-47D16	42-76037		Sq. #17, Ward's Drome(?)
P-47D21	43-25623		LytleSq. #18 "My Texas Gal"
P-47D23	42-27890		Sq. #21, MID 1944
P-47D23	42-27894		Sq. #8',
P-47D23	42-27897		Sq. #20, MID 1944
P-47D23	42-27899		DikovitskySq. #3
P-47D23	42-27901		Sq. #15 MID 1944
P-47D23	42-27905		Burt " "
P-47D23	42-2800		3HowlandMIA 10/9/44
P-47D23	42-28020		PetersonMIA 2/2/45
P-51K10	44-12031		Sq. #27, Ie Shima July 1945
P-51K10	44-12033		Sq. #33, Ie Shima July 1945

REPRESENTATIVE AIRCRAFT OF THE 348TH FIGHTER GROUP

341ST FIGHTER SQUADRON

Type	Serial	Pilot	Remarks
P-47D2	42-8082		#34 Finschhafen era
P-47D2	42-8096	Rowland	#31 "Miss Mutt"
P 47D2	42-8099	Henderson	KIA 12f27/43, Arawe, N.B.
P-47D2	42-8117	Jacoby	KIA 10/22/43
P-47D16	42-76046		Garst MIA 3/22/45
P-47D4	42-22623		#37

P-47D4	42-22641	Weeks	
P-47D4	42-22669		#29
P-47D4	42-22684	Rowland	#31"Miss Mutt II"
P-47D4	42-227891		#32Ditched off Noemfoor
P-47D4	42-227893		#44
P-47D4	42-227983		#44
P-47D23	42-27635		
P-47D23	42-27613		
P-47D23	42-27983	Thomas	MIA 12/8/44
P-47D23	42-27596	Moore	MIA 10/8/44
P-51D15	44-15120	Erickson	Trns. from 3AC Group. Blue nose and tail. Erickon Missing in action, 1/9/45.
P-51D15	44-15136	Mix	#60, Trns. from 3AC, Mix MIA 2/21/1945
P-51D15	44-14956		#49, Trns. from 3AC,
P-51D20	44-63566	Redner	MIA 3/8/45

REPRESENTATIVE AIRCRAFT OF THE 348TH FIGHTER GROUP

342ND Fighter Squadron

Type	Serial	Pilot	Crewchief	Remarks
P-47C	41-5975	Eastham		"Miss Mary Jane"
P-47C	41-6564	O'Neill		As a result of the 3/ 1943 dive the ailerons were bent, landing gear doors buckled, air duct bulged and wings and empennage highly overstressed.
P-47C	" "	Gallagher		"City of Hartford"
P-47D2	42-8059	Desilets		MIA 8/16/43 Sq. #59
P-47D2	42-8152	Gallagher		"Cabby"
	"42-8054			Sq. #61
	"42-8067	Dunham	Stanton	Sq. #68
P-47D2	42-8095	Pratt		MIA 12~26/43
P-47D2	42-8119			Sq. #60
P-47D2	42-8145	Ness		MIA 10/22/43
P-47D2	42-8130			Sq. #67
P-47D4	42-25406	Popek	Franzen	
P-47D4	42-25640	Knapp		
P-47D4	42-22694			Sq. #64
	42-27865	Overbey		MIA 12/11/44
	42-75920	Larrimore		MIA 12/19/44
	42-75940	Frankfort		MIA 5/27/44

P-51	44-12085	Davis	Sq. #84
P-51	44-12076		Sq. #72
P-51	44-12054	Kooper	MIA 3/12/45
P-51	44-12581	Popek	"Rollicking Rogue"
P-51	44-6136_		Squadron #60
P-51	44-63275		Squadron #83
P-47D23	42-27612	Hartman	Ditched off Leyte, 12/1/44
P-47D23	42-28071		Sq. #80, Late 1944 Markings

AIRCRAFT OF THE 348th FIGHTER GROUP

460th Fighter Squadron

Type	Serial	Pilot	Remarks
P-47D23	42-27637	McClendon	Shot down by friendly aircraft
P-47D21	42-25637		to 342nd Squadron Nov. 1944
P-47D21	42-25624	" "	
P-47D21	42-25485	" "	
P-47D23	42-27706		to 96 Service Sq., Nov. 1944
P-47D23	42-27853	" "	
P-47D21	42-25493		lost on operations, 12/30/44
P-47D23	42-27617		to 58th FG, January 1945
P-47D21	43-25646		to 311 FS, 58 FG, Feb. 1945
P-47D23	42-27884	1945	Dunhamto 58th FG, March
P-47D21	43-25643		to 100 Service Group, March 1945
P-47D21	42-25395		to 58th FG, March 1945
P-47D21	43-25629		to 58th FG, March 1945
P-47D21	42-25412		to 58th FG, March 1945
P-47D21	42-25403		to Depot #3, March 1945
P-47D21	42-24381		to 58th FG, March 1945
P-47D21	42-27851	""	
P-47D21	42-27881	""	
P-47D21	42-27991	""	
P-47D21	42-27988	""	
P-47D21	42-27901	""	
P-51D	44-12015		to 100 Service Group March 1945
P-51D	44-12091"		
P-47D23	42-28011		to 58th FG, April 1945
P-51D20	44-63320		Economocoff lost in combat, 5/14/45
P-51D20	44-64064		Sq. #128, sent to service squadron in June 1945
P-51D20	44-64025		Millerlost with pilot, 8/6/45

Appendix B

348th Fighter Group Casualties

This is a partial listing of group casualties in combat or while on duty in a combat related situation or training exercise. The scattered nature of casualty records makes this listing as complete as possible while presenting the possibility of additional names not yet revealed.

2Lt Charles G. Hay (340) Crashed at Westover in adverse weather.

March 1, 1943 — 2Lt Stanley Jankowski (342) P-47 (Ser. unk) Reported lost in a training accident.

April 12, 1943 — 2Lt Gordon H. Kimpel
2Lt Elrod G. Howard (341) P-47 (Ser. unk) Reported to have collided over the village of Appenang.

August 15, 1943 — 2Lt John H. Schrik caught in a fatal crosswind at Port Moresby. He was from Oak Park, Illinois.

August 16, 1943 — 2Lt Leonard Leighton (341) P-47 (unk) Reported MIA during escort of transports to the Marilinan area. Believed to have bailed out, and his body was recovered by an Allied patrol some months later.

August 18, 1943 — F/O Wilfrid J. Desilets (342) P-47D2RE, 42-8059. Assigned to the 342nd on March 31, 1943. He took off at 1145 AM from Horanda Strip in a sixteen plane formation escorting transports to Wau. The formation went through heavy overcast that ranged from 6,000 feet to 12,000 feet. He and another pilot, Cyril C. Andrews were missing after the formation cleared the overcast. Andrews bailed out and returned to base, but Desilets was never seen again.

September 16, 1943 — Lt. Fred A. McNich (340) P-47 (unk) Killed on takeoff from Jackson Drome while towing target.

September 27, 1943 — Lt. Charles A. Matson (340) (unk) Crashed on landing at Baker's Drome

October 22, 1943 — Lt. Harold Jacoby (341st) P-47D2RE, 42-8117. He was reported MIA after a stiff air battle during B-25 escort to Wewak.

October 22, 1943 — Lt. Ernest R. Ness (342) P-47D2RE, 428145. Was last seen by his element leader, Lt. Charles Whistler with a Tony fighter on his tail during the escort to Wewak.

October 29, 1943 — Corporal Robert S. Johnson (340) Killed in an accident on his way back from work.

December 26, 1943 — Lt. James E. Pratt (342) P-47D2RE, 42-8095. During the action off Cape Gloucester Pratt's P-47 was seen to be hit by friendly anti-aircraft fire and he crashed with his fighter.

December 27, 1943 — Lt. Milburn Henderson (341) P-47D2RE, 42-8099. He was last seen by his wingman a few miles south of Arawe, New Britain in no apparent trouble. He was listed MIA when he failed to return.

348th Fighter Group Casualties

There were no reported casualties in Squadron or group records for January 1944.

February 18, 1944 — Lt. David J. Riley (340)
Lt- Walter S. Monroe, Jr Collided during local patrol. Crashed 5 miles NE of Finschhafen Strip. Observers saw both planes fall into the sea. Both men well-liked veterans.

March 5, 1944 — Colonel Neel Ernest Kearby (HQ) P-47D4, 42-22668. One of the few casualties lost to enemy fighters. It was an ironic note that the rules he instilled so well into his men and that were responsible for many of those pi lots' surviving during combat missions should be broken by him and cause his own death (see text).

April 13, 1944 — Lt. Robert M. Stroud (341). Operational Flying accident. May 23, 1944 Sgt. Adolph F. Majohrzak (340) Accidentally killed by guard on Wakde Island.

May 27, 1944 — Lt. Wynans E. Frankfort (342) P-47D 42-75940. He had gone down in the New Guinea jungle the previous year and walked back. This time he was on another mission in the Biak area and simply disappeared.

June 4, 1944 1 — Lt Sam Galik (341). Landing accident at Wadke.

June 26, 1944 1 — Lt John B. Yearby (340) Killed in a takeoff accident at Wakde when his P-47 caught fire and crashed into the sea.

June 8, 1944 1 — Lt James L. Rowe (340). On detached service to Wing. Co-pilot on B-25 flight and listed as MIA.

348th — Fighter Group Casualties

September 6, 1944 — 2Lt Miles B. McDougal (340) (unk) Hit by anti-aircraft fire during bombing run at Kahoe, Halmaheras. Crashed in Wasile Bay.

October 8, 1944 — Major John T. Moore (341, HQ) P-47D 42-27596. Let down through cloud to find bombing target on Ceram Island. Never heard from again.

October 9, 1944 — 1Lt. Warren H. Howland (340) P-47D 42-28003. MIA on divebombing mission to Liang Airdome, between Amboina and Ceram.

October 24, 1944 — Lt. Malcolm Rand (342) p-47D (unk) Attacked Japanese aircraft on ground at Babo, Dutch New Guinea. He volunteered the attack and it is believed he flew into an anti-aircraft trap. He was from Mexico, Maine, and was a well-liked flight leader from the beginning of 348th operations.

November 4, 1944 — SSgt Richard N. Van Nostrant (460) Reported KIA by a Japanese daisy cutter bomb during raid at Tacloban.

November 10, 1944 — 2Lt Andrew A. McClendon (460). P-47D 42-27637 several miles behind his formation enroute to Leyte and was shot down in error by P-38. He was last seen over the Mindanao Sea and his formation was covering a B-25 strike on Japanese shipping.

November 29, 1944 — Lt. Robert P. Smith (460) P-47D (unk). He was on Lynn Parson's wing when the two of them went down to strafe a destroyer. Smith was either hit by antiaircraft fire or struck the destroyer and crashed.

November 30, 1944 — 2Lt Perry M. Tobre (460) (P-47D) (unk). Reported KIA during the day's mission.

December 8, 1944 — Cpl Daniel V Murello
Cpl Milton Sova (341) These two enlisted men were on guard duty during the night of December 7/8 and were ambushed by a fifteen man Japanese patrol during the early morning hours.

December 8, 1944 — 2Lt Cletus J. Thomas (341) P-47D 42-27983. Reported MIA during a mission to north central portion of Leyte.

December 11, 1944 — Lt. William M. Overbey (342) P-47D 42-27865. On mission #2-911 that took off at 3 o'clock in the afternoon to cover a shipping strike northwest of Leyte, Overbey was an element leader. His flight sighted eight A6m5 Zeros below and dived to the attack. His wingman lost sight of him in the maneuvering split-s and rolls and he was not seen again.

December 24, 1944 — 1Lt James B. Morris (341) P-47D MIA over Clark Field target area. He was from Kentucky.

December 24, 1944 — 2Lt August P. Svancarek (341) P-47D MIA over Clark Field. He was from Illinois.

December 24, 1944 — 2Lt Kenneth F. Saunders (460)P-47D At tacked on the way back from Clark by an enemy fighter. No parachute was seen before his P-47 hit the water.

348th Fighter Group Casualties

December 25, 1944 1Lt Charles P. Murray (340) P-47 (unk). He was circling downed plane when apparently he lost control and crashed into the sea.

These names are also listed in one document or another and appear to be casualties by the end of 1944:

340th

7 December 1944 1Lt Alexander M. Ritsch.
2Lt Patrick J. Lambert. Both men were flying an A-20 when it apparently suffered mechanical failure and crashed into the sea.

342nd

Early 1944 SSgt Edsel Ford was working on a truck on a Finschhafen strip when the vehicle slipped into the whirling propeller of a P-47. Before he was able to stop the truck, Ford was crushed between the door and the moving prop blades.

Circumstances unknown:

2Lt Joseph H. Freeman
2Lt Fred V. Bright
2Lt James F. Lyons
2Lt Jack Winokur
2Lt William E. Luton (342) joined the 342nd in January 1944 and listed MIA by October 1, 1944

SSgt Gerald J. Charlier
PFC William F. Grege

Lt. Albert Newman
Lt. Douglas Matthews
Lt. Samuel Kilgore
All three were in the 342nd and lost on December 1, 1944.

Joseph Jekielek MIA December 4, 1944
FO James D. Larimore (342) Reported MIA in P-47D 42-75920 on December 19, 1944

348th Fighter Group Casualties

January 8, 1945 2Lt Randall W. Tuttle (460) MIA during strafing at Mactan Island.

January 9, 1945 Lt. Charles D. Erickson (341) P-47 44-15120 Listed as MIA, probably on strafing mission.

January 12, 1945 Lt. Paul McMath (460). Lost to antiaircraft fire over Luzon's Central Valley.

January 26, 1945 Lt. David McMahon (460). Injured in a takeoff accident. Died of burns on January 29.

January 29, 1945 Lt. Ralph Prouty (341). Reported MIA in operational accident while flying with 340th Squadron on cover mission over a convoy. He was the Squadron assistant armament officer since October 1944.

February 1, 1945 Lt. William Anahu (342). Assistant Operations Officer. Snaprolled on landing at Elmore Field, Mindoro after cover mission.

February 2, 1945 Lt. Herbert Peterson (340) P-47D, 42-28020. MIA while covering convoy.

February 20, 1945 Lt. Earl T. Loucks (342). He was making an emergency landing at San Narcisso, Luzon during a slow-time test mission when his P-47 hit the water, overturned and sank. His body was later recovered for burial.

February 21, 1945 Lt. Earl F. Mix (341) P-51D, 44-15136. MIA, probably on ground attack mission.

March 8, 1945 Lt. Robert Redner (341) P-51D, 44-63566. MIA on unspecified flight.

March 12, 1945 Lt. Clark Kooper (342) P-51D, 44-12054. Claimed a Ki-84 Frank fighter, but his fighter was last seen trailing smoke by wingmate Lt. Robert Dow. Kooper bailed out and was sighted in his dinghy, but was never recovered.

March 15, 1945 2Lt. Roy F. Martin (340). Crashed on a local test hop.

March 18, 1945 2Lt. Robert 0. McPeak (340). Operational accident. He lost control of his aircraft when it developed engine trouble.

March 22, 1945 Lt. Richard C. Garst (341) P-47D, 42-76046. MIA on unspecified operational accident.

March 20, 1945 Lt. Ferdinand Peterson (342). Reported to have crashed 8 miles south of Nichols Field.

March 26, 1945 F/O James W. Clements (342).Crashed on takeoff from Magaldan Strip during a cross country flight.

March 30, 1945 F/O Samuel Macken (340). Local Patrol. P-51 was seen to crash and explode in the water about twenty miles west of base. Wreckage recovered by crash boats.

348th Fighter Group Casualties

April 3, 1945 Lt. George Goddard (342) P-51D, 44-63275. Listed as MIA, probably to training or operational accident.

April 3, 1945 Sgt Thomas Harper (340) Ordnance Section. Hit by truck on his way back from work.

April 11, 1945 Lt. Charles L. Nickell (342). MIA due to groundfire during strafing.

April 11, 1945 1Lt Walter A. Abraham (460). Bomb run 1500 yards E. of Santa Maria river. Suddenly pulled up to 3,000 feet, spun in and crashed.

Mid-April 1945 Lt. Truman Ragsdale (342) MIA due to groundfire.

Mid-April 1945 2Lt Richard Wolffe (341). Lost on ground attack to groundfire.

April 27, 1945 Lt. Richard McAfee (341?) P-51D, 44-14930. Probably lost in an operational accident.

April 27, 1945 TSgt Louis E. Conerly (342) Reported killed in an accident on this date.

May 13, 1945 1Lt Wayne S. Randolph
2Lt Leonard C. Novick (340) MIA mid-air collision returning from mission over central Luzon.

May 14, 1945 Lt. Gerald Economocoff (460) P-51D20, 44-63320. Aircraft disintegrated in mid-air east of Manila.

June 1, 1945 2Lt Charles Dilts (340). During a bomb run on the Bontoc area he never pulled out of his dive.

June 10, 1945 1Lt Floyd H. Stone (460). Struck by 2Lt James Hamilton's wing and prop in mid-air collision over San Julian, Luzon. Hamilton parachuted safely but Stone was MIA.

June 8, 1945 Lt. Robert Dow (342). Crashed into Roadgrader on takeoff for escort mission.

July 25, 1945 2Lt Burton E. Bennell (341). He was a new pilot, MIA on one of his first missions.

July 26, 1945 1Lt Bernard Kane (460) P-51D20, 44-64114. Cover B-25s and A-26s bombing Kanoya East Airdrome. Wing came off, probably due to AA fire. Crashed near Kanoya town.

July 15, 1945 Lt. Merle M. Miller crashed on takeoff for PBM cover mission.

August 6, 1945 Lt. Richard Miller (460). Developed a coolant leak and parachuted into the ocean. He was seen in his dinghy, but was later listed as MIA.

August 11, 1945 Capt. George Elvey
Lt. Wilbur Frable (460) P-51D, 44-63294 & 44-15008
These two pilots were involved in a mid-air collision and were evidently the last 348th casualties of World War II.

Appendix C

348th Fighter Group Aerial Victory List

The following list was compiled from final Far East Air Forces tabulations and was compared with unit mission reports and individual pilot combat reports. Air Force Study 85 seems fairly consistent with this list and scattered Japanese records are available to provide some comparison. Time and area are those reported in pilot combat reports.

Date	Time	Pilot	Type	Area
8/16/43	1500	Max Wieck	Zero(Oscar?)	Near Marilinan
	1530	L. Leighton	Oscar	Marilinan
9/4/43	1430	Neel Kearby	Betty & Oscar	14 mi S Hopoi
9/13/43	1043	William Banks	Zero (Oscar?)	NE Marilinan
	1100	Lawrence O'Neill	Beny	5 mi NE Marilinan
9/14/4	1045	Neel Kearby	Dinah	Near Malahang
9/22/43	1245	John Moore	Zero	Near Finschhafen
	1245	Charles Cronk	2 Bettys	Finschhafen
	1245	Walter Benz	Dinah	S. of Finschhafen
10/11/4	1115	William Dunham	Tony	Wewak
	1115	Neel Kearby	4 Oscars & 2 Tonys	Wewak
	1130	John Moore	2 Tonys	Wewak
10/12/43	1300	Robert Rowland	Dinah	Wewak
10/16/43	1100	Thomas Barber	Zero (Oscar?)	Alexishafen
	1100	Guy Johnston	Tony	Alexishafen
	1100	Andrew Lytle	Tony & Hamp	Alexishafen
	1100	Max Wieks	Zero & Hamp	Alexishafen
	1100	William Dunham	2 Hamps	3 mi S. of Madang
	1100	James Pratt	2 Hamps	3 mi S. of Madang
	1100	Willis Cooley	2 Hamps	3 mi S. of Madang
	1125	Neel Kearby	Zero (Oscar?)	Wewak
10/19/43	1100	Neel Kearby	2 Petes	Wewak
	1100	William Dunham	Pete	2 mi E. Wewak
	1100	Franklin Love	2 Pete	2 mi E. Wewak
	1100	Theodore Wood	Pete	2 mi E. Wewak
10/22/43	1030	Walter Benz	Tony	5 mi E. of Dagua
	1030	Edward Popek	Tony	5 mi W. of Kairiru Is.
	1030	Wynans Frankfort	Hamp(Oscar?)	W. Kairiru Is.
10/23/43	1040	Samuel Blair	Hamp	Near Finschhafen
	1040	Kenneth Briggs	Zero	Near Finschhafen
	1040	Samuel Galik	Zero	Near Finschhafen
	1040	Gene Spencer	Zero	Finschhafen
	1045	James Rowe	Hamp	Near Finschhafen
11/5/43	1105	Robert Rowland	2 Tonys	Near Wewak
	1105	Francis Oksala	Tony	Near Wewak
	1105	EdwardRoddy	Tony&Hamp	Near Wewak

Date	Time	Pilot	Type	Area
	1105	Samuel Blair	Tony	Near Wewak
11/7/43	0855	Francis Oksala	Hamp (Oscar?)	NW of Lae
	0855	Robert Rowland	2 Hamps (Oscars?)	Near Saidor
	0855	Samuel Blair	Hamp(Oscar?)	Near Nadzab
11 /15/43	1115	Walter Benz	Oscar	Wewak
	1130	Robert Martin	Oscar	Wewak
	1130	William Banks	2 Oscars	Wewak
	1130	Robert Sutcliffe	Oscar	Wewak
11/25/43	1010	WilliamBanks	Dinah	SEWewak
12/1/43	1245	Wilburn Henderson	2 Tonys	Near Wewak
	1245	George Della	Tony	Near Wewak
	1245	Clarence Blend	Tony	Near Wewak
12/3/43	1050	Neel Kearby	3 Zeros (Oscars?)	20 mi NW Wewak
	1100	Meade Brown	Tony	Wewak
	1115	Francis Oksala	Tony	Near Wewak
12/16/43	1645	Edward Roddy	2 Zeros	Arawe
	1655	Franklin Love	Zero	Arawe
	1655	Robert Gibb	Zero	Arawe
	1700	Marvin Grant	Kate	Arawe
12/17/43	0815	Frank Morrison	2 Vals & 1 Oscar	Near Arawe
	0815	Robert DuCharme	Val	Near Arawe
	0815	Harvey Chapman	2 Vals	Near Arawe
	0815	Sam Blair	Val & Oscar	Near Arawe
	0815	Ed Roddy	Dinah	Near Arawe
	0815	Francis Donar	Val	Near Arawe
	1430	Howard Tuman	Val	Near Arawe
12/20/43	0800	William Banks	Dinah	20 mi NW Arawe
12/21/43	1630	Robert Gibb	2 Vals	Arawe
	1645	William Dunham	3 Vals	Arawe
	1645	Randall Hilbig	2 Vals	Arawe
	1650	Frank Russo	Val	Arawe
	1720	Guy Roberts	Hamp	Arawe
12/22/43	1320	Clarence Blend	Zero (Oscars?)	Near Wewak
	1320	Samuel Blair	Zero (Oscar?)	Near Wewak
	1320	Neel Kearby	Zero (Oscar?)	Near Wewak
12/23/43	1030	Neel Kearby	Tony	NearWewak
12/26/43	1700	Winans Frankfort	Tony	30 mi NW Umboi Is.
	1700	Raymond Gallagher	Betty	Cape Gloucester
	1700	Marvin Grant	Betty	5 mi NW Umboi Is.
	1700	Lawrence O'Neill	4 Bettys	5 mi NW Umboi Is.
	1700	George Orr	2 Bettys	30 mi W. Umboi Is.
	1700	Ed Roddy	2 Bettys	5 mi N Umboi Is.
	1700	Robert Sutcliffe	2 Bettys	30 mi NW Umboi Is.
	1700	Edward Wyroba	Betty	5 mi N. Umboi Is.
	1700	Robert Rowland	Betty	Cape Gloucester
	1700	James Pratt	Tony	Cape Gloucester
	1740	Walter Benz	Beny	2 mi NW Sakar Is.
12/27/43	0830	Richard Lake	Zero & Tony	Arawe
	0800	John Lolos	2 Zeros Near	Arawe
	0830	Robert Anderson	Zero Near	Arawe
	0835	Harvey Carpenter	Val	Arawe
	0840	Meade Brown	Val, Zero	Arawe
	0840	Richard Frost	Zero S of	Arawe
	0840	Myron Hnatio	2 Vals & 1 Zero	Near Arawe
	0840	Joel Pitchford	Val	Arawe
	0840	Lloyd Zaage	Val	Arawe
	0855	Richard Fleischer	2 Vals Near	Arawe
	0900	William Foulis	Zero	Near Arawe
	0900	John Moore	2 Zeros	Near Arawe
	0900	Frank Morrison	Oscar	Arawe

Date	Time	Pilot	Type	Area
	0900	Merle Zeine	Zero	Near Arawe
	0900	Arthur Weeks 2	Zeros	Near Arawe
	0900	Robert Rowland	Zero	20 mi W Arawe
	0900	James Rea	Zero	Near Arawe
	0900	James Lynch	Oscar	Near Arawe
		Stanley Souders	2 Zeros	Near Arawe
		Jerome Fischer	Zero	S. of Arawe
12/28/43	0830	John Moore	Kate	Cape Gloucester
12/31/43	1315	Robert Gibb	2 Vals	Arawe
	1315	Theodore Wood	Val	Arawe
12/31/43	1315	Malcom Rand	Zero	Arawe
	1315	Edward Popek	Zero	Arawe
	1315	Robert Knapp	2 Vals	Arawe
	1315	George Davis	Val	Arawe
	1325	Lyle Dowsett	Val	Arawe
	1325	Richard Lake	Val	NearArawak
	(1315)	(Winans Frankfort)	(Tony)	(probable?)
1/3/44	1015	Neel Kearby	Sally	Near Wewak
	1455	Neel Kearby	Zero(Oscar?)	Near Wewak
1/9/44	1215	Neel Kearby	2Tonys	Near Wewak
1/18/44	1100	Myron Hnatio	Zero	Wewak
2/3/44	1140	George Davis	Tony	Wewak
		Malcom Rand	Tony	Wewak
		William Wallace	Tony	Wewak
	1115	Michael Dikovitsky	Tony Hamp (Oscar?)	Wewak
	1115	Lyle Dowsett	Tony	Wewak
	1115	Richard Fleischer	Hamp (Oscar?)	Wewak
		Charles Allen	Tony	Wewak
2/4/44	1535	Edward Roddy	Helen	Wewak
2/7/44	4090	William Banks	Tony	Cape Gloucester
2/27/44	1700	Robert Rowland	Sally	Cape Hoskins
3/2/44		Francis Fredenburgh	Zero	Near Lou Island
		Wilfrid Joyal	Hamp	Near Lou Island
	1230	John Lolos	Hamp Near	Lou Island
	1230	John Moore	Zero	Manus Is.
		James Nixon	Zero	Near Momote
		Glenn Perryman	Hamp	Manus & Lou Is.
3/5/44	1710	William Dunham	Nell, (Lily?) Oscar	Wewak
	1720	Samuel Blair	Nell (Lily?)	Wewak
		Neel Kearby	Nell (Lily?)	Wewak
3/11/44		Thomas Barber	Oscar	Wewak
		William Bennett	Tojo	Wewak
		Hervey Carpenter	2 Oscars	Wewak
		William Chase	Oscar	Wewak
	1100	Michael Dikovitsky	Oscar	Wewak
	1100	Lyle Dowsett	Oscar	Wewak
	1105	Richard Fleischer	2 Oscars	Wewak
	1105	Myron Hnatio	Zero (Oscar?)	Wewak
	1105	Andrew Lytle	Oscar	Wewak
		Gerald Woodruff	Oscar	Wewak
		Lloyd Zaage	Oscar	Wewak
5/27/44	1630	Charles Nickell	Oscar	Biak
	1635	George Burgess	2 Oscars	Biak
	1635	Marvin Grant	Tony	Biak.
	1645	Robert Sutcliff	Oscar	E. Bosnek, Biak
5/29/44	0825	Albert Newman	Zero	Biak.
		George Orr	Oscar (Mk 1)	Biak
		Robert Knapp	Zero	20 mi SW Mokmer AD
6/3/44	1120	Max Wieks	Hamp	Biak
	1120	Richard Fleischer	Oscar	Biak

Date	Time	Pilot	Type	Area
	1120	Ralph Heiden	Zero	Biak
	1120	Noble Jones	2 Zeros	Biak
	1120	Roy Martin	Oscar	Biak
6/4/44	1740	George Burgess	Zero	40 mi E. Bosneck
		Marvin Grant	2 Zeros	40 mi E. Bosneck
		William Overby	Kate	W. Koeroedoe Strait
6/12/44	1030	Marvin Grant	2 Kates	SE Biak
	1030	William Overby	Kate	SE Biak
	1030	Edward Popek	3 Kates	SE Biak
	1045	Franklin Love	Tony	N. end Sarendidori St.
	1045	George Orr	Kate	Biak
6/16/44	1050	Robert Martin	Dinah	50 mi W. Mokmer, Biak
11/12/44	1440	Richard Frost	Zero	San Jose, Leyte
11 /18/44	0740	Wiiliam Thompson	Tony	Camotes Sea
	0740	William Dunham	Zero	Camotes Sea
11/19/44	1515	George Della	Zero	Camotes Sea
	1625	Paul McGuire	Zero	Poro
11/24/44	1515	Edgar Stoudt	Jack	10 mi s. Pacijan
	1552	George Della	Jack	Camotes
11/29/44	0925	Thomas Sheets	Oscar	15 mi E. Cebu
11/30/44	1520	Dewitt Searles	Oscar	Port Carmen, Cebu
	1520	Samuel Denmark	Oscar	Port Carmen, Cebu
12/6/44	0815	Howard Minnick	Dinah	Negros
127/44	0950	William Aswell	Sally	N. Ponson
	0950	George Grace	Nick	N. Poro
	0950	Thomas Sheets	Sally	N . Ponson
	1400	William Dunham	2 Zeros	Between W. Cebu-San Isidro
	1415	William Dunham	2 Oscars	Palompon-W. Camotes
	1400	Boris Popov	Zero	Camotes Sea
	1400	Frank Russo	Zero & Sally	N. San Isidro Bay
	1400	Howard Minnick	Zero	W. Cebu-San Isidro
	1400	John Smith	Zero	W. Cebu-San Isidro
	1403	Gerald Economoff	Zero	N. tip Cebu
	1425	Gerald Economoff	Oscar	N. Camotes Is.
	1544	William Foulis	Dinah	Calangaman
12/10/44	0820	Lynn Parsons	Sally	S. of Ormoc Bay
	0940	William Wallace	Dinah	Ormoc Bay
	1145	James Curran	Tony	NW Camotes
	1145	Edward Demetor	Tony	W. Tip Cebu
	1210	John Mastilock	Tony	Apale Pt., Ormoc Bay
	1630	George Davis	2 Tonys	Cebu and Negros
	1645	Samuel Denmark	Sally	S. of Baybay, Leyte
	1645	Richard Frost	Sally	Baybay
	1645	Robert Smith	Sally	SW coast Baybay
	1700	Truman Ragsdale	Zero	Dulag, Leyte
12/11/44	1220	Robert Smith	Zero	5 mi S. Carnasa
	1315	William Banks	Zero	Carnasa
	1530	Walter Benz	Oscar	Cebu
	1540	Gerald Sheely	Oscar	Cebu
	1625	Robert LeBounty	2 Zeros	Cebu
	1630	Michael Dikovitsky	Zero	Ormoc Bay
	1630	Charles Murray	Zero	Ormoc Bay
12/14/44	0705	William Dunham	Sally	offTalisay
	0705	DeWittSearles	Sally	S. of Bagasay
	1030	Wallace Harding	Tony	S. Silay strip, Negros
	1110	Meade Brown	Tony	TalisayA/D, Negros
	1110	Andrew Mix	Zero	Cebu City
12/15/44	0900	Walter Benz	Zero	Semirara Is.
	0910	Roy McCord	Zero	Mindoro
	0950	David Mumper	Zero	Mindoro

Date	Time	Pilot	Type	Area
12/18/44	1115	Gerald Economocoff	Judy	Gigante Is.
	1220	DeWitt Searles	Sally	S. San Augustin, Mindoro
	1230	Lyman Peck	Zero	5 mi S. tip Mindoro
12/20/44	1130	Walter Benz	2 Zeros	Mindoro
	1130	George Davis	Zero	Mindoro
	1130	William Krueger	Zero	Mindoro
12/20/44	1130	John Pate	Zero	Mindoro
	1130	Charles Whistler	Zero	Mindoro
	1135	David Eastham	2 Zeros	Mindoro
	1135	Robert Knapp	2 Zeros	Mindoro
	1145	Richard Watrous	Dinah	Mindoro
12/22/44	1025	David Mumper	U/I SEF	10 mi SE Clark (Frank?)Fld.
	1035	Bert Lee	Zero1	2 mi E Clark Fld.
	1055	Louis Rekers	Tony	5 mi E Clark Fld.
	1100	William Foulis	Tony	6 mi E Clark Fld.
	1100	Michael Dikovitsky	Zero	Clark Fld.
	1100	Lyle Dowsett	Oscar	Clark Fld.
	1100	Harry Mansfield	Zero	Clark Fld.
	1100	Robert McNulty	Oscar	Clark Fld.
	1100	Andrew Mix	Zero1	2 mi E Clark Fld.
12/24/44	1015	William Banks	2 Zeros	N Clark Fld.
	1015	Gerald Excell	Zero	N Clark Fld.
	1015	Wallace Harding	Zero	N Clark Fld.
	1145	Wallace Harding	Zero	N Clark Fld.
	1045	William Anahu	Zero & Oscar	Manila, Luzon
	1045	Jack Quinlan	Oscar & Tony	W Clark Fld.
	1045	Meade Brown	2 Zeros	Clark Fld.
	1050	John Doenges	Oscar	NearClark Fld.
	1050	Francis Hall	Zero	Clark Fld.
	1050	Noble Jones	Zero	Clark Fld.
	1055	George Davis	2 Zeros	Manila, Luzon
	1055	Clark Kooper	Zero	Manila, Luzon
	1100	Robert Redner	Tojo	14 mi NW Clark Fld.
			Zero	15 mi N Manila City
	1100	Floyd Stone	Zero	N Clark Fld.
	1105	William Foulis	3 Oscars	10 mi NW Clark Fld.
	1105	Ollie Miller	2 Oscars	10 mi NW Clark Fld.
	1105	William Schlegel	2 Tojos	E Clark Fld.
	1110	James Mullen	Zero	15 mi NW Clark Fld.
	1110	Louis Rekers	Zero	10 mi NW Clark Fld.
	1115	George Della	2 Zeros	N Clark Fld.
	1115	Robert Smith	2 Zeros	20 mi N. Clark Fld. & 30 mi NE Clark Fld.
1/3/45	1630	John Smith	Zero	NW Negros Is.
3/11/45	1105	Bert Lee	Betty	75 mi E. Poulo Canton Is.
3/13/45	1110	Robert Dow	Frank	Samah A/D, Hainan Is.
	1110	Clark Kooper	Frank	Samah A D, Hainan Is.
3/15/45	1115	Albert Gould	Tojo	Hong Kong
	1130	Ruben Moskaloff	Jack	Hong Kong
8/1/45	1015	William Dunham	Frank	Take Is., Kyushu
	1015	Edward Popek	2 Franks	Off SW Kyushu
	1015	Thomas Sheets	Frank	Take Is., Kyushu
8/6/45	0935	Charleton Ambler	Zero	Saishu A/D
	0935	Charles McDonald	2 Zeros	Saishu A/D
	0935	Cliff McMillin	Zero	Saishu A/D
8/8/45	1030	George Elvey	Zero	Kyushu
	1010	Reid Tait	Jack	Tsuiki, Kyushu
	1120	Jack Quinlan	2 Zeros	Tsuiki A/D, Kyushu
8/11/45	1120	David Standiford	Frank & Zero	Tsuiki A/D, Kyushu
8/12/45	0830	Kermit Allen	George	

Nose Art

Josie!

Cozy
Cookie

Betty
Lou

"BATTLIN"
BEAUT
28

Missy
II

HOOSIER
HOT SHOT

Lady Eleanore

"Little Chum"
2nd

Much Muggin'

JAIL BAIT

CAROLINA
WENCH

MISS VIRGINITY
NEVER
BEEN PLUCCED
OR FORCED DOWN

"The Duchess"
5th

Little
Bess

MY
TEXAS
GAL

Aircraft

Fiery
Ginger
IV

Fiery
Ginger

Fiery
Ginger
IV

Fiery
Ginger
IV
Good luck Jack

Bonnie

CREW CHIEF
ARMORER
PILOT
Major "Bill" Dunham
P47-D-23-RA

120
227884

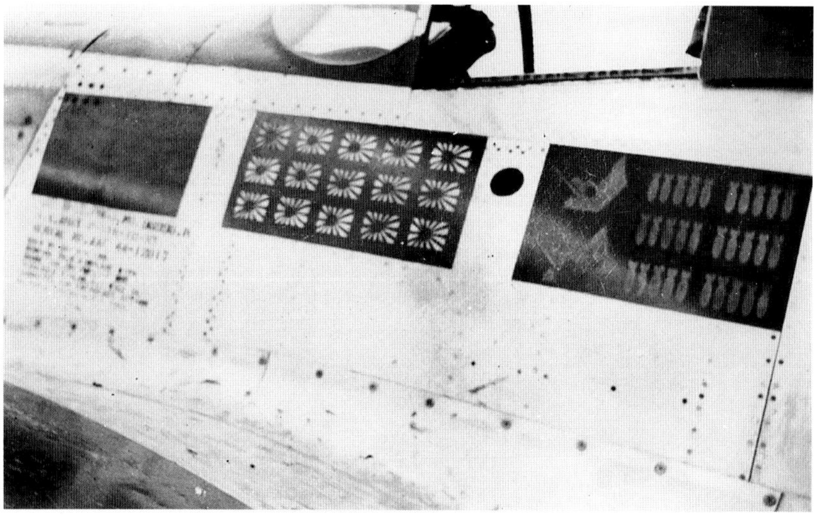

SUNSHINE
100
41

SUNSHINE
412073

SUNSHINE

Miss Mutt
PRIDE
OF
LODI
OHIO

Miss Mutt
31

MISS
MUTT
II
31

MISS
MUTT
II

MISS
MUTT
II
31
222684

PRIDE
OF
LODI
OHIO
435

DIRTY
DICK
IV

Pilot
Col. "Dick" Rowland

Dirty
Old Man

Dirty
Old Man

Dirty
Old Man
96

DIRTY
OLD MAN

38

Racine Belle

Sylvia

Little
Bess

Little
Bess

THE ROLLICKING ROGUE

CLEVELAND
CLEAVER

CLEVELAND
CLEAVER
3

JOSIE

JOSIE

Kathy
VIDI!
VICI!

99
222903

DIANE
10

20

29

Helene
70

79
222510

NIP
NIPPER

12
28077

34

275905

HOOSIER
HOOTY

80
228011

BOOTSIE

44

Miss JEANIE
33

031

41

44
52

"Mrs. Bonnie"

"Mrs. Bonnie"

83

Index

Also from the publisher

ATTACK & CONQUER: THE 8TH FIGHTER GROUP IN WORLD WAR II

STANAWAY & HICKEY.

The 8th fought the best Zero pilots, and took the war to the enemy with P-38s over Rabaul and Hollandia.

Size: 8 1/2" x 11" over 500 photos
320 pages, hard cover
ISBN: 0-88740-808-7 $45.00

POSSUM, CLOVER & HADES • THE 475TH FIGHTER GROUP IN WORLD WAR II

John Stanaway.

The epic story of one of the highest scoring fighter units in the southwest Pacific. Aces included McGuire, Loisel, MacDonald, Roberts and Bong.

Size: 8 1/2" x 11" 336 pages over 700 b/w and color photographs, color profiles; hard cover

ISBN: 0-88740-518-5 $45.00